SPACED OUT

ALASTAIR GORDON

SPACED OUT

RADICAL ENVIRONMENTS OF THE PSYCHEDELIC SIXTIES

RIZZOLI
NEW YORK

“YOU DON’T NEED TO KNOW THAT MUCH
YOU JUST NEED TO GO AHEAD
AND TRY IT OUT.
BUT THEN YOU HAVE TO DO
OTHER THINGS.”

—STEVE BAER

FOR IONA

CONTENTS

OPPOSITE
Domes, *Manera Nueva, New Mexico (Photo: Jack Fulton).*

INTRODUCTION

"THERE ARE NO LIMITS TO CREATIVITY,
THERE IS NO END TO SUBVERSION."
–RAOUL VANEIGEM, 1967

It begins to feel as if some spirit force were pushing my rented Capri up toward the black mesa. The sun has just set behind the outlying malls with a garish display of crimson and ochre streaks. Farther out from Phoenix there are blobbish silhouettes of Big Horn and Cypress Butte dissolving into desert mist. I am driving straight from the airport, north on Route 17. "Purple Haze" begins to play on the radio, and by the time I reach the rutted turnoff to Cordés Junction, Jimi Hendrix's words sound like predestination.

On first impression Arcosanti looks like a ruin, all starts and stops and unfinished business. There's only a single lightbulb glowing, but I can make out a few vague shapes, the looming silhouette of a tower, and a crescent-shaped berm. I am greeted on the ramp by a skunk, who flashes his tail and scurries into the shadows. A willowy new ager appears out of a doorway and shines a flashlight on my face. "We've been expecting you," she says with a sleepy smile. Her name is Sandy and she's wearing a breezy cotton dress—not hippie at all—with blonde hair cropped short. Everyone at Arcosanti is apparently asleep, so she speaks in a whisper that only adds to the spaciness of my arrival. I follow her past a cluster of dwelling pods burrowed into the side of a canyon and along a terrace that seems to be leading directly toward the twinkling stars of Ursa Major.

The concrete has been cast into capricious vaults with one level appearing to push through the next. I have the impression that there are other such vaults, many more layers, stacked and crumbling. We reach an esplanade that slopes inward with flowers and ornamental trees growing from concrete containers. The walls are streaked with red and yellow as if they had been tie-dyed. I never visited Arcosanti during its heyday in the early 1970s, but I had several friends who came as "workshoppers" to mix concrete and help make these organic forms. Paolo Soleri intended it to be a concentrated living node without cars, a "prototype town" for seven thousand people, self-sufficient and sustainable. Unlike most visionaries, however, the Italian-born architect actually came to the desert and started to build the thing with his own hands.

We come upon a fork in the pathway. One branch descends, the other snakes through a colonnade of sloping columns. Sandy guides me up another set of steps and we arrive at the Sky Suite perched at the top of the complex. I was hoping she might stay and chat, but she hands me a candle and a blanket and slips back into the night. The room is saturated with familiar smells: musty and nutty but sweet like incense and sage, and something slightly stale like old beeswax. I'd expected something much more funky and cluttered, not quite so Spartan. I imagine the earliest occupants crawling around like modern aborigines waiting for the sun to rise, cross-legged or making love on the floor. I want to call my wife and let her know I've arrived but I'm out of cell phone range. A part of me wants to check in to the nearest Marriot, but another part of me feels at home, even *safe*, in the giddy sky nest. I'm glad I came. I lie on the bed beneath an eye-shaped window and gaze out at the stars.

"Why bother with that hippie crap?" said one friend just before I left New York. I certainly hadn't anticipated this sense of well-being. There are the smells and the sense of intimacy—so familiar—and the untethered sense of space, psychedelic, sexual, hallucinatory, and drifting. For a moment it all comes back: the feeling that you are everywhere yet *nowhere* at the same time. I thought I was pretty well

OPPOSITE
Apse, *Arcosanti, Arizona (photo: Terrence Moore).*

grounded against the old spatial flux but can feel something slipping, loosening within the soft recesses of my frontal lobe. What is this adolescent feeling of heightened expectation, of believing that anything is possible? We felt it at rock concerts, love-ins, group gropes, and sensitivity-training sessions, chanting and dancing, drumming together as one mindless organism, when the flash of insight, acid premonition, group mind, and astral telegram were the operative modes of communication in place of today's IMs or text messaging. The sudden revelation of personal experience, what Raoul Vaneigem called the "revolution of everyday life," was more subversive than the big revolution that everyone was waiting for. In fact, there were thousands of overlapping revolutions and uprisings happening at once, thousands of different storms rising and joining forces with other storms, massing themselves along separate fronts. Yes, drugs were a major part of it, but they were just a means to another place, another reality, not an end in themselves. When Aldous Huxley's "doors of perception" crashed open, they led to the most extraordinary garden of possibilities.

At the time it was easy to dive into the blob of hairy humanity. It felt so good, being absorbed in amoebic solidarity, swelling and spreading: "Got a revolution!" sang the Jefferson Airplane, turning noun into verb. It seemed like a real war for a while—them against us, armed with verbs—and somehow, we would win. Then, that soulful sense of gathering passed as suddenly as it had begun.

The music and drugs have been well documented, but the fractured sense of space, the softened corners, the communal élan are less easily reclaimed. They were there in the stroboscopic light shows, crash pads, painted busses, and head shops—flashing and peeling away in overlapping veils of color—but where are the landmarks and monuments of the psychedelic revolution, and how do we go back if we don't even know where to begin?

Tim Leary spoke about a Magic Theater and the Beatles sang of Strawberry Fields. Carlos Castaneda, in his best-selling peyote fable, wrote of the *sitio,* a place of psychic strength. But Griffin, a wandering hippie mystic, got it right when he said: "All the lines and dots intersect at any dot."[2] No matter where you are, you're always at the center of the web. So all those landmarks and monuments are meaningless after all.

The psychedelic sensoriums closed their doors and most of the domes, yurts, tepees, and hand-built shelters burned or rotted into nothingness. A few of the sixties communes still exist, but the brightest stars—places like Drop City, Morning Star, and New Buffalo—vanished long ago. That's the wonder of this place. The biomorphic sinews of Soleri's desert outpost have somehow survived into the opening decade of the twenty-first century. It seems like a good place to start. At least it's still here and from what I've heard, it's starting to come back into its own.

I feel oddly torn but surprisingly calm. I see the constellations and a wavering line on the horizon where a distant butte rises from the earth, but it's too dark to see much else. I hum the throbbing Hendrix riff, *Duhn, dihn... Dunh, dihn...,* and drift into sweet, numinous sleep.

OPPOSITE
Handmade door, Arcosanti (photo: Alastair Gordon).

1 ENCHANTED LOOM

"WE ARRANGED THE ROOM IN SACRED DESIGN. INCENSE CANDLES."

—TIM LEARY[1]

Psychedelic explorers of the early sixties noted a transformation of conventional space into vibrating space harmonies.[2] Edges softened. Corners vanished. Boundaries dissolved along with the simultaneous dissolution of ego. Rooms were seen to rearrange themselves, breathe, flutter, and pulsate with mystic emanations, or explode with preternatural color. "One has the impression of *mouches volants*, a gentle flowing of boundaries and substances," wrote psychologist Rolf Von Eckartsberg after his first LSD trip.[3] Traditional hierarchies of space were upturned, polarities flipped. "A push from the inside is a pull from the outside, and vice versa," wrote Alan Watts, Anglican priest turned Zen geographer of inner space.[4] "My left side is now my right side and my right side is my left side," noted psychiatrist Art Kleps.[5]

"The walls of the room no longer seemed to meet in right angles," wrote Aldous Huxley after ingesting half a gram of mescaline.[6] He stared at a chair, admiring the supernatural smoothness and "tubularity" of its legs.[7] Draperies became "living hieroglyphs," while the flannel folds of his own trousers appeared as a labyrinth of mythic complexity. "This is how one ought to see," concluded Huxley. "This is how things really are."[8] Psychologist Stanley Krippner, while on psilocybin, compared his living room to a three-dimensional Vermeer.[9] Timothy Leary, of Harvard's Center for Personality Research, saw the walls glow phosphorescent yellow, "electric vibrating."[10] British psychiatrist Humphrey Osmond observed how the walls of a room bulged with a sense of imminent collapse: "I knew that behind those perilously unsolid walls something was waiting to burst through."[11] But what exactly was waiting to burst through and what was one to make of these early acid apparitions? Basic assumptions about man's place in the universe were changing, and the effects of this new awareness would soon make themselves felt in a much broader cultural context.

Psychedelics undermined the notion of Renaissance space and all the certainties that it held. "[The] perspective looked rather odd," noted Huxley, while others described how foreground and background elements merged into a singular softness.[12] "The usual *gestalt* mode of perception, where the figure is noticed and the ground ignored, seems to be modified," wrote psychologist Ralph Metzner, who watched with bemused detachment as the walls of his bedroom dissolved into infinite refractions.[13] As early as 1882, William James made note of similar shifts in perception while under the influence of nitrous oxide: "The centre and periphery of things seem to come together," he wrote, seeing how time and space were inextricably interwoven and wondering if this quality of unbroken continuity was, indeed, the true essence of being.[14] LSD-25, psilocybin, and mescaline took the mind even further and liquefied all psychic barriers, offering a space that was flowing, nonhierarchical, and in a constant state of mutation—a space that had more to do with center than circumference, a space "in which to create new selves," as one tripper put it.

Self-medicating psychologists went to great lengths describing the effects of the new alkaloids, but a surprising number began with a disavowal: that the writer in question was powerless to communicate the depth of his or her experience, that such all-consuming synchronicity defied description. Narrative structure seemed to erode. "Words were useless;

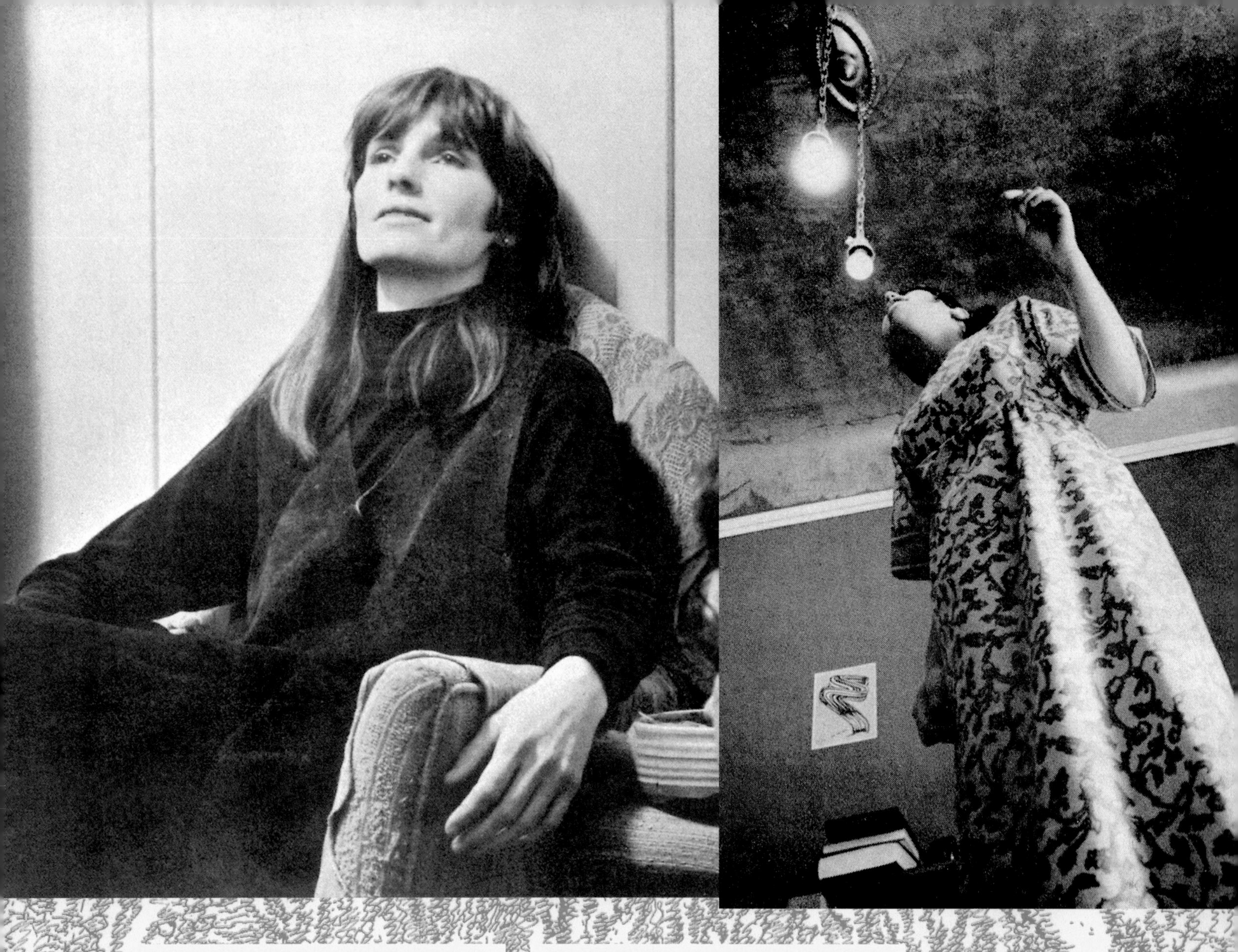

speech was a waste of time," wrote Krippner, who felt that only a vague approximation was possible at best.[15] Osmond, who coined the term "psychedelic," felt that an accurate account required a "language which does not exist."[16] Even the most poetic imaginations struggled to find the right words. When Belgian writer Henri Michaux tried to translate his mescaline impressions into a coherent narrative he felt blocked.[17] At one point he gave the swarming spatial experience a proper name, "Anopodokotolotopadnodrome," but it was an improbable word construction that collapsed from the weight of its twenty-five characters.[18] During another vivid trip, Michaux described a range of hallucinatory mountains that sprang up "sharply pointed . . . idiotic but immense," and as he wrote, the double "m's" of the word "immense" dragged his pen toward the bottom of the page, creating an unintentional pictogram. The downstrokes of ink became the fingers of a glove, then a noose, then the arches of "unthinkable, baroque cathedrals."[19] How was one expected to proceed given such a calamitous sequence of non sequiturs? No surprise that the psychedelic period left so few notable works of literature.

Frequently, the experience was characterized as a mental geography or "mindscape" through which the subject progressed in a pilgrimage of revelatory pathways and detours—as if such random psychotropic events existed as three-dimensional shadow plays, complete with their own topography and spectrum of dazzling colors. Somehow, the human mind found ways to translate the stimuli into a sequential journey of self-discovery with a beginning, middle, and end. (Hence, the popular usage of a "trip" with white light as its Holy Grail.)

To some, it took on architectural form, a house or palace with halls and twisting passageways, a "magic theater," a "cerebral museum."[20] Others described a pathway, a perplexing labyrinth, a "tender garden of

divine bliss," an "artificial paradise."[21] Still others encountered wildly allegorical landscapes with fountains and "pearly depths of the infinite."[22] Huxley compared the placeless place to a terra incognita: "Like the earth of a hundred years ago, our mind still has its darkest Africas, its unmapped Borneos and Amazonian basins.... We are out of the Old World, and exploring the antipodes."[23]

But modern times and modern drugs demanded modern metaphors. The psychedelic experience went beyond conventional notions of geography or architecture and suggested something closer to a web of energy. Osmond wrote of a "shimmering filigree of the finest silver mesh," while behavioral psychologist Heinrich Klüver described a "lattice" or "honeycomb."[24] Michaux characterized it as a "crumblejumble" of gestation, transformation, and multiplication.[25] While less picturesque than a castle or a garden pathway, this kind of imagery was better suited to the turbulent impressions that writers found so difficult to describe. Alan Watts saw LSD's multisensory effect as a unified field in which organism and environment somehow wove themselves together in what he called an enchanted loom. "Light, sound, touch, taste, and smell become a continuous warp," wrote Watts. "Shape becomes color, which becomes vibration, which becomes sound, which becomes smell, which becomes taste, and then touch, and then again shape."[26]

Watts's associates at Harvard's Center for Personality Research agreed. Synchronicity was the password of the day. Each and every sensation appeared interlocked in a "billion-fold avalanche of neurological activity," wrote Leary.[27] "Symbolic thoughts fuse with somatic-tissue events. Ideas combine with memories—personal, cellular, evolutionary, embryonic—thoughts collapse into molecular patterns."[28] Watts even tried to demonstrate what these interwoven veils looked like by illustrating his psychedelic memoir, *The Joyous Cosmology*, with close-up photographs of crystal formations, the skeletal structure of a leaf, and the spiraling strands of a clematis plant in fructification.[29] About the same time, Michaux, conceding the limitations of prose, began to set down his mescaline impressions in a wordless writing, using pen-and-ink hieroglyphs and repetitive scratchings on paper—some surprisingly similar to Watts's imagery—while Leary illustrated his essays with dense, cellular patterns to help his readers comprehend the varying levels of somatic energy experienced on LSD.

TIME CHAMBER

One thing became clear during the early period of psychedelic experimentation: extraordinary experiences demanded extraordinary settings. The return to normalcy after a psychedelic journey was something of a shock, and there was good reason that the end of a trip came to be known as *crashing*. Even the most clinical researchers understood the importance of "set and setting." How was one expected to return to the routines of everyday life after a journey to the deepest recesses of inner space? The sense of communal oneness was gone, synchronicity and cosmic connectivity broken. "The satori doesn't

ABOVE LEFT: *Alan Watts, geographer of inner space.*

RIGHT: *Fructification of Clematis, illustration in Watts's* The Joyous Cosmology.

PREVIOUS PAGES
P. 16: *Solar, cellular, somatic and sensory levels of energy (Leary).*
P. 18 UPPER: *Visiting the "cerebral museum"*; LOWER: *Henri Michaux,* Mescaline Drawing, *1955.*
P. 19: *Time Chamber, Newton Center, Massachusetts, 1963.*

seem to last," said Leary, wondering how such revelatory states might be prolonged. "How could I be consumed by ecstasies undreamed of by oriental kings and return to my Harvard square office the next morning?"[30]

Up to that point, test subjects had been treated like lab rats, strapped to a cot, injected with liquid LSD, and placed under observation beneath bright fluorescent lighting. Harsh settings would alienate the subject and provoke paranoid reactions. "The atmosphere should be homelike rather than clinical," wrote Watts, who felt that the new drugs should be treated as religious sacraments.[31] He envisioned a specially designed building, a kind of retreat house, far removed from the precincts of the hospital, a place where subjects felt sheltered and safe.

Alfred M. Hubbard, a former Office of Strategic Services (OSS) agent turned psychedelic missionary, was one of the first to explore the possibilities of setting. As early as 1958 he was treating patients in a specially designed session room that came to be known as a "Hubbard Room." It was furnished with throw pillows, a comfortable couch, low levels of lighting, and a hi-fi system to play soothing music.[32] Hubbard selected suggestive imagery in accordance with the personality of each subject. "Someone uptight may be asked to look at a photo of a glacier, which would soon melt into blissful relaxation," he explained.[33] A copy of Salvador Dalí's *Last Supper* hung on one wall, and Gauguin's *Buddha* on another. There was also a small altar at one end, with candles and a statue of the Virgin Mary. The religious imagery helped Hubbard guide his subjects toward a deeper therapeutic experience.

Leary and his colleagues in the Harvard Psilocybin Project were reaching the same conclusions. They started running controlled sessions in aesthetically pleasing surroundings that were free from accidental interruption and "secular distraction."[34] "If your concept of 'real estate' is neurological rather than mammalian, then your habitat defines your launching pad," wrote Leary. Conventional furniture was replaced with low, softly contoured seating. Candles replaced electric lighting.

The new radical consciousness cried out for a different approach to space, so Leary and his research team moved their experiments off campus into a rambling old house in Newton Center, a suburb of Boston. In the fall of 1962 they began to experiment with multifamily living.[35] There were twelve full-time residents, including Leary, his two children, Richard Alpert, and Ralph and Susan Metzner. Several other friends, including Alan Watts, Charles Olson, Allen Ginsberg, and heiress Peggy Hitchcock, came and went like spirits in the night. Leary described their homestead as a *psychlotron*, a place where social conditioning and past histories could be effectively obliterated. "That place to which you return becomes neurologically engraved in your subsequent consciousness," he wrote. "It is a new 'home'—a new neurological center."[36]

Traditional concepts of "room," "home," "family," and "community" were reconfigured. Walls were adorned with Rorschach ink blots and collages done under hallucinogenic influence. Red velvet cushions were scattered across the floor. Guests would take LSD and sit in a circle on a grass-green rug. A statue of the Buddha—donated by Peggy Hitchcock—sat at one end of the room. A flickering Moroccan lamp became an object of particular fascination. "[The lamp] glowed and radiated and people would get hung up looking at it," recalled one Newton Center regular.[37] The environmental experiments went beyond throw pillows and flickering lights, however.

"The size and shape of the room make a difference," noted Leary after a particularly rewarding session when everyone sat closely around the kitchen table throughout a blizzard.

LIFE
THE EXPLODING THREAT
OF THE MIND DRUG
THAT GOT OUT
OF CONTROL
LSD
TURMOIL IN A CAPSULE
One dose of LSD is enough
o set off a mental riot
of vivid colors and insights
or of terror and convulsions
MARCH 25 · 1966 · 35

n a bad trip, a boy cries in defiance—or for help.

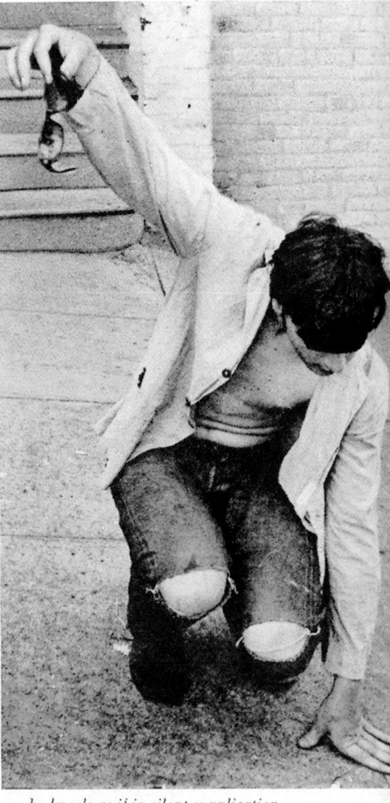

. . . he kneels as if in silent supplication.

Young people must pass through a Superior Court ro
to reach David Smith's makeshift offices at San Fr
cisco General. They are terrified by the sternness t
see in the California and American flags on the wal
and by themselves. Smith knows their terror. Insteac
frightening them further into withdrawal, he slo
pushes his patients to face themselves.

If a user is still "high" on a lingering bad trip, Sm
administers antipsychotic (chlorpromazine) or a
anxiety (chlordiazepoxide) tranquilizers to help l
down. He also treats the physical disorders commor
drug cultures and communal living: upper-respirato
tract infections, hepatitis and VD. Then, he talks, try
to turn the young from the myth that drugs solve eve
thing toward a belief in the active struggle to grow.
patient cannot find reality, Smith urges him to feel
to walk in the park, touching trees if he cannot to
human beings. If he needs further help, the doctor co
sels him as an out-patient or refers him to a psychiat
or state medical facility. His method may be the l
available, but it does not always work. Too many yo

aturday Evening Post · August 12, 1967 · 35c

POST

NAZI LEADER'S SON
WHO BECAME
A PRIEST

TWIGGY SPEAKS O
ON LIFE AND LOVE

DIVING FOR
PIRATE TREASURE

THE
NEWLY
DISCOVERED
DANGERS
OF
LSD
TO THE MIND
TO THE BODY
TO THE UNBORN

The Saturday Evening POST

THE HIDDEN EVILS OF LSD

ew research finds 's causing genetic damage at poses a threat of havoc now nd appalling abnormalities or generations yet unborn.

y Bill Davidson
otographs by Don Ornitz

☐ In Oregon, a young mother brought her newborn baby in to be examined. The child had a defect of the intestinal tract and its head was developing grotesquely—one side growing at a much faster rate than the other.

☐ A mental patient in New York and six young men in Oregon were found to have extensive damage of their heritage-carrying chromosomes—damage of the type that is known to result in misshapen and defective babies.

☐ Two of the young men in Oregon also were found to have a chromosomal abnormality that seems to be identical with the first stages of leukemia, the incurable blood cancer that proliferated at Hiroshima after the bomb fell.

☐ A graduate student in Los Angeles has twice undergone typical epileptic *grand mal* convulsions—one time with seizures so violent that he broke two vertebrae.

The young mother, the mental patient in New York, the young men in Oregon and the graduate student—along with several thousands of new mental-hospital inmates—all have one thing in common. They all took LSD.

The baby, of course, hadn't taken much of anything—except, perhaps, the consequences.

The scientific evidence linking LSD with the baby's deformities,

OPPOSITE
The dangers of LSD as depicted in the popular press.

He envisioned a setting that would guide group consciousness away from the "mundane-local" and push it into more expansive directions.[38] It would be a softly contoured enclosure—something like a submarine or a communal spaceship—with curving walls to foster what he called hive consciousness. Everyone would be drawn together in intimate union, "fighting the pull of the expanding, disintegrating universe."[39] A small room was converted into the "Time Chamber." Doors and windows were sealed off. The walls and ceiling were draped with Indian paisley print bedspreads of "cellular design." The only way to enter was from the basement, through a hole in the floor. One visitor described it as a "gypsy tea-leaf reader's tent," while Leary thought of it as a psychedelic version of Tom Sawyer's clubhouse.[40] Individuals who tripped in the Time Chamber reported losing their sense of time and place. "It was easy to forget, on drugs or straight, where you were in the house or indeed the planet."[41]

But Leary was starting to think even more expansively, dreaming of a psychedelic community where fellow seekers could gather without fear of harassment. It would be a free-form tribe, a "transpersonative" commune in the spirit of Pala, the tropical utopia of Huxley's novel, *Island*. "Like spiritual pilgrims of the past we needed a deserted spot where life would be inexpensive and free from religious persecution," wrote Leary.[42] In January 1963, sensing that their days at Harvard were numbered, he and Alpert founded the International Federation for Inner Freedom (IFIF), a nonprofit organization with the stated goal of encouraging, supporting, and protecting research on psychedelic substances. "Who controls your cortex? Congress shall make no law abridging the individual's right to seek an expanded consciousness."[43] A string of IFIF cells would be established around the world to train guides in the arts of cosmic consciousness. In May 1963 Leary and Alpert were officially fired from Harvard, and a month later, the first issue of the *Psychedelic Review*, IFIF's house organ, was published.

That summer, Leary and his Cambridge castaways moved to Zihuatanejo, a small fishing village on the Pacific coast of Mexico, where they rented a beachfront hotel and turned it into the IFIF Psychedelic Training Center. "The place trembled with old vibrations," wrote Leary. "You felt flesh, seed, and nameless forces."[44] The old Hotel Catalina, renamed the "Freedom Center," sat at the end of a winding dirt road. The central building was surrounded by small stucco bungalows terraced along the side of a hill overlooking La Ropa beach. An IFIF manual outlined the aims of the center: "to liberate members from their webs so that they can soar, at will, through the infinite space of their consciousness... IFIF has come four thousand miles to get away from YOU!"[45] The first group of thirty-six trainees included psychologists, psychiatrists, one stockbroker, a TV actress, a French author, and an actual yogi. (Two weeks of bed and board cost two hundred dollars plus an extra six dollars for every dose of LSD.)

Apart from regularly scheduled acid sessions, there were mind games, midnight bonfires, and sensitivity training sessions in which participants were encouraged to experience oneness with a leaf, a seashell, a pinecone. But the most important ritual at Zihuatanejo was the "transcendental watchtower," a twenty-foot-high wooden structure built near the water's edge. The structure could be seen from every point on the grounds and acted as a focal point of higher consciousness.[46] The idea was to have someone in the tower tripping at all times. A lone tripper would climb the rope ladder, sit on a palm-thatched platform, and stay there in isolation for twelve hours, gazing out toward the ocean. The tower became such a charged symbol that simply walking near it was said to make people high.

SEAL OF THE LEAGUE

To avoid suspicion, the hotel staff was told that the tower was a lifeguard station.

But IFIF's tropical paradise wouldn't last long. When Mexican authorities got wind of bizarre happenings at the Hotel Catalina, they shut the place down and canceled all visas. The group returned briefly to Massachusetts and then ventured to the Caribbean island of Dominica with plans to build an "intellectual avant-garde tourist center."[47] Just as in Mexico, the local government suspected trouble and deported them. A stopover on Antigua also fell through and soon the group found itself back in Massachusetts, deeply in debt and wondering what IFIF's fate might be. In the period of only three months, its leadership managed to get thrown out of Harvard University and three different countries. "We were learning a most interesting lesson in applied cultural anthropology," wrote Leary. "Without a power base (territorial, political, financial) social innovations are relentlessly harassed by all existing bureaucracies."[48]

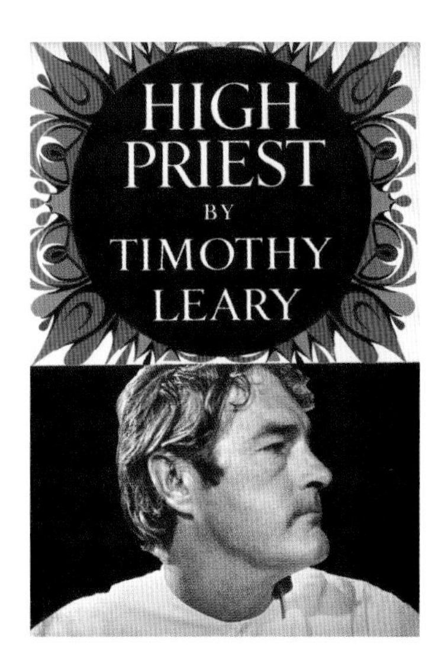

CASTALIA

In the fall of 1963, William and Thomas Mellon Hitchcock, twin brothers of heiress Peggy Hitchcock, invited the fugitives to settle at their sprawling estate in Millbrook, New York. It was the perfect setting. A medieval stone tower, complete with portcullis, stood guard at the entrance. From there, a mile-long driveway wound past maple trees and sweeping lawns up to the Bavarian Baroque mansion. "*Der Alte Haus*," as the original owner called it, was built in the 1890s with sixty-four rooms, two turrets, and several massive chimneys.[49] "The Big House, all boarded up, loomed Transylvanian under its two high turrets and steep gables," wrote Leary, describing his first impression.[50]

At first, it was seen as a temporary way station in the quest for the ultimate island-style utopia, but Leary and his colleagues soon settled in and made Millbrook their official headquarters. Life was ritualized, and the hive dynamic that started at Newton Center and Zihuatanejo was now transferred to the rambling old manse, where it blossomed into an ever-expanding circle of reciprocity. The name of the group was changed from IFIF to "The Castalia Foundation" after the monastic colony of intellectuals in Hermann Hesse's novel *Das Glasperlenspiel* (*The Glass Bead Game*). The big house was cleared out. Old furniture was either delegged and brought closer to the ground plane, or replaced with "harem-style" furnishings, low couches, and silken pillows. The top of an old oak table was removed and set on the floor. One of the living rooms became the main session room. Cushions were arranged in a circle around a candle while LSD tablets were ceremoniously carried into the room on a silver platter and passed around like communion wafers. "It was an ambience designed for soft landings," wrote Leary.[51]

Bedrooms were turned into womb rooms. Bed frames and box springs were thrown out and the mattresses placed on the floor. "On a group trip everyone had decided to throw all the beds out for aesthetic reasons," explained one visitor.[52] Leary took up residence in the turret room that soon became known as "Merlin's Tower." Alpert, the

OPPOSITE
LOWER LEFT: *Timothy Leary holding court at the League for Spiritual Discovery, Perry and Hudson streets, Greenwich Village, New York, 1966 (photo: Ben Martin);*
UPPER RIGHT: *Leary sitting beneath the sacred birch at Millbrook, New York.*

Metzners, and Michael Hollingshead made their own nests on the second floor. Jazz musician Maynard Ferguson and his family occupied a suite of rooms just below the tower room while Art Kleps, psychiatrist and founder of the Neo-American Church, made his home in the medieval gatehouse.

Walls were covered with psychedelic paintings and mandalas. The stuffed head of a tiger—an artificial pink flower in its mouth—stood guard on the newel post. A walk-in closet was padded with fabric and turned into an isolation chamber. Speakers and microphones were hidden in the walls. A disembodied voice might whisper instructions from the *Tibetan Book of the Dead*: "Remember: This is the hour of death and rebirth," or it might quote a passage from the *I-Ching.*

The two-thousand-five-hundred-acre estate became a never-never land of myth and allegory. Weekend sessions spilled outside to a stand of oak trees known as the "sacred grove," where there was chanting and moon gazing. An old tennis building was converted into a meditation house while the chalet-style bowling alley was used for multimedia events. "The bowling alley and the stark pines looked like an illustration from a book of fairy tales," noted one visitor.[53] Further afield was a mile-long lake and a waterfall. During the summer months, trippers could be found swimming in the lake, prancing beneath the waterfall, or climbing the twin hills called, respectively, "Lunacy" and "Ecstasy." "On this space colony we were attempting to create a new paganism and a new dedication to life as art," wrote Leary.[54]

One Millbrook regular who took this statement to heart was Allen Atwell, an artist who arrived in 1964 and tripped with Ralph Metzner in the tower room.[55] A few weeks later, he was painting directly onto the walls of the big house: mystical allegories springing directly from his hallucinatory sessions. "LSD has made me more apocalyptic," he confessed.[56] There were still vestiges of the figurative—torsos, limbs, faceless heads—but these soon melted into a shallow, swirling miasma without foreground or background, what one visitor described as "hot molten fantasia."[57] Atwell's investigations in the big house expanded into a project called the "Psychedelic Temple," an all-around mural that exploded with vortices of color and energy, swirling in eddies and washes, congealing here and there, drifting into corners, up across the ceiling, and pushing into adjacent hallways. The painting would have gone on and on if Atwell hadn't eventually run out of room.[58] But it wasn't just space, or lack thereof, that held him back. While he applied color as energetically as possible, he was trying to capture something so fleeting, so maddeningly ineffable that the medium itself failed him. Paint was too static, too slow to replicate the all-is-one synesthesia that Atwell strived for.

Around the same time, there were glimmers of a different art form emerging at Millbrook. A photographer named Arnie Hendin was working with multiple slide projectors, bouncing images of mirrors to create what one viewer described as "graceful gymnastics of color."[59] Sometimes Hendin blurred the slides in and out of focus or overlapped the imagery to create bizarre juxtapositions—a New York street scene against a field of cows, for instance. "Arnie changed our session room from the inside of a cigar box to the inside of a diamond," recalled Michael Hollingshead, who helped organize the audio-visual events at Millbrook known as "Tranart," short for transcendental art, with the intention of "re-creating an acid experience without the drugs."[60]

At first, these "phantasmagoric illuminations" were little more than parlor tricks, but they grew more sophisticated as other

OPPOSITE
The Alte Haus, Millbrook, New York, adorned with Tantric imagery.

FOLLOWING PAGES
P. 28: *Allen Atwell's Psychedelic Temple.*
P. 29 UPPER: *Lightshow at Millbrook by Jackie Cassen and Rudi Stern, 1966;*
LOWER: *Paul Ortloff, "Exhalation," 1965.*
P. 30–31: *Isaac Abrams, "All Things Are Part of One Thing," 1966.*

multimedia artists came to visit and shared their ideas. A collaborative group called USCO (The Company of Us) used strobe lights, kinetic sculptures, prisms, smoke, and loud screeching sounds to create states of sensory overload. "We try to vaporize the mind by bombing the senses," said one light artist.[61] Rudi Stern and Jackie Cassen were also regular visitors and they combined 35mm slides and super-8mm films in a spacey rush of imagery mixed with vibrating patterns. The frenetic overlay of light and sound came closer to simulating the effects of LSD than any of Atwell's murals. "It's no longer just a question of wielding a brush," said Gerd Stern of USCO. "You can't do it all yourself."[62]

LA HONDA

Meanwhile, out on the West Coast, a different kind of acid cult was starting to gather momentum. Ken Kesey had been introduced to LSD while still a graduate student in Stanford's creative writing program. Following the success of his first novel, *One Flew Over the Cuckoo's Nest* (1962), he purchased a property in La Honda, fifteen miles from Palo Alto, and gave it over to total, living-in-the-moment excess. A wooden bridge led over the stream to a big log house surrounded by redwoods. Inside there was a stone fireplace and a yellow chandelier hanging from the ceiling. Kesey retreated there with his wife, Faye, and his three children—Shannon, Zane, and Jed. A whole gang of friends from Stanford's creative writing program started drifting in—Robert Stone, Ed McClanahan, Jane Burton—and everyone was entranced with the soaring redwoods and moss-covered rocks of Kesey's hideaway. There were also edgier, less intellectual types like Ken Babbs, who had flown combat missions in Vietnam, and beatnik legend Neil Cassady. They began to gather in La Honda around the same time that the Castalia group was settling in at Millbrook, but there was a wild-west anarchy at La Honda that surpassed all the moonlight ravings of Leary's group.

There were no guides or *Tibetan-Book-of-the-Dead* incantations, no group discussions, no proper way to lose one's mind. If, in some ways, La Honda was a back-to-nature pastoral, it was Walden on acid, part of Kesey's "neon renaissance." Ornette Coleman and the Beatles blared through hi-fi speakers planted on the roof. The trunks of redwood trees were streaked with fluorescent paint and the figure of a hanged man dangled above the stream. Sculptor Ron Boise fabricated bizarre metal creatures in the woods. Mike Hagen built a funky lean-to lined with scraps of carpeting and mattresses called the "Screw Shack." Others slept in tents or crawled inside the hollowed-out trunks of redwoods. "I remember that I was up there tripping out and I became conscious that I was actually humping a tree," recalled Steve

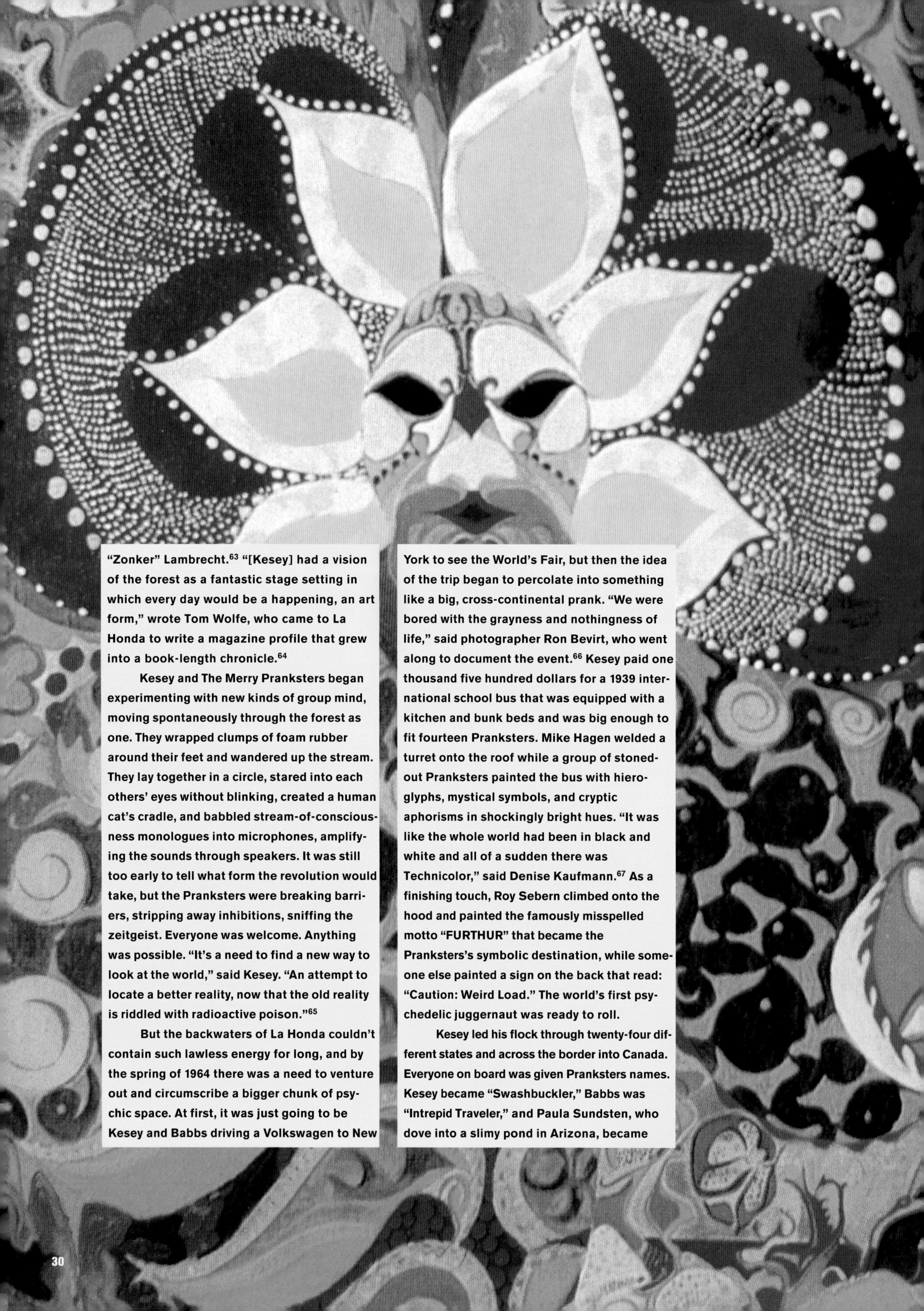

"Zonker" Lambrecht.[63] "[Kesey] had a vision of the forest as a fantastic stage setting in which every day would be a happening, an art form," wrote Tom Wolfe, who came to La Honda to write a magazine profile that grew into a book-length chronicle.[64]

Kesey and The Merry Pranksters began experimenting with new kinds of group mind, moving spontaneously through the forest as one. They wrapped clumps of foam rubber around their feet and wandered up the stream. They lay together in a circle, stared into each others' eyes without blinking, created a human cat's cradle, and babbled stream-of-consciousness monologues into microphones, amplifying the sounds through speakers. It was still too early to tell what form the revolution would take, but the Pranksters were breaking barriers, stripping away inhibitions, sniffing the zeitgeist. Everyone was welcome. Anything was possible. "It's a need to find a new way to look at the world," said Kesey. "An attempt to locate a better reality, now that the old reality is riddled with radioactive poison."[65]

But the backwaters of La Honda couldn't contain such lawless energy for long, and by the spring of 1964 there was a need to venture out and circumscribe a bigger chunk of psychic space. At first, it was just going to be Kesey and Babbs driving a Volkswagen to New York to see the World's Fair, but then the idea of the trip began to percolate into something like a big, cross-continental prank. "We were bored with the grayness and nothingness of life," said photographer Ron Bevirt, who went along to document the event.[66] Kesey paid one thousand five hundred dollars for a 1939 international school bus that was equipped with a kitchen and bunk beds and was big enough to fit fourteen Pranksters. Mike Hagen welded a turret onto the roof while a group of stoned-out Pranksters painted the bus with hieroglyphs, mystical symbols, and cryptic aphorisms in shockingly bright hues. "It was like the whole world had been in black and white and all of a sudden there was Technicolor," said Denise Kaufmann.[67] As a finishing touch, Roy Sebern climbed onto the hood and painted the famously misspelled motto "FURTHUR" that became the Pranksters's symbolic destination, while someone else painted a sign on the back that read: "Caution: Weird Load." The world's first psychedelic juggernaut was ready to roll.

Kesey led his flock through twenty-four different states and across the border into Canada. Everyone on board was given Pranksters names. Kesey became "Swashbuckler," Babbs was "Intrepid Traveler," and Paula Sundsten, who dove into a slimy pond in Arizona, became

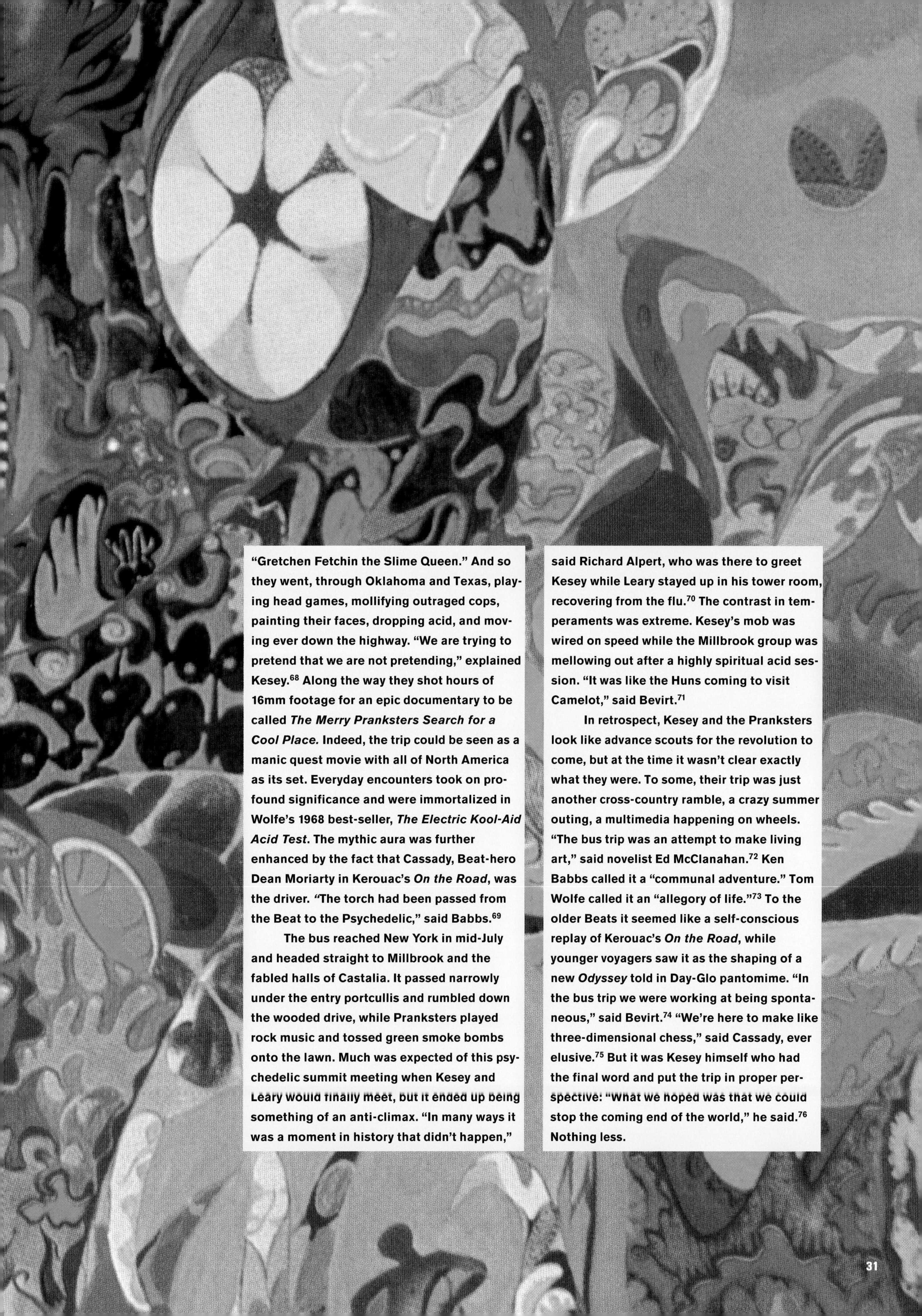

"Gretchen Fetchin the Slime Queen." And so they went, through Oklahoma and Texas, playing head games, mollifying outraged cops, painting their faces, dropping acid, and moving ever down the highway. "We are trying to pretend that we are not pretending," explained Kesey.[68] Along the way they shot hours of 16mm footage for an epic documentary to be called *The Merry Pranksters Search for a Cool Place.* Indeed, the trip could be seen as a manic quest movie with all of North America as its set. Everyday encounters took on profound significance and were immortalized in Wolfe's 1968 best-seller, *The Electric Kool-Aid Acid Test*. The mythic aura was further enhanced by the fact that Cassady, Beat-hero Dean Moriarty in Kerouac's *On the Road*, was the driver. "The torch had been passed from the Beat to the Psychedelic," said Babbs.[69]

The bus reached New York in mid-July and headed straight to Millbrook and the fabled halls of Castalia. It passed narrowly under the entry portcullis and rumbled down the wooded drive, while Pranksters played rock music and tossed green smoke bombs onto the lawn. Much was expected of this psychedelic summit meeting when Kesey and Leary would finally meet, but it ended up being something of an anti-climax. "In many ways it was a moment in history that didn't happen," said Richard Alpert, who was there to greet Kesey while Leary stayed up in his tower room, recovering from the flu.[70] The contrast in temperaments was extreme. Kesey's mob was wired on speed while the Millbrook group was mellowing out after a highly spiritual acid session. "It was like the Huns coming to visit Camelot," said Bevirt.[71]

In retrospect, Kesey and the Pranksters look like advance scouts for the revolution to come, but at the time it wasn't clear exactly what they were. To some, their trip was just another cross-country ramble, a crazy summer outing, a multimedia happening on wheels. "The bus trip was an attempt to make living art," said novelist Ed McClanahan.[72] Ken Babbs called it a "communal adventure." Tom Wolfe called it an "allegory of life."[73] To the older Beats it seemed like a self-conscious replay of Kerouac's *On the Road*, while younger voyagers saw it as the shaping of a new *Odyssey* told in Day-Glo pantomime. "In the bus trip we were working at being spontaneous," said Bevirt.[74] "We're here to make like three-dimensional chess," said Cassady, ever elusive.[75] But it was Kesey himself who had the final word and put the trip in proper perspective: "What we hoped was that we could stop the coming end of the world," he said.[76] Nothing less.

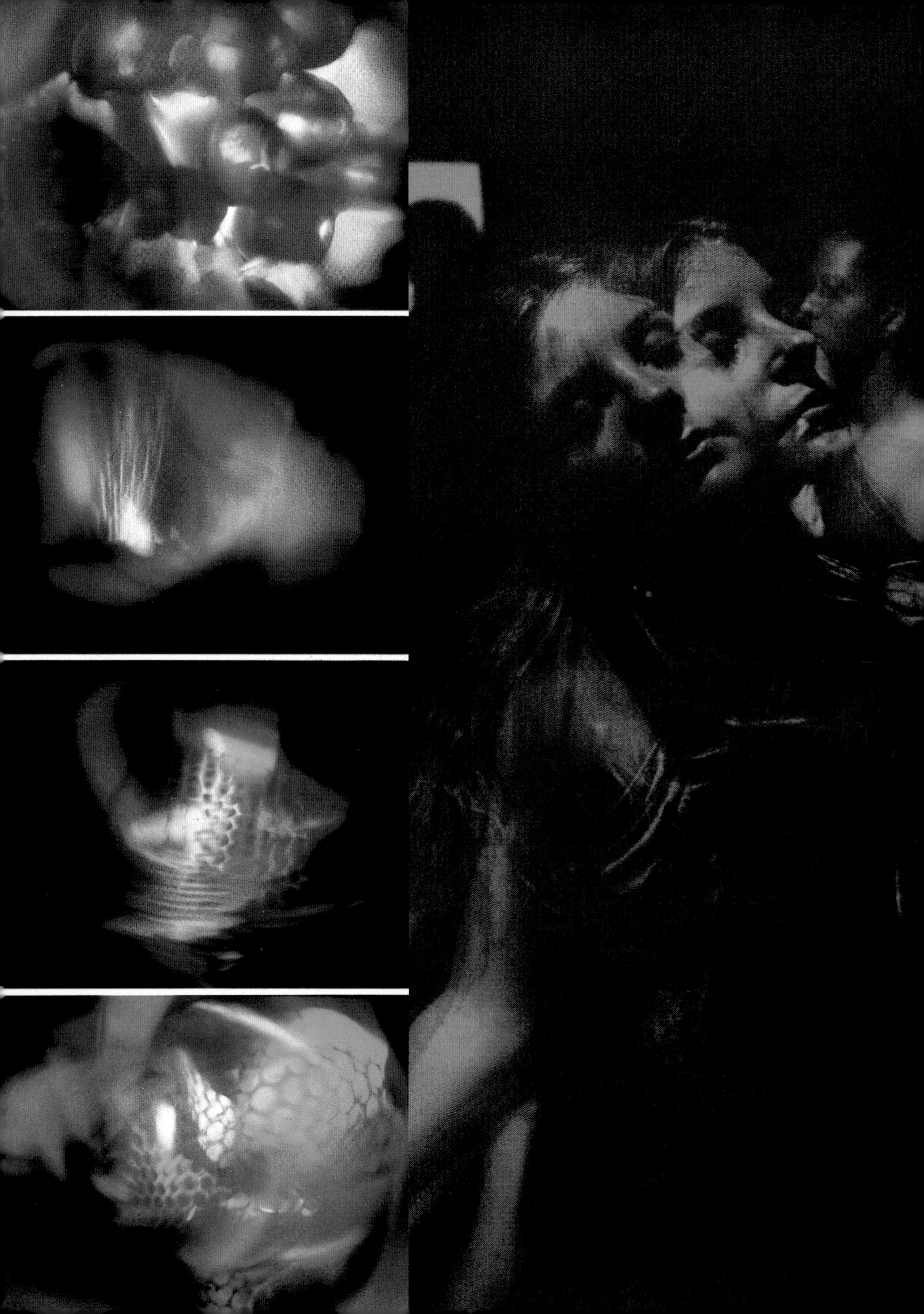

2 INFINITY MACHINES

"WE ARE ALL ONE, BEATING THE TRIBAL DRUM OF OUR NEW ELECTRONIC ENVIRONMENT."

—USCO, 1966[1]

The September 9, 1966, cover of *Life* magazine carried the image of a half-naked man wearing bug-eyed goggles, leaning back in a chair, his face and body streaked with reflected color. The caption read: "LSD ART: New Experience that Bombards the Senses," but what was this strange man doing on the cover of America's family magazine, assuming a place normally reserved for presidents and astronauts? His name was Richard Aldcroft and he was a new kind of American hero, an *inner astronaut,* explained the editors of the magazine. Aldcroft's heightened state of awareness was achieved not with drugs but through the barrage of spectral colors that shot out of his own "Infinity Machine," a metal box—crudely fabricated, but highly effective. The hemispheric goggles were designed to disrupt normal binocular vision. The brain, attempting to fuse the disparate images, produced a spacey sense of disorientation similar to the effects of LSD. The experience could be ecstatically beautiful, or, according to *Life,* terrifying. "The voyager who wants to blast off into inner space has the choice of many routes."[2]

The outer/inner space paradigm was hard to resist. It fit the heady mood of exploration that John F. Kennedy instigated with his to-the-moon speech of May 25, 1961, in which the youthful president committed the nation to a new frontier, one that refocused the nation's imagination away from nuclear brinkmanship toward a "Space Race." There was an eerie parity to the fact that NASA's early space probes and Tim Leary's mind probes were happening at the same time. As Buckminster Fuller proclaimed, cryptically: "We are all astronauts. Always have been."[3] Images sent back from Apollo spacecraft inspired a generation to reimagine the world as a unified entity, a lovely blue orb, undivided by political strife.[4] The space program's goal was to gain the high ground, while the psychedelic movement's stated goal was to reach higher consciousness and open the way to the next phase of human evolution.

The idea of an infinite "mindscape" of interplanetary travel also provided a news hook for the press. *Life*, the publication that had introduced the American public to the space program, would now do the same for inner space, running numerous spreads on the psychedelic subculture. In the beginning, its reporting was surprisingly objective, at times even enthusiastic, compared to negative coverage in magazines like *Look* and the *Saturday Evening Post.* (This may have had something to do with the fact that Time/Life founder Henry Luce and his wife, congresswoman Clare Booth Luce, both experimented with psilocybin in 1958.)

"LSD enables everyone to become an astronaut of himself," wrote Alan Harrington in "A Visit to Inner Space" (1966), a vivid account of the universe he found through LSD.[5] This idea of inner exploration helped to legitimize psychedelic research, making it sound timely, even heroic. Philosopher and acid pioneer Gerald Heard referred to trippers as "intranauts" and believed that proper training was as crucial for them as it was for real astronauts. "One has to have the health and the resistances which are necessary to probe through into a world with which we are not wholly familiar."[6] Leary referred to his subjects as *neuronauts,* hero-explorers, and explained how they should be briefed with all available facts, and then "expected to run their own spacecraft, make their own observations, and report back to ground control."[7]

Allan Watts imaged ways to map the uncharted inner cosmos that surrounded the original nuclei of the world—what he called the "center of centers"—that was as "remotely distant on the inside as the nebulae beyond our galaxy on the outside."[8] In other words, infinity stretched both ways, outward and inward, between galactic and molecular scale, simultaneously, a *zoomy* distance for any human brain to grasp. This may explain the sense of empowerment on one hand—anything was possible—combined with bewilderment and blown minds on the other. "A billion stars in a billion galaxies of space and time is the form of your power, and limitless is your name," proclaimed an underground broadsheet of 1967.[9]

Aldcroft's Infinity Machine was, in effect, a souped-up kaleidoscope with mirrors, prisms, and a lens at one end. A bright bulb shone through a Plexiglas cylinder filled with celluloid strips, shards of colored glass, and strips of shiny metal suspended in mineral oil. The cylinder, powered by a small servo-motor, would rotate at varying speeds while the reflective objects would tumble and dance in the light, mimicking the shimmering filigree of an acid hallucination while suggesting "infinity of mind."[10]

There was something of the alchemist about Aldcroft. He worked alone, tinkering with controls, adjusting his instrument to achieve the optimum effect. "He became the projector," recalled one colleague. "He became the light."[11] Several competing light artists tried to copy his patented system but failed. (In one attempt, the oil cylinder overheated and exploded.)[12]

Aldcroft was one among a growing tribe of "psychic artists" who were employing all technical means to forge cosmic consciousness in real time and real space, extending the body and expanding the mind with all manner of lights, mirrors, goggles, prosthetic head expanders, and other contraptions rigged for optic and aural exploration. It was an unexpected twist in the late industrial age: art and technology combining to produce a new kind of mysticism, echoing and confirming McLuhan's aphorism that electric light equaled pure information.[13] "These Zarathustra machines generate a high through the focusing mechanisms of corneas, through irises dilating and contracting with 3,500 to 8,000 angstroms," wrote Leary. "[They reach] cerebral zones that have never been activated with such Niagras of exploding colors and wiggling patterns."[14] Indeed, the light shows of the 1960s were the first authentic expression of the cellular consciousness that Leary and Watts had been anticipating.

"There are moments when I feel I am witnessing the beginnings of new religions," said Jonas Mekas, director of the Film-Makers' Cinematheque, where so many multimedia artists previewed their work. "Something is happening and is happening very fast," he said. "It has everything to do with light—and everybody feels it and is in waiting—often, desperately."[15] But what accounted for this sense of urgency? Mekas and his friends were flirting on the edge of theology, playing the role of Gnostic initiates who had witnessed the light and now wanted to guide others along the same path. "We must expand our horizons beyond the point of infinity," said one missionary of light. "We must move from oceanic consciousness to cosmic consciousness."[16]

The emerging counterculture would frequently be characterized as a tribe of back-to-the-land neo-Luddites. But while mistrusting the way technology could be exploited for power and profit—to bomb Vietnam or pollute planet Earth—they were not opposed to technology per se. In fact, it was a key ingredient of the new tribalism. "Mysticism is upon us," wrote critic Gene Youngblood. "It arrives simultaneously from science and psilocybin."[17] Norman Mailer saw it in the motley armies of

night who gathered at the Pentagon in October 1967 to exorcise the demons of war. "The new generation believes in technology more than any before, but the generation also believes in LSD, in witches, in tribal knowledge, in orgy, and revolution," he wrote. "Belief is reserved for the revelatory mystery of the happening where you do not know what's going to happen next."[18] The quest for logic was replaced by a faith in the revelatory mystery that came from living in the present, a present that was largely defined by technology.

Boundaries fell between disciplines as everything merged into one fertile swamp of possibility called "mixed media" or "multimedia." Artists incorporated new techniques into their work from strobe lights, fiber optics, and synthesizers to laser beams and an emerging field of research called cybernetics. Billy Kluver, an engineer at Bell Laboratories, produced *9 Evenings: Theatre and Engineering*, a collaboration between engineers and artists held at New York's 69th Regiment Armory in 1966. It was a three-ring circus of interactive art and science. Despite technical glitches, *Nine Evenings* exposed a much broader audience—more than ten thousand—to what one participant called the "initiation rites for a new medium," taking them out of the funky storefronts and lofts of the avant-garde and setting the stage for a more popular kind of spectacle.[19]

Artists such as Alan Kaprow and Robert Whitman had been exploring multimedia effects since the late 1950s, incorporating flashing lights, random projections, mirrors, and smoke in their open-ended happenings. (Kaprow's seminal "18 Happenings in 6 Parts," took place in October 1959 at the Reuben Gallery in Manhattan.) There was also groundbreaking work being done on the West Coast by Seymour Locks, a professor at San Francisco State University, who was conducting experiments with overhead projectors and liquid dyes.

Another precursor was the architect Ken Isaacs who built something called the "Knowledge Box" in 1962. "I wanted an environment that was constructed out of pure information," said Isaacs, who used twenty-four projectors to saturate every inch of the twelve-foot-square box with a sequence of imagery, words, and patterns. In theory, the barrage of information would be transferred subliminally to the brain of the viewer.[20] In one sequence, images of Brazilian peasants were mixed with glamour shots of Elizabeth Taylor. At the same time, an integrated speaker system played sounds of wind, the clanking of agricultural tools, and voices from a group-therapy session. First-time users claimed to experience a sense of infinite depth: "Into the blackness comes a square of cross-hatched lines," wrote *Life* reporter Paul Welch. "Looming, converging lines invite you to follow them out to the end of time and space."[21]

Experimental filmmakers were beginning to produce similar effects in their own medium—loosely termed "expanded cinema"—in films without plots, beginning or end, but rather as non-narrative streams of imagery penetrating the threshold of inner space. This was achieved through a variety of means that included multiple projection, double exposure, and handmade animation, as well as scratching, dyeing, or hand painting the film stock, frame by frame, and even burning it. "I like the ideas of infinity, space, and instant change," said Stan VanDerBeek, who wanted to break away from the spatial restrictions of conventional cinema, away from the "window effect" of the rectangular screen that he found suffocating. "The visual boundaries, the surfaces of the stage, [are] always inhibiting," he said. "My ideal theater is to be of infinite space with no 'edge' to the screen...a total Envelope-Environment."[22] Inspired by a visit to Isaac's Knowledge Box, VanDerBeek built a domed structure in 1964 called the "Movie-Drome" on

All manner of goggles, prosthetic head expanders, and other contraptions were rigged for optic and aural exploration.

ABOVE: *Stan VanDerBeek in front of the Movie-Drome, Stony Point, New York, 1964.*

OPPOSITE
Ken Isaacs and the Knowledge Box, 1962.

PREVIOUS PAGES
P. 34 UPPER LEFT: *Richard Aldcroft gazing through hemispheric goggles, as seen on the cover of* Life *(September 9, 1966)*; LOWER RIGHT: *Haus-Rucker-Co.,* Fly Head, *1968;* BOTTOM: *Liquid light effects by Aldcroft's Infinity Machine.*

FOLLOWING PAGES
P. 38 UPPER: *USCO,* The Tabernacle, *floor plan, 1966;* P. 39 MIDDLE: *USCO (Bob Dacey),* Tie-Dyed Cave, *1966.*

his property in Stony Point, New York, and equipped it with a battery of projectors. People would lie around the periphery of the space and watch the molten imagery of the VanDerBeek's "newsreel of dreams," a collage of incongruous imagery—dead Vietnamese peasants, abstract colors, Karl Marx, a jazz musician—culled from pop culture and the evening news, all churning across the curved surface of his Movie-Drome. (Photographic imagery was sometimes mixed with a kind of hand-drawn animation that VanDerBeek learned while working on the "Winky Dink and You" program for CBS Television.) The senses were overwhelmed in order to penetrate unconscious levels and reach for the "emotional denominator of all men, the nonverbal basis of human life," said VanDerBeek, who proposed a vast network of similar structures to be built around the world and connected by satellite.[23]

The poet Gerd Stern first dropped LSD in Mill Valley, California, in 1963, and it opened up an unforeseen well of creativity. "I became less hysterical for one thing," confessed Stern.[24] As Michaux had learned on mescaline, Stern found his writing became more visceral. "[My poems] started to run off the paper into collage and lights and sounds," he said.[25] Words became objects, cut and pasted, or projected onto walls, stripped of conventional meaning. Inspired by the ideas of Marshall McLuhan, Stern began to experiment with random flows of information rather than traditional narratives. He created his first kinetic environment—"?Who R U & What's Happening?"—in 1963 at the San Francisco Museum of Art. This, in turn, led to the formation of USCO (The Company of Us), a multimedia collaborative that included Stern, painter Steve Durkee, engineer Michael Callahan, filmmaker Jud Yakult, Stewart Brand, and others. "We're going forward to where we were in the beginning... the circle is coming full around," said Stern.[26] They sublimated their artistic egos in

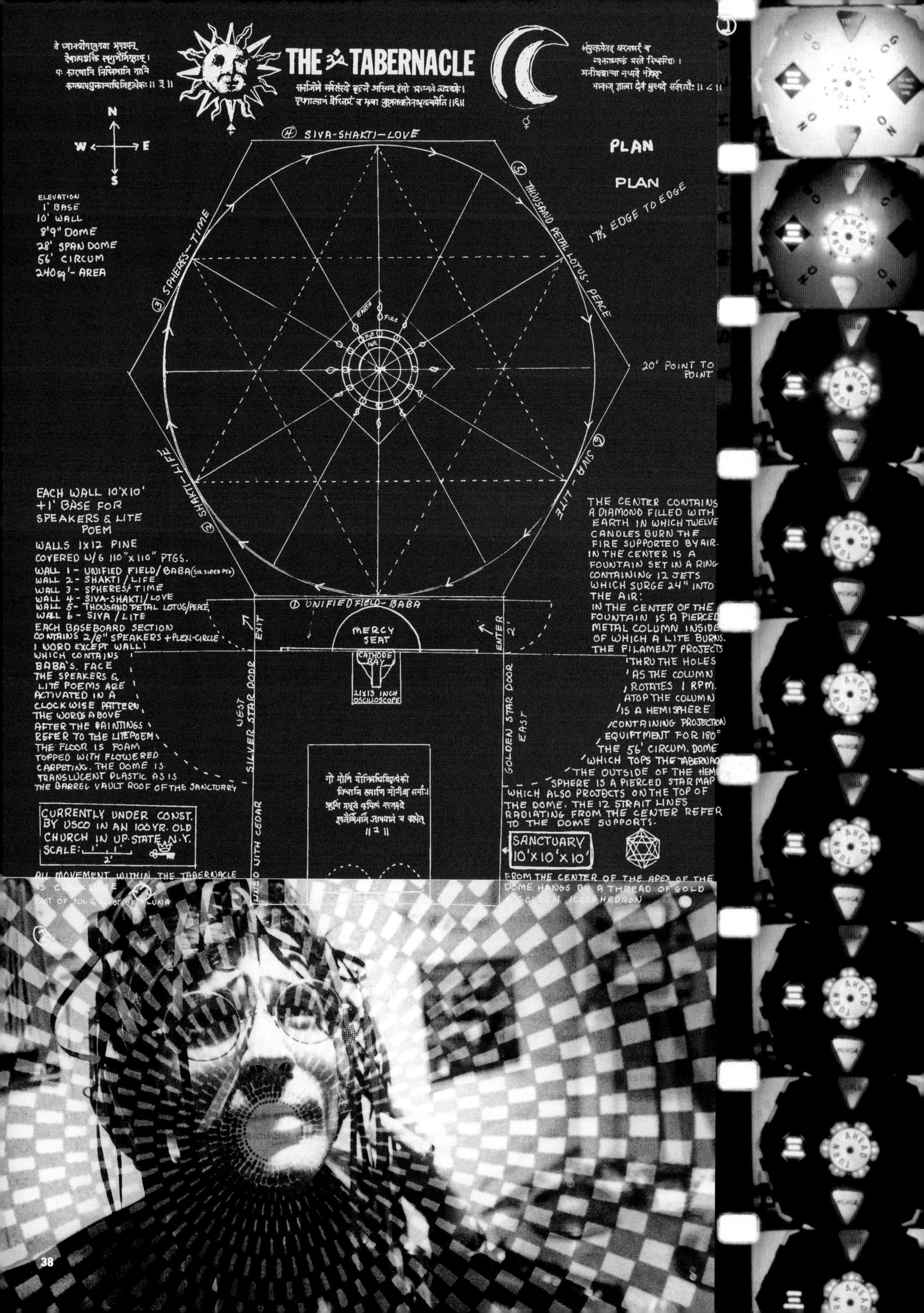

THE TABERNACLE
N
W
E
S
ELEVATION
1' BASE
10' WALL
8'9" DOME
28' SPAN DOME
56' CIRCUM
240 sq'- AREA
(4) SIVA-SHAKTI-LOVE
PLAN
PLAN
(5) THOUSAND PETAL LOTUS-PEACE
17½' EDGE TO EDGE
(3) SPHERES-TIME
EARTH
FIRE
H2O
AIR
20' POINT TO POINT
(2) SHAKTI-LIFE
(6) SIVA-LITE
EACH WALL 10'X10' +1' BASE FOR SPEAKERS & LITE POEM
WALLS 1X12 PINE COVERED W/6 110"X110" PTGS.
WALL 1 - UNIFIED FIELD/BABA (SIX SIDED PTG)
WALL 2 - SHAKTI/LIFE
WALL 3 - SPHERES/TIME
WALL 4 - SIVA-SHAKTI/LOVE
WALL 5 - THOUSAND PETAL LOTUS/PEACE
WALL 6 - SIVA/LITE
EACH BASEBOARD SECTION CONTAINS 2/8" SPEAKERS + PLEXI-CIRCLE 1 WORD EXCEPT WALL 1 WHICH CONTAINS BABA'S FACE
THE SPEAKERS & LITE POEMS ARE ACTIVATED IN A CLOCKWISE PATTERN
THE WORDS ABOVE AFTER THE PAINTINGS REFER TO THE LITE POEM
THE FLOOR IS FOAM TOPPED WITH FLOWERED CARPETING. THE DOME IS TRANSLUCENT PLASTIC AS IS THE BARREL VAULT ROOF OF THE SANCTUARY
(1) UNIFIED FIELD-BABA
EXIT
ENTER 2'
MERCY SEAT
CATHODE RAY
21X13 INCH OSCILLOSCOPE
WEST SILVER STAR DOOR
GOLDEN STAR DOOR EAST
LINED WITH CEDAR
THE CENTER CONTAINS A DIAMOND FILLED WITH EARTH IN WHICH TWELVE CANDLES BURN THE FIRE SUPPORTED BY AIR. IN THE CENTER IS A FOUNTAIN SET IN A RING CONTAINING 12 JETS WHICH SURGE 24" INTO THE AIR:
IN THE CENTER OF THE FOUNTAIN IS A PIERCED METAL COLUMN INSIDE OF WHICH A LITE BURNS. THE FILAMENT PROJECTS THRU THE HOLES AS THE COLUMN ROTATES 1 RPM. ATOP THE COLUMN IS A HEMISPHERE CONTAINING PROJECTION EQUIPTMENT FOR 180° THE 56' CIRCUM. DOME WHICH TOPS THE TABERNACLE THE OUTSIDE OF THE HEMISPHERE IS A PIERCED STAR MAP WHICH ALSO PROJECTS ON THE TOP OF THE DOME. THE 12 STRAIT LINES RADIATING FROM THE CENTER REFER TO THE DOME SUPPORTS.
CURRENTLY UNDER CONST. BY USCO IN AN 100 YR. OLD CHURCH IN UP STATE N.Y.
SCALE: 2'
SANCTUARY 10'X10'X10'
ALL MOVEMENT WITHIN THE TABERNACLE IS CLOCKWISE
EAST OF SOL & WEST OF LUNA
FROM THE CENTER OF THE APEX OF THE DOME HANGS BY A THREAD OF GOLD A GOLDEN ICOSAHEDRON
TURN AHEAD

favor of the group soul and lived together in an old church in Garnerville, New York.

USCO's pioneering infusions of psychedelia, eastern mysticism, and communal living would propel their work beyond the confines of the avant-garde into a broader stream of cultural rebellion. "We are all one, beating the tribal drum of our new electronic environment," read an USCO manifesto of 1966.[27] Under the persuasive influence of McLuhan, they embraced the idea that society was moving away from Renaissance individualism back to a kind of electronic tribalism. (One of their first mixed-media events had, in fact, been performed with McLuhan at the University of British Columbia in 1964.)

Like Stern, they all reached new levels of awareness through hallucinogens. "When you take LSD, all these synapses start firing simultaneously," said Durkee, and this was exactly what USCO wanted in its work, to push spatial and audio stimuli to a point of overload, so that the mind lost focus and began filtering on other levels—as with interactive pieces like "Hubbub" (1965) or "We Are All One" (1967). The goal was a state of synesthesia, the simultaneous perception of harmonic opposites, a state in which sound became color and color became sound.

"In the breaking down of conditioned responses, your habitual patterns of association no longer operate," explained Durkee. "Where you once heard a baby cry before, now you hear five hundred different things."[28] (USCO got so good at this kind of audio-visual bombardment that they were asked to develop an overload program for a group of doctors at John Hopkins who were studying sensory deprivation.)

In May 1966, USCO created a series of psychedelic environments at the Riverside Museum in New York.[29] "Tie-Dyed Cave" was made with color-blot prints on the ceiling and floor. "The cave is where we first lived, and we were trying to go back into that place where all these things were blurred together," said Durkee. "[We wanted] to turn people back into their subconscious—into non-discrimination." The enveloping walls of the cave were painted with retina-wrenching graffiti-vague figures, ghosts, divinities—and at the center was a padded chair, a mechanical hassock, in which people spun themselves to get the full effect. As the chair turned, the imagery on the walls would melt into a hypnotizing blur.

Everything in the domed space of the "Tabernacle," another USCO installation, was illuminated by pulsating rhythms of red and purple lights revolving on the top of a metal column. One wall had a nine-foot-high image of Shiva, the Hindu god of creation. The figure of Buddha was superimposed over Shiva, and lines of energy emanated from their common center. Tape loops played the sound of "Om" overlaid with the beating of a human heart. "It was all construed symbolically and metaphysically on every level," said Durkee.[30]

In 1966 USCO collaborated with Tim Leary on a "brain-activating" light show at the New Theater in New York. Suggestive imagery was projected through vials of colored gelatin, tumbling crystals combined with a cacophony

SPEED
CHECKED
BY
RADAR

TURN ON LOVE·LITE
PEACE
LITE
guidanceecounsellingnavigationand control
is our business

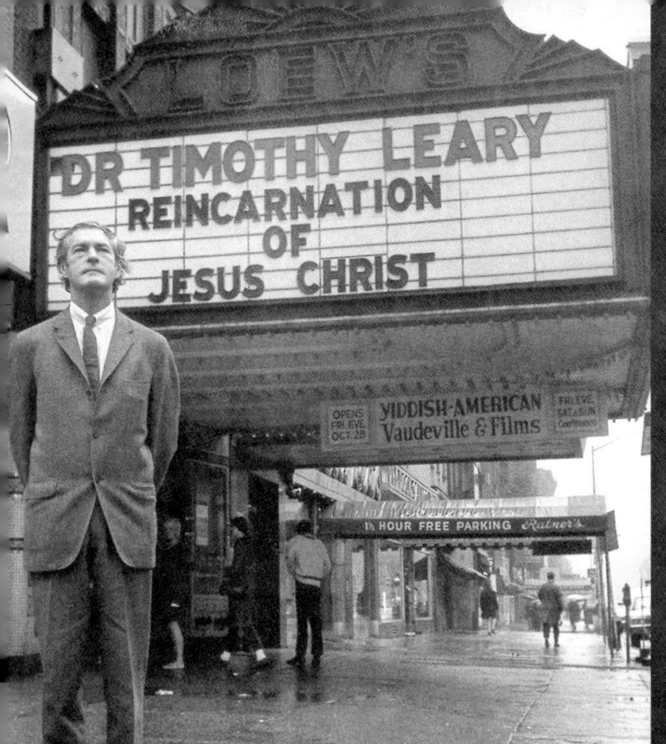

of random sounds, but Leary felt uncomfortable with USCO's free-form anarchy. (Among other unscripted moments, they played a screaming Antonin Artaud tape while Leary was trying to deliver his "Tune in, turn on" homily.) USCO, for its part, felt Leary was locked into old patterns of thought. "He wanted to do things like the life of Buddha and the life of Christ and we said no thanks," recalled Gerd Stern. "We don't do linear."[31]

By the summer of 1966, Leary and his crew were preparing to mount a series of "Psychedelic Religious Celebrations" at the Village East Theater on Second Avenue. This time they chose to work with light artists Jackie Cassen with Rudi Stern (no relation to Gerd Stern), who were more accommodating to Leary's style of performance. The theme of the first evening was "Death of Mind," based on Hermann Hesse's novel *Steppenwolf* and the passages about a magic theater: "entrance not for everybody... price of admittance your mind." The house lights dimmed, and Leary strode onto the stage wearing an all-white Indian tunic, his trademark white sneakers, and a string of beads. Cassen and Stern projected imagery onto three diaphanous veils of scrim, while Leary wandered about the stage, allowing his shadow to flutter against the screens. Ralph Metzner played the part of Harry Haller, the protagonist of Hesse's novel. (The themes of the next two celebrations were *The Reincarnation of Christ* and the *Life of Buddha*.)

As *Village Voice* critic Jill Johnston wrote at the time: "The name of the game is dislocation."[32] Dozens of mixed-media operatives were exploring similar kinds of psychedelic mysticism, attempting to break away from conventional parameters of space and time. "Become one with eternity," wrote Japanese artist Yayoi Kusama, who flirted with the infinite in such mirrored environments as the *Infinity Mirror Room* of 1965 and *Peep-Show: Endless Love Show* of 1966. Austrian artist Walter Pichler produced total-experience contraptions to expand the mind such as "Intensiv-Box" (1967) shaped like a bathysphere and equipped for sensory saturation.

The French group GRAV (*Groupe de Recherche d'Art Visuel*) created "Labyrinths," a sequence of interactive environments that were meant to provoke an altered state of consciousness. Spectators walked or crawled through mazelike spaces while assaulted by flashing lights, mirrors, kinetic-light murals, and other devices designed to disorient, break scale, and create what GRAV referred to as *l'instabilité*.[33]

Following their work with Leary, Stern and Cassen designed a sequence of architectural spaces called Vibrations, which pushed GRAV's idea of interactive labyrinths even further. The galleries of New York's Architectural League were transformed with fiber-optic constructions and light-activated sound patterning to create what one critic described as a "shimmering universe."[34] Walls were draped with Mylar and shiny silver

ABOVE: *Tim Leary plays the Yiddish-American Theater, New York, NY, October 1966.*

OPPOSITE
"Death of the Mind," Leary's Psychedelic Religious Celebration #1, audio-visual effects by Cassen & Stern.

PREVIOUS PAGES
PP. 40–41: *USCO's audio-visual experiments in electronic tribalism.* P. 40: *Gerd Stern and Michael Callahan at work;*
P. 41 UPPER: *The Tabernacle;*
MIDDLE: Seven Diffraction Hex, *1967.*

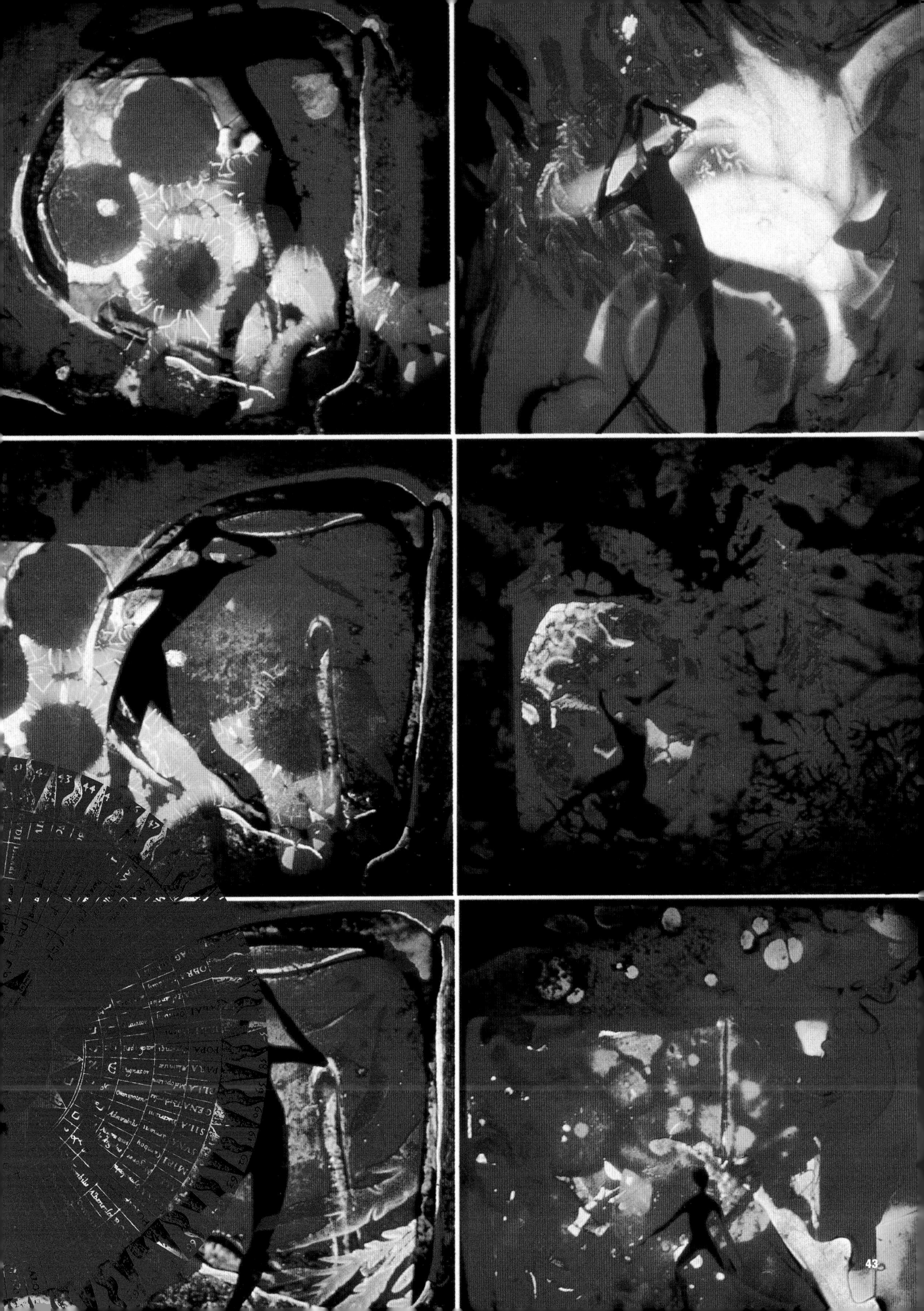

globes. A strobe-lit fountain splattered droplets of water that appeared suspended in midair. Floors were carpeted with foam rubber mats so that spectators could lie down and meditate at any point along the way.

By 1968 these kinds of flickering, cosmic passageways were becoming a part of mainstream culture. Even Hollywood offered a version of psychedelic infinity in the "Stargate Corridor" sequence at the end of *2001: A Space Odyssey*, Stanley Kubrick's 1968 film that became a touchstone for inward explorers. Astronaut David Bowman heads toward Jupiter but finds himself swept into a mysterious force field that hurls his spacecraft into another galaxy. Special-effects engineer Douglas Trumbull used a slit-scan projection system and a stream of colorful defractions to convey Bowman's journey beyond the infinite, replicating a technique pioneered by Aldcroft and other psychedelic artists. The sequence culminates when Bowman is transformed into a higher consciousness, an embryo floating freely in the universe (without umbilical cord) to the strains of Richard Strauss's *Also sprach Zarathustra*. As Kubrick explained: "[Bowman] is reborn, an enhanced being, a star child, an angel, a superman, if you like, and returns to earth prepared for the next leap forward of man's evolutionary destiny."

On May 13, 1968, an event called the Magic Theater opened at the Nelson-Atkins Gallery of Art in Kansas City and was enthusiastically hyped by the national press. It was, explained *Time*, a "trip that will becloud the boundaries separating reality and illusion [and] return the traveler momentarily to his primal, psychic self—all without benefit of hallucinogens."[35] Like Leary's Death of Mind celebration, the exhibition was based on the Magic Theater allegory in Hermann Hesse's *Steppenwolf.* Billed as an exhibition of "psychic art," the show featured a series of eight environments installed within the neoclassical galleries of the Nelson-Atkins. All were designed to disorient and create what one journalist described as a "journey through time to a period before we were ourselves."[36] Terry Riley's "Time-Lag Accumulator" was a mysterious octagon of semitransparent glass equipped with flashing strobes and microphones that reorchestrated random noises—conversations, chatter, whistles—and played them back as indecipherable "sound webs."[37] Robert Whitman's Vibrating Mirror Room was made from elasticized bathing suit material and Mylar walls that oscillated at varying speeds. But it was Stanley Landsman's "Walk-In Infinity Chamber" that produced the closest thing in the show to a total out-of-body hallucination. Thousands of tiny lightbulbs were set into the chamber's mirrored walls, and visitors reported the sensation of floating untethered in outer space and experiencing profound insights. The critic for *Art International* described Landsman's box as "a sky of nameless fear which predates God."[38] Some visitors left in haste, complaining of headaches and vertigo. One person fainted, while another fell into a catatonic trance and had to be carried out by security guards.

The passage through the Magic Theater presented a sequence in which pure sensation, disorientation, and hallucination replaced the time-honored hierarchies of conventional architecture, suggesting a radically new kind of spatial experience. There was a good deal of speculation in the press about how all of this would filter into everyday life—at first the possibilities seemed limitless—but as with the drugs that inspired so many of these spaces, the effects wore off. (How often could one subject oneself to the optic abuse of strobes or screeching audio overload before growing blind, deaf, or, for that matter, just getting bored?) The mind-blowing originality was gone. Optic sensations that had once verged on the sacred could now be found around the block at a new breed of commercial discotheque. The ineffable was becoming another commodity.

EXPERIENTIAL ENCLAVES

"It's a psychedelic experience," read the advertisement for a total-environment club called Cheetah that opened in New York in 1966. The cavernous club included a library, a TV room, and a theater for screening experimental films, but the biggest draw was the eight-thousand-square-foot dance floor and the mind-blowing lighting effects that reminded one visitor of "Broadway signs gone berserk."[39] A giant wheel with three thousand colored lights hung from the ceiling and was electronically keyed to the music so that high notes produced a yellowish hue, while bass notes produced a wash of purple. A device billed as the "Depth Perception Machine"—another adaptation of Aldcroft's Infinity Machine—created an array of spectral illusions: shooting stars, color explosions, and other effects.

As the multimedia frontier pushed outward, it pulled a broader, mass-market audience into the fold, and Cheetah was just one example of a new entertainment hybrid that combined live music, dancing, and light shows. Critic Robert Christgau, struggling for the right expression, referred to the new discotheques as *filmotheques*. "[They] blast their habitués eyes as well as their ears. They are designed to add the inebriation of light to that of sound."[40] *Life* magazine, always on the prowl for the latest trend, compared the experience to an "electronic earthquake" and ran a splashy cover story—"New Madness at the Discotheque"—in its May 27, 1966, issue that featured Cheetah and other clubs like Bob Goldstein's "Lightworks" in New York, Le Bison in Chicago, and the Whisky a Go Go in Los Angeles. "You had better wear ear plugs, dark glasses, and shin guards. Otherwise, you may be deafened, blinded, and bruised."[41]

Michael Myerberg, producer of Walt Disney's *Fantasia,* bought three old airplane hangars at Roosevelt Field on Long Island and turned them into a gigantic "flashing bedlam" called The World. USCO was brought in to create a fully integrated audio-visual system using twenty-one different screens and a variety of projection techniques.[42] Most of the imagery on the slides featured abstract details taken from Old Master paintings, while the movies were a montage of 1950s horror movies mixed with experimental footage by filmmaker Judd Yalkut. Projectionists stood on a platform suspended high above the dance floor and directed the sequence of imagery to suit the music and mood of the dancers who consisted mainly of young, restless suburbanites.

ABOVE: *Bob Goldstein's Lightworks Discotheque, New York, NY, 1966;* RIGHT: *Slides from USCO's lightshow for The World Discotheque, 1966.*

PREVIOUS PAGES
P. 45 UPPER: *Ugo La Pietra,* Tubular Environment for Contemplation, *1969;* LOWER: *Stanley Landsman,* Infinity Drawing, *1968.*

SAT
ACT
IS

LIFE
INSIDE DEFIANT RHODESIA
MANHUNT AT SHADE GAP
New Madness at the Discothèque
t 'The World'
ancers gyrate amid
ar-out movies and
ashing lights
MAY 27 · 1966 · 35¢

The World Discotheque, Garden City, NY, 1966.

By 1967 the clubby, teenaged atmosphere of places like the World and Cheetah was turning into something much less wholesome. The music became more percussive and introspective. Hair grew longer, while the clothing went from Barnaby Street gear to loosely flowing garments. Lighting effects turned into blistering bubbles and burning auras. There was on-stage improvisation with trancelike repetition, long drum solos, and meandering guitar riffs. Audience members became more self-involved, giving over their minds and bodies to the music, while their movements on the dance floor were no longer the calculated Bandstand moves of the Frug or Watusi, but a totally no-name, free-form anarchy with arms flailing and heads jerking as if partially detached from the spinal chord.

To the uninitiated it seemed unsettling: so many kids dancing by themselves with a vacant, zombie look in their eyes. The sense of anatomical (and psychic) dislocation was exaggerated by flashing strobes that created the illusion of staccato movements and disjointed limbs.[43] Rapid flashing could also produce "Fechner Color," the optical illusion of a colored aura, triggering in some a trance state, or in extreme cases, an epileptic seizure. "A hand may appear to be simply suspended in space," noted a visitor to one psychedelic club.[44] "Half-blinded, [I] saw nothing till the next flash came, revealing the dancers in a new position, instantly rearranged with no transition apparent."[45] Wildly frenetic gestures were frozen in a kind of jellied suspension, an effect known in scientific parlance as "temporal aliasing." The shorter duration the flash, the slower the body appeared to be moving until it neared a point of stasis.

Journalists and academics came to the new clubs, gawked at the mini-skirted girls, and took notes. What was going on here? In the midst of so much movement there appeared to be a sense of slow-motion hypnosis, even death. "We note the glazed stares and numb, expressionless faces of youthful dancers," wrote sociologist Alvin Toffler.[46] What had started with the avant-garde was growing into a spectacle of extreme unpredictability that merged high with low culture, arcane mysticism with pop consumerism. "Society will seek its communal mythic experience in elaborate intermedia environments," predicted critic Gene Youngblood, while Toffler envisioned a kind of "experiential enclave" in the not-too-distant future that would be managed by a "psych-corps" of special engineers.[47] But Youngblood's and Toffler's enclaves were already shaping themselves on the strobic dance floors of New York and San Francisco.

"A whole Pop industry... snowballed into mass-manufacturing the light show paraphernalia and blow-your-mind stuff," said Andy Warhol, whose Exploding Plastic Inevitable (EPI) was a link in the transition from small-scale happening to mass-market mind blow.[48] (EPI opened in April 1967 and took place nightly in an old ballroom on St. Mark's Place.) New levels of audio-visual synergy were also being reached at UFO, a club on London's Tottenham Court Road, where Pink Floyd and Jimi Hendrix often performed. In Los Angeles there were clubs like The Trip and others along the Sunset Strip that catered to the psychedelic scene. But it was farther north, in San Francisco, where the art form truly flourished. As Bill Ham, a pioneer of West Coast psychedelia, put it: "San Francisco was the Paris of lightshows."[49] Every acid rock concert was accompanied by a lightshow, and some of the groups, such as Ham's own Light Sound Dimension (L.S.D.), were as much of a draw as the bands.

The best lightshow artists achieved a kind of poetic luminosity. Tony Martin, a painter in his own right, developed a unique overlay of color and imagery for the Fillmore

Auditorium between 1965 and 1967. Along with other effects, he worked with two-inch-by-two-inch glass slides painted and scratched by hand. In some cases, he would sandwich found materials—string, tobacco, lace, butterfly wings—between the glass plates like biology specimens.[50] Mark Boyle and Joan Hills incorporated burning slides, live worms, and acid poured over zinc in their wildly combustive performances in London. One American team boasted that it could "peel the paint off the wall" with ten thousand watts of projected light.[51] Some groups were very casual about the sequence of their shows, while others had tightly scripted routines and worked with customized control panels to orchestrate a range of effects. Single Wing Turquoise Bird worked with thirty-six different projectors, including a giant xenon-arc film projector with asynchronous color and strobe wheels attached. The Joshua Light Show worked a complicated rear-projection system backstage at the Fillmore East in New York. Others used smoke machines, oscilloscopes, black lights, color wheels, liquid crystal projectors, and homemade kaleidoscopes. Overhead projectors, like the Dukanes 7800, allowed light artists to improvise freely with the musicians onstage. "The difference with the overhead projector is that you can work in the present [and] that's a whole other trip," said Ham, who would mix vegetable dyes, mineral oil, and soap detergent in shallow glass bowls and jiggle them to create blooming, protoplasmic imagery. "Time-lapse clouds run across magenta bull's eyes," read an account of one particularly lyrical display. "Horses charge in slow motion through solar fires.... Flashing trapezoids and rhomboids whirl out of Buddha's eye.... White translucent squids wrestle with geometric clusters."[52]

Jerry Brandt, a savvy young agent at William Morris wanted to go beyond the thrills of a mere discotheque and create what he called "*Ultra*-media," a far-out (and profitable) fusion of lights, music, and live performance. It would be a new-age circus, an Electric Circus. Advertising leaflets read: "Electric Circus. Come. (Stoned.)"

Besides live music by the Velvet Underground and Soft White Underbelly, the Circus featured an in-house astrologer, a clothing boutique, and something called the Great Expectations Room, where patrons could have their faces painted with Day-Glo colors. There were also juggling midgets, fire-eaters, and trapeze artists who would perform between sets. Ivan Chermayeff and Tom Geismar designed the graphics while Tony Martin choreographed the lighting effects. Architect Charles Forberg softened the boxy interior with white nylon stretched from ceiling to floor in softly sculpted folds. The semi-translucent membrane of this stylized circus tent provided a two-sided foil. Slide and movie projections were directed through apertures in the fabric to create a dreamlike overlapping of imagery: a recurring red squid, a giant armadillo, and old black-and-white footage garishly branded with blobs of exploding color.

When it opened in July 1967, the Circus proved to be a success with a well-heeled crowd that ventured downtown to immerse itself in the trippy atmosphere. ("Hippies are almost as scarce as Negroes," noted *New York Times* writer John Leo who was there for the opening.) While the four-and-a-half dollar entry fee did keep out many, management lured offbeat patrons with a fifty-cent admission price for anyone coming barefoot.[53] Park Avenue heiresses could rub shoulders with acid freaks and street urchins dancing in the six-thousand-square-foot womb space.

At its loudest and brightest, the Circus transcended the average discotheque and

The best lightshow artists achieved a poetic luminosity.

OPPOSITE
LEFT, UPPER: *Joshua White's lightshow team, Fillmore East, New York, NY, 1969;* LOWER: *USCO's custom-built control panel, inside and out;* LINE ART: *Tony Martin's "Game Room," interactive installation, 1968.*

FOLLOWING PAGES
P. 52: *Ivan Chermayeff and Tom Geismar, poster for Electric Circus, New York, NY, 1967;*
P. 53: *Tony Martin, "Ultramedia" light show,* Electric Circus, *fabric tent by Charles Forberg.*

YELL
RED
BLUE
MAVERICK SYSTEMS
CLOCK RATE

DARLING DAUGHTERS
SWEET MOTHERS DANCE
BLACKLIGHT DYNAMITE
ACROBATS ASTROLOGERS
JUGGLERS FREAKS CLOWNS
ESCAPE ARTISTS VIOLINISTS
GROK GRAPES GRASS
UPS DOWNS SIDEWAYS
AIR-CONDITIONED
IN MORE WAYS THAN ONE
THE ULTIMATE LEGAL
ENTERTAINMENT EXPERIENCE
THE ELECTRIC CIRCUS
OPENS JUNE 28, 1967
23 ST. MARKS PLACE, N.Y.C.
EAST VILLAGE
THINK ABOUT IT.

ut in their ghetto this
The white p
are wagin
the Inner Sel
THIS SIDE UP

OPPOSITE

Tony Martin, composite multi-projector images for Fillmore West and the Electric Circus, 1966–1968.

PREVIOUS PAGES

Tony Martin, hand-made glass 2"x 2" slides, mixed media: string, tobacco, lace, butterfly wings, etc., used in combination with eight electronically controlled slide projectors for the Electric Circus, New York, NY, 1967–1968.

FOLLOWING PAGES

PP. 58–59: *"McLuhan geisha house," Cerebrum club, New York, NY, 1968. Tripped-out clients wear translucent togas and gaze at glowing orbs.*

verged on ritual. When a theologian named James Lapsley visited the club in 1968 he had an epiphany. There, beneath the strobes and molten magic, were hundreds of long-haired aborigines—hot-blooded proof of McLuhan's "world soul"—who appeared to be groping toward group consciousness. Lapsley sat beside the dance floor and tried to make sense of the audio-visual chaos. Surely those pulsing blobs had deeper, nonsecular meaning. Here was a generation of guilt-free children conditioned to participate rather than merely observe (as Lapsley himself was doing). Through layers of color and noise the dancers appeared to be lifted onto a higher plane of experience. "It is a place where Marshal McLuhan meets Sigmund Freud," wrote Lapsley in the "psycho-theological" treatise he later wrote about his experiences.[54]

No one was quite sure what to call Cerebrum when it opened in New York in the summer of 1968. Was it a participatory nightclub? A pleasure dome? A sensory-stimulation laboratory? It certainly wasn't a nightclub in the normal sense. There was no dance floor, no live music, no alcohol. Upon entering an unmarked storefront at 429 Broome Street, patrons encountered a small black room in which a disembodied voice invited them to remove their clothes and don translucent togas. They then proceeded down a ramp into a cavernous space with imagery streaking across the walls. The main space was designed to disorient the spectator, obliterate the normal body-to-ground relationship, and open a door to new sensations. "One is now suspended in space-time," explained the architect John Storyk.

The floor was made from a series of fourteen raised platforms, like narrow, padded walkways, totally undermining the normal body-to-floor relationship. Sexy young women passed out plastic pillows, stereo earphones, glowing orbs, and prisms. Musical instruments were played. Clouds of strawberry-scented fog rose up from openings in the floor.[55] Needles of light pierced the fog like electrons in a cloud chamber. "At Cerebrum one is voyeur, exhibitionist, and participant," wrote critic Gene Youngblood. "One is both male and female. One is a walking sensorium."[56] Participants sucked on mint-flavored ice balls and gathered in circles as guides squirted cream over their intertwined fingers. A weather balloon was filled with helium and released into the air. People gathered beneath the silken fabric of a parachute and waved their arms up and down like birds.

The press came out in force on opening night. *Life* called Cerebrum a "cabaret of the mind" and *Time* called it a "McLuhan geisha house."[57] "The place speaks to the ancient human desire to shed the burden of consciousness, to plug into some warm large Other, to regain the indiscriminate bliss of babyhood," wrote Dan Sullivan, reporting for the *New York Times*.[58] Sociologist Alvin Toffler devoted a section of his best-selling *Future Shock* to the spacey encounters he had that night. "Bubbles drift down.... Hostesses float through.... Random images wrap themselves around the walls,"[59] wrote Toffler, predicting that this kind of simulated environment would eventually take the place of actual experience.

But instead of being the precursor of some virtual utopia, Cerebrum signaled the end of a certain moment. The novelty soon wore thin, and the club closed after only nine months. Perhaps things had gotten too passive or there were too many spaced-out characters lying around, staring at the lights. As *Time* noted, Cerebrum had taken the sensation of being "turned on" to the point of being turned off. Some of the other psychedelic clubs were also slipping into decline. On March 22, 1970, a bomb exploded on the dance floor of the Electric Circus and injured seventeen people, effectively putting an end to an era.[60]

3 CRASH PADS

"A GOOD PAD IS WHERE YOU CAN LIVE-IN AND LOVE-IN AND TURN ON WITH YOUR OWN COMMUNAL 'FAMILY.'"

—*LOOK*, AUGUST 22, 1967[1]

It started somewhere in a whorl of swirling lines and color emanating from the source, pulsating, protoplasmic, spiraling outward like one of Jung's mystic mandalas. Suddenly the air was charged with an ineluctable sense of gathering as in a storm brewing or the threads of a fable being woven around an ancient fire. Through acid and pot, chanting or magic incantation, the most banal corner of the universe seemed charged with Technicolor meaning. Random waves of energy coalesced and transformed themselves into enclaves of bohemian promise and free space. Thousands of young people, "refugees from suburban internment camps," were drawn toward a common purpose, realizing that they weren't alone, making the scene in the East Village and Haight-Ashbury, the campuses of Berkeley, NYU, Ann Arbor, and other places.[2]

Energetic young warriors were gathering in the wings, no longer just errant academics, bohemians, and visionaries, but an international love bomb spreading by contact high and instantaneous absorption by the press. In 1966 *Life* magazine estimated that one million Americans had tried LSD. By 1967 more than four million had seen the light. The revolution was already underway.

"They are predominantly white, middle-class, educated youths, ranging in age from 17 to 25," reported *Time*, hoping to explain how so many disaffected youths had come to scorn money and all forms of ownership, how they shunned work and status and hoped to generate a new society rich in spiritual grace and "old virtues of agape and reverence."[3]

But it didn't make sense. As Bob Dylan sang: "Something is happening here and you don't know what it is. Do you Mr. Jones?" John Gruen, writing in the *Village Voice*, called them the "Combine Generation," which never caught on, while others wrote about "new bohemians" and "neo-beatniks." But this generation was different. Its members weren't wearing the existentialist black turtlenecks of the Beats. Their hair was longer. Their body language was looser. They believed in free love, turning on, and garbing themselves in brightly colored outfits, sandals, and Edwardian finery. (Allen Ginsberg called them the "costumed ones.") "Flower Children" and "Love Generation" came closer to the point, but it was another word, *hippie*, that stuck, covering everyone from fourteen-year-old runaways to fifty-year-old mystics. The term was first used in print on September 6, 1965, when the *San Francisco Examiner* ran a story about a new coffeehouse in Haight-Ashbury that referred to the clientele as "hippies."[4] (While defining a genuine cultural revolution, the word would also limit the parameters of that same revolution. As soon as it had a name, the movement would be scrutinized and, ultimately, trivialized.)

Clothing was free-flowing, diaphanous, and revealing: hand-stitched embroidery with rainbow swirls and tie-dyed sunbursts. Victorian rags were mixed with funky military uniforms salvaged from thrift shops, patchwork jeans, wooly Afghan vests, and strings of beads. But the truest expression of hippie sensibility was wearing nothing at all.

Along with the hair and nudity came a new relationship to space that was at once allegorical, embracing, and nonhierarchical. It was there in the free-form ecstasies and spacey guitar riffs, in the spectral Day-Glo walls of head shops, in throbbing psychedelic posters and tie-dyed patterns, leading the mind away from preconditioned responses past sensual overload.

One thinks back to the early chroniclers of psychedelia, to those effervescent webs and how the quotidian envelopes of architectural space were always bulging or turning themselves inside out. Space, or the idea of space, became elastic, almost acrobatic. A short passageway might be stretched to infinity. A desert expanse might seem miniscule. Old standards of measurement no longer made sense. Old monuments and institutions were meaningless. Anywhere became everywhere.

The new mental landscape had more to do with origins than endings. It was about freedom to move anywhere unhindered by spatial restrictions or boundaries. There was constant talk of centering, getting centered, finding the center. "Hold on to the center," said Lao-tzu, while the ancient *I-Ching* spoke of innumerable centers in its enigmatic hexagrams, vague enough to serve every occasion from quiet introspection to armed revolt, but always grounded, somehow, in the mythic, providing soft parameters and points of reference. The corrupt middle-class landscape of picket fences and two-car garages was replaced with something more elemental: mountain, lake, fire, wind. "Fire in the lake: the image of REVOLUTION. Six in the second place means: When one's own day comes, one may create revolution. Starting brings good fortune. No Blame."[5]

No blame indeed. Insights from acid and hash made everyday space seem sublime. Small gulags of hipness seeded themselves within the workaday grid: gathering, grounding, nesting, and remodeling "found space."

America's Outlaws.

BELOW LEFT: *Topless women, San Francisco, 1966 (photo: Gene Anthony/ Wolfgang's Vault);* RIGHT: East Village Other.

OPPOSITE
Crash pad scene in the East Village and Haight Ashbury.

PREVIOUS PAGES
P. 60: *"Grok," Galahad's communal crash pad, the East Village, 1967 (photo: Ben Martin).*

FOLLOWING PAGES
PP. 64–65: *Electric Lotus Head Shop, East Village, New York, NY (photo: Don Snyder).*

Finast
APPLE JUICE
TIME
CHART
AQUARIAN AGE
BEGINS
AGE OF KRONOS
PHILOSOPHY WILL BE ONE
1940 A.D. WORLD WAR II
ALANTIC PEACE TREATY
1580 AD. ELISABETH I
1220 MAGNA CHARTA
800 A.D. NICHOLOS THE GREAT
500 A.D. PISCEAN ERA-CLOVIS
20 A.D. CHRIST
CEASAR
220 B.C. PUNIC WAR
GREECE CONQUERED
580 B.C. BUDDHA
LAO-TZU CONFUCIUS
ZOROASTER
940 B.C. TROJAN WARS
1300 B.C. RAMSES II MOSES
1660 B.C. ARYAN INVASION
2020 B.C. HAMMURABI
2380 B.C. DYNASTY OF UR
2740 B.C. SARGON-MINOS
WORSHIP OF BULL
3100 B.C. RISE OF ASSYRIA
VEDA
PISCEAN
AGE OF HERA
ALANTIC
Renaissance
MEDIEVAL
ROME
GREECE
EGYPT
WESTERN EUROPEAN
MEDITERRANEAN
MARS SHEEPFOLK
ARIES AGE OF APHRODITE
BABYLON
IRAN
BACK TO GEMINI - AGE OF HERMES - INTELLIGENCE
INDIAN VEDAS - BAHRAT - GANGES - BURMA
4000-5980 B.C.
BACK TO CANCER - AGE OF ARTEMIS - MOONSTUFF

Even the streets of New York were ritualistically reclaimed and brought within the circle. There was a flamboyant scene along St. Mark's Place, with alternative establishments like the Peace Eye bookstore and the Electric Lotus Head Shop, the Psychedelicatessen, and a store called Paranoia that featured a "trip room" in the back. The air was filled with incense and patchouli oil as hunkering bands of gypsies gathered in the parks.

There was a vibrant underground press—*East Village Other*; the still-radical *Village Voice*; the *Rat Subterranean News*; *Other Scenes*; *Inner Space*—all covering the street scene and news about the Fugs, Velvet Underground, and other local bands. On June 1, 1967, the Grateful Dead played a free concert in Tompkins Square Park that was followed by a "psychedelic block party" on St. Mark's Place.

New York's avant-garde was expanding beyond a small circle of insiders to large-scale multimedia spectacles by E.A.T., Robert Whitman, and Japanese-born artist Yayoi Kasama (maker of the *Infinity Mirror Room*), who stimulated the streets with "Body-Festival" happenings. Young, good-looking hippies danced naked to live rock music while Kasama painted their nipples with fluorescent polka dots. "Since people in New York are so conservative, so narrow-minded about sex, I want to overturn the conventions through my demonstrations," said Kasama.[6]

On Easter Sunday 1967, the city turned into a tie-dyed encampment as Central Park was claimed by hordes of flower children—more than ten thousand by one estimate—gathering on Sheeps Meadow. They came laden with daffodils, "ecstatic in vibrant costumes and painted faces," reported the *Voice*. "Rhythms and music and mantras from all corners of the meadow echoed in exquisite harmony, and thousands of lovers vibrated in the night."[7]

Several hippies stripped off their clothes and ran through the gathering. Some climbed into treetops and played flutes. Others gathered in groups and chanted *Hari Krishna, Hari Rama,* while Allen Ginsberg, elder guru of new consciousness, floated past, playing finger cymbals. Bonfires were lit on the hillside. Banners fluttered in the wind. The great meadow turned into a mudslide as hundreds joined hands in a circle and then flopped together on the ground.[8] Even the police felt the love that day, surrounded by the non-violent mob chanting, "We love cops.... Turn on Cops." Officers left the park with daisies in their holsters.

But New York was never destined to be a free-love utopia. Life in this city was more about surviving than grooving. Food and shelter were expensive, the weather extreme. "This neighborhood is a bad place to get your initiation into pyschedelics," warned Southey Swede, a hippie entrepreneur who ran the Psychedelicatessen on Avenue A.[9] The trend was moving westward, toward California, to Haight-Ashbury, an "abstract vortex for an indefinable pilgrimage," or what Leary called, oddly, the "largest undergraduate college in the psychedelic movement."[10]

ABSTRACT VORTEX

Haight-Ashbury was the prosaic intersection of two streets in a shabby neighborhood of San Francisco, but it was more than that. By the summer of 1966 it was estimated that more than fifteen thousand hippies were already living there, and thousands more were streaming in. It was easier to survive here than on the streets of Manhattan. The weather was forgiving, and there were lovely parks and low-rent crash pads in the old wood-framed houses of the neighborhood. A village-green sense of place spiraled out from the intersection of Haight and Ashbury streets to Golden Gate Park and the eight-block-long Panhandle. (Another area of the park, a place of communal synergy, was known as "Hippie Hill.")

The "abstract vortex" of Haight-Ashbury.

OPPOSITE
UPPER LEFT: *Haight-Ashbury free clinic.* LOWER LEFT & RIGHT: *The Panhandle, 1967.*

FOLLOWING PAGES
P. 70: *Avalon Ballroom;* P. 61: Berkeley Barb, *Nov., 1967.*
P. 72: *Multi-colored façade in Haight Ashbury.*

There was also the Blue Unicorn Café, the I and Thou Coffee Shop, the Diggers' Free Store; hip boutiques like Mnasidika and Wild Colors; Happening House and the Psychedelic Shop on Haight Street, which for a while became the symbolic oasis of the community.

"Like, wow! There was an explosion," said Jay Thelin, who opened the shop in January 1966. "People began coming in from all over and our little information shop became a sort of clubhouse for dropouts," he said. Homeless hippies were allowed to hang out while tripping. Others just needed a quiet place to lay low. "It was the only place on the street where they could get good vibrations," said Thelin.[11]

There was a series of well-publicized happenings, Be-Ins, street fairs, rallies, and gatherings that helped to further galvanize the feeling of group mind and hippie solidarity. Ever since returning from their cross-country excursion, Kesey and the Pranksters had been concocting new kinds of audio-visual anarchy, applying what they learned on the bus to a series of "Acid Tests" that were, in the beginning, little more than unstructured parties with loud music and free acid. Segments of the bus movie would be shown while the Grateful Dead played, Allen Ginsberg or Neil Cassady babbled into a microphone, and Roy Seburn projected liquid-light ectoplasms onto a wall. The Acid Tests (there were eight in all) evolved into bigger, more organized spectacles like the Trips Festival that took place over a three-day period in San Francisco's Longshoreman's Hall (January 21–23, 1966). While Kesey and the Pranksters were the inspiration, it was Stewart Brand, Ramon Sender (cofounder of the San Francisco Tape Music Center), Ben Jacopetti (founder of the Open Theater), and other Bay Area artists who turned it into a unique kind of psychedelic circus.

Bill Graham, manager of the San Francisco Mime Troupe, was there to help coordinate events and collect admission. (Tickets cost two dollars per night and five dollars for the whole weekend.) The Pranksters directed a barrage of sound and imagery from a tower of steel scaffolding. Kesey himself, wearing a silver space suit and bubble helmet, stood on the highest level, projecting cryptic messages onto the walls:

"Can you die to your corpses?
Can you metamorphose?"

More than six thousand witnessed such oddities as Ben Jacopetti's "God Box"; Elizabeth Harris and her twelve-foot light sitar; Ron Boise's Thunder Sculptures; the "Wainwright Masturbation Sermon"; and something called the "Stroboscopic Trampoline." While these sideshows were entertaining, they were overshadowed by the heaving mob dancing to the Grateful Dead and other local bands, while free tabs of LSD were passed around courtesy of Augustus Owsley Stanley III, a Berkeley chemistry major who was now manufacturing his own brand of high-grade acid. The small, free-form acid happening was morphing into something bigger, mass market, and well promoted. Indeed, the Trips Festival was the first psychedelic event to have a professional advertising firm on its payroll.[12]

The Haight era, for better or worse, was launched that weekend and the kind of rock emporiums that followed were, in some ways, organized versions of the Trips Festival.
A few weeks later, Bill Graham, recognizing

the profit to be made off of acid culture, opened the Fillmore Auditorium at the intersection of Fillmore Street and Geary Boulevard and started holding weekly concerts. Chet Helms and his Family Dog Productions organized similar concerts in the Avalon Ballroom at 1268 Sutter Street. There was also the Matrix, the Winterland, and other venues that started to cater to the emerging San Francisco sound.

The Haight had its own eclectic cast of locally based gurus, shamans, and provocateurs like Ronny Davis of the San Francisco Mime Troupe; Stewart Brand, publisher of the *Whole Earth Catalogue*; Emmett Grogan of the Diggers, the first true political party of the psychedelic nation; poet Richard Brautigan; and Stephen Gaskin, who held "Monday Night Classes" at the Avalon Ballroom where he espoused his own brand of Acid/Yoga wisdom. The *City of San Francisco Oracle,* the world's first psychedelic newspaper, was "a rainbow of beauty and words" that covered all the latest in the drug/rock/free-love sector, its pages filled with a collage of overlapping imagery.

Agitprop groups like the San Francisco Mime Troupe and the Artist's Liberation Front charged the streets with outspoken dissent. "The foundation of a civilization is growing here," said Peter Berg, a radical activist and founding member of the Diggers, which broadcast its radical ideologies through a series of Dada-style street actions and public confrontations. Diggers organized free food and housing programs and operated the Free Store at 901 Cole Street. Indeed, they developed a total philosophy of "free." "You Are a Free City!!!!" proclaimed one of their posters.[13] "Realize your spine. Man, woman, reborn Free. Grow into a Free Form. A Free City is a gathering of free people."

For the most part, the Diggers remained anonymous, preferring to stimulate social change through a series of cryptic statements and mini manifestos stapled to trees and telephone poles around San Francisco. (These were often disseminated by Chester Anderson and his enigmatic Communication Company.) One broadsheet encouraged the masses to meet at the corner of Haight and Masonic streets and obstruct traffic by walking, crawling, or hopping back and forth across the intersection in a funky communal dance: "umbrella step, stroll, cake-walk, sombersault [sic], finger-crawl, squat-jump, pilgrimage, philly dog, etc." By about six in the evening, six hundred were blocking the intersection and disrupting traffic. The police arrived on the scene and arrested several participants, including five Diggers.

On another occasion the group presented the mayor of San Francisco with a five-point course of action demanding that all uninhabited buildings be turned into free housing; that all parks and other public spaces be returned to the people for "free life acts"; and that all current park restrictions be rescinded immediately.[14] "Freedom, revolution, liberation pops the cork of imagination," said Berg. "Our part now coming up is to communicate in direct spinal language... to move our minds as sensuous instruments."[15]

The furry clans wove their own sense of solidarity, even a kind of nationhood, when several thousand hippies attended a Love-Pageant Rally in the Panhandle in October 1966 to protest a state law banning LSD. Ken Kesey, who was by then a fugitive from justice, made a surprise appearance and then slipped quickly back into hiding.

Thousands more would gather on the Polo field in Golden Gate Park and celebrate a "union of love and activism" called the Human Be-In.[16] (Astrologer Gavin Arthur chose January 14 as the most auspicious date because Venus, planet of love, would be in the constellation of Aquarius.)

The idea, promoted by the *Oracle*, was to unify the disparate elements of the underground:

Berkeley Barb
204
PEACE
LOVE
LAY, Don't Slay!
NOT POLICE
SEE PAGE 3
PEACE WITH HONOR
LOVE
Peace
PEACE
LOVE
PEACE
LOVE
peace
not
police
PEACE
police
LOVE
LOVE
PEACE
not
police
LOVE
SHERIFF
CONTRA COSTA COUNTY
© W.S. METCALF 67

love-generation hippies, Berkeley radicals, acid heads, college students, spiritual seekers, even Hells Angels. "Members of the new nation will be coming to Celebrate and Prophesy the Epoch of Liberation, Love, Peace, Compassion, and Unity of Mankind."[17]

They came from all over the city, drifting on a cloud of hash smoke, dressed in flowing robes and feathers, talismans, plumes, and bells.

Some carried banners and peace signs, others waved prayer flags. Naked children ran through the crowds. The Diggers supplied free turkey sandwiches. Owsley handed out tabs of White Lightning. The Hells Angels provided security and emergency medical care. The best Bay Area bands—Quicksilver, the Dead, Big Brother, Jefferson Airplane—played for free. Tim Leary spoke. Gary Snyder blew a conch shell. There was no particular agenda. Allen Ginsberg led a sacred chant to the god Shiva. Lenore Kandel read from her *Love Book.*

But it wasn't about the performers on the stage. It was about being there among so many other freaks—as many as fifty thousand by some estimates—feeling a collective sense of identity. "It was the first time the San Francisco hippies walked out of their apartments, walked out into the middle of that big green grassy polo field, and saw each other all together at once in one place," wrote Stephen Gaskin, who, upon approaching the park, was so shaken that he had to lean against a tree and gather his strength before joining the great gathering. "The energy and vibrations were so strong that I trembled and my knees shook."[18]

Rumors had been spreading all week that a flying saucer would be landing in the middle of the Be-In, heralding news of the Aquarian era. A small airplane circled overhead. A parachutist wrapped in white bandages jumped out of the plane and, for a moment, the focus of the group shifted to this apparition floating through the cloudless

YEP, IT'S GOOD TO BE ALIVE

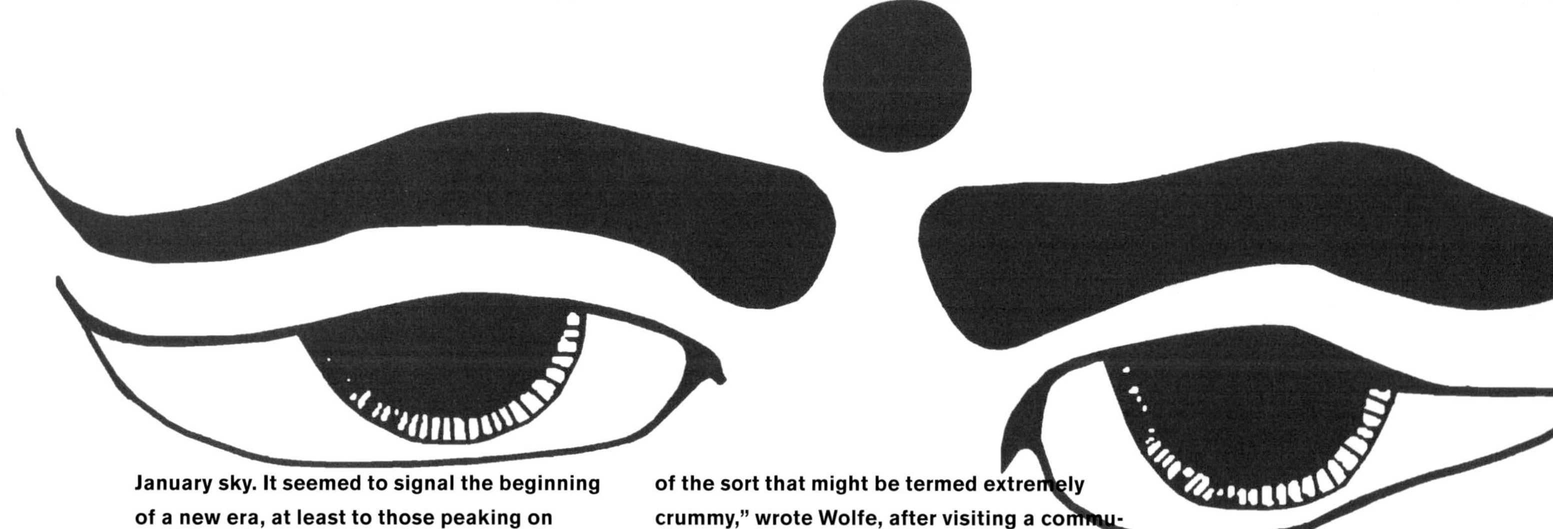

January sky. It seemed to signal the beginning of a new era, at least to those peaking on White Lightning. "We all looked up into the sky with a single ripple of turned heads," wrote one eyewitness. "We wanted to believe in magic that would match the day; and the man floating down on a white cloud was clearly a fairy-tale happening."[19]

The day attained mythic status within the counter culture. "The Human Be-In is the joyful face-to-face *beginning* of the new epoch," reported the *Oracle*. In other ways it may have signaled the beginning of the end since the national press came out in force and soon turned the hippie phenomenon into a titillating, front-page drama. Scott McKenzie's "San Francisco" was released shortly after the Be-In and became the number one pop song in the country: *"If you're going to San Francisco / Be sure to wear some flowers in your hair..."*

After this, the deluge.

CRASH PADS

Meanwhile, the domestic movement was downward. Everyone wanted to sit, squat, kneel on the floor, join hands in a circle, assume the lotus position, sleep, or make love on the floor. This was a major shift, one of the first actions taken in the transformation toward Aquarian living. It signaled a return to primitive origins, to Mother Earth and the beginnings of environmental consciousness as well as a more tribal mindset that would shape so many environments of the sixties. What had started with Hubbard Rooms and time chambers spread into urban crash pads and rural acid retreats. Pillows were scattered across the floor. Legs of tables and chairs were sawn off in what Tom Wolfe described as the "amputated" look. Unnecessary furnishings were limited or done away with altogether, and the floor itself became the primary piece of furniture. "The apartment is all one room, of the sort that might be termed extremely crummy," wrote Wolfe, after visiting a communal crash pad in the East Village.[25] Like many journalists, he was shocked by the ratty decor, the cockroaches, and the broken windows, but, worst of all, by the "flipnik litter" that was strewn across the floor.[20]

The downbeat funkiness of the hippie scene seemed to pose the biggest threat to the established order, even more than the hair and drugs. *Look* magazine characterized one of the Haight's communal pads as being a "filthy, litter-strewn, swarming dope fortress." Walls were covered with psychotic drawings and spooky religious symbols. Rock music was howling full volume from a stereo, and flies swarmed through clouds of pungent marijuana smoke. When sociologist Lewis Yablonsky visited an East Village crash pad he was horrified by the "young zombies" he met there. "Rodents and roaches swarmed all over the mess."[21]

And it was true. Most of the communal pads were crude affairs with drippy candles, broken windows, and backed-up toilets. "Everything was crumpled and tattered," wrote Jess Stearn in *The Seekers,* a sensationalized account of hippie squalor. "Clothes, food, and books littered the floor in all three rooms."[22] Another writer described one hippie hideout as "wall-to-wall greasy mattresses."[23]

How could it be that nice middle-class kids were willing to live in such funk holes? "Why did they give up a three-bedroom house in the suburbs for a mattress in a commune?" asked one mystified journalist.[24] It was even more confusing to non-hippie neighbors. As a Puerto Rican resident of the East Village put it, "We *have* to live in this shit. They don't."[25]

But for many young seekers, the crash pad was a first step toward independence, a place to begin new lives and overcome old taboos of ownership and personal hygiene. Living in such nonmaterialist settings was, in and of itself, a moral statement for those who

"The joyful beginning of a new epoch..."

PREVIOUS PAGES
PP. 74–76: *Human Be-In, Golden Gate Park, San Francisco, California. January 14, 1967;*
P. 77: *Hanging out on hippie hill, Golden Gate Park.*

saw themselves as refugees from the psychic oppression of American society, its obsession with domestic cleanliness, its whiter whites and brighter brights. It was also a *fuck you* to parents and institutions, a move toward self-empowerment, as well as a kind of boot camp in the move toward retribalization. One was forced to give up adolescent selfishness and possessiveness because everything—absolutely everything—was shared, from food to drugs, clothes, beds, bedbugs, toothbrushes, and lovers. However unsanitary it may have seemed to an older generation, a younger generation saw the crash pad as a fresh start.

Wall-to-wall mattresses.

ABOVE: *Painted partitions at the Sans Souci Temple, Los Angeles, Califorina, 1967.*

OPPOSITE
Haight-Ashbury housing with a mandala from the San Francisco Oracle: *"The Meaning of Life Is the Celebration of It."*

Of course it was nothing new. As a place, it had evolved in its own messy way from opium dens, artists' garrets, bohemian digs of the twenties, and the "unshaven rooms" of the Beatnik fifties, but LSD brought a bolder sense of color.[26] "The Hashbury's pads are something else," reported *Time* in 1967. "Most of them sport gaudily painted doors and rainbow window shades."[27] (Some of the national magazines had only recently introduced full-color printing and found that barefoot flower children and their habitats made an ideal counterbalance to the grim realities of war reports from Vietnam.)

It was something of a coup for journalists to gain access to a hippie pad and file behind-the-scenes accounts. One writer gained entry to a communal pad only after hiring a street hippie to serve as his underworld guide.[28] Katie Kelly, a reporter for *Time,* attempted to blend in with scruffy East Village runaways by donning a thrift-shop mini-dress and an old raincoat. William Hedgepeth, an editor at *Look*, went even further and masqueraded as a wandering love child with a Mexican blanket

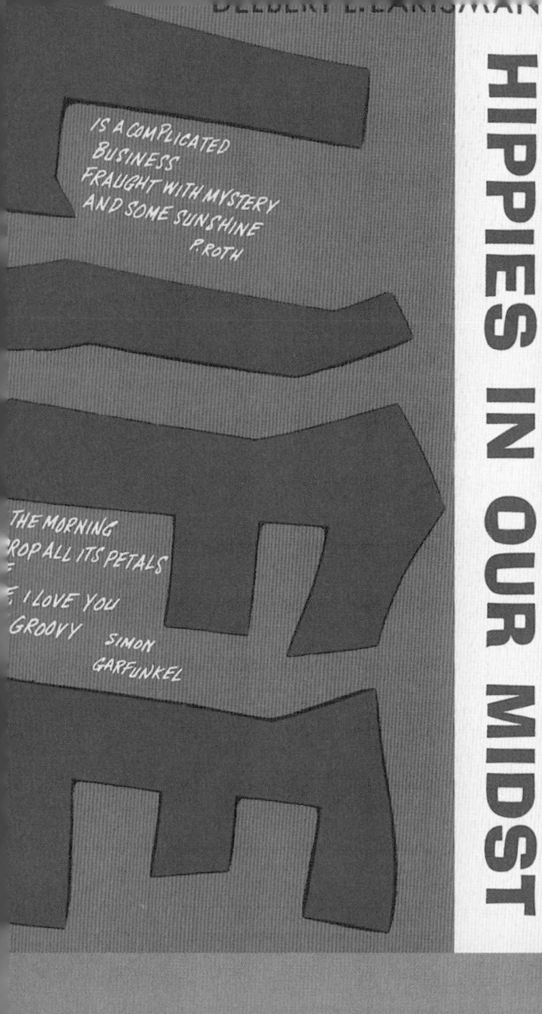

A good pad
is where you can live-in and love-in and turn on with yo
own communal "family."
Editor Hedgepeth (holding hat) is shown with those of his
who were not immersed in the
flowers of the park or panhandling on Haight St.

THE HIPPIES

BURTON H. WOLFE

WHO THEY ARE
WHERE THEY ARE
WHY THEY ACT THAT WAY
W THEY MAY AFFECT OUR SOCIETY

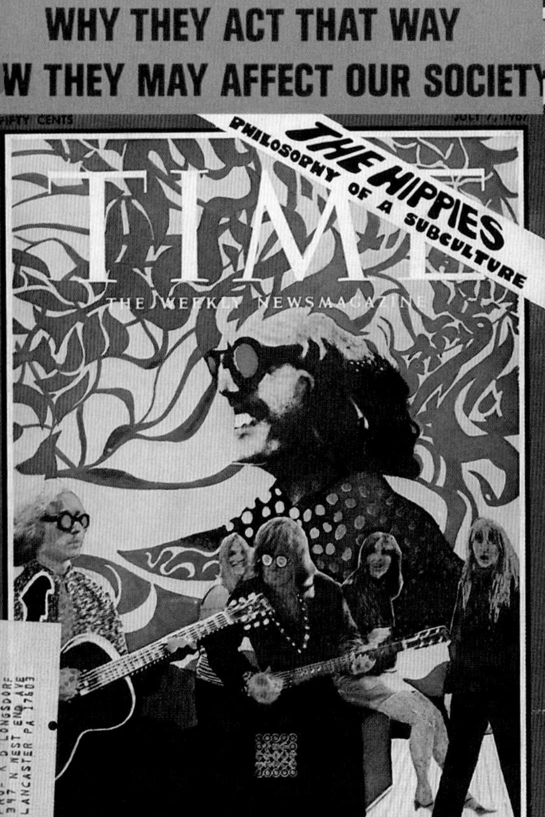

INSIDE THE HIPPIE
REVOLUTION

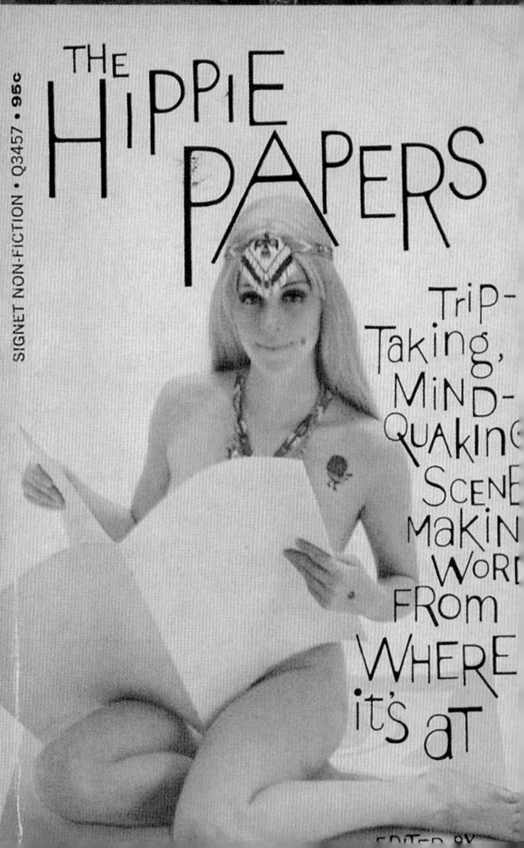

OPPOSITE
Media coverage of the hippie phenomenon.

FOLLOWING PAGES
PP. 84–85: *Galahad's Crash Pad, East Village, New York, NY, 1967 (photos: Ben Martin).*

thrown over his shoulder. For several weeks he lived undetected in a Haight-Ashbury group dwelling, where he shared the floor with an odd variety of hippies drifting in from the streets. One stoned-out character named "The Bat" wore a black cape and squealed throughout the night. "In the darkened bedrooms, blank-faced males and females sat stupefied on the floors," noted Hedgepeth.[29]

In Gerald Moore's front-line report for *Life,* the primitive setting was as much a part of the story as the acid parties and bad trips.[30] Accompanying photographs showed a teenage girl staring wide-eyed at a bare lightbulb, while another crouched in a fetal position on the filthy kitchen floor. The *San Francisco Chronicle* ran a front-page story about a ten-room warren at 408 Ashbury Street and how its walls were painted with bizarre murals. "Although there was little furniture, the flat was populated by fifteen men, nine girls, three cats, two dogs, and two hamsters," reported the *Chronicle.*[31] Joan Didion visited similar digs in her Haight-Ashbury roundup for the *Saturday Evening Post.* "It is three o'clock and Deadeye is in bed," wrote Didion, describing the disheveled apartment of a former Hells Angel turned love child. "Somebody else is asleep on the living-room couch, and a girl is sleeping on the floor beneath a poster of Allen Ginsberg.... The room is overheated and the girl on the floor is sick."[32]

One writer estimated at least fifty communal "tribes" in a five-block area of the East Village, but it was impossible to know exact numbers. Most of the younger street hippies were transient, often squatting illegally or crashing for a few nights and then moving on. Of all East Village pads, Galahad's was the best known, filling three floors of an old tenement building on East 11th Street. Galahad, a twenty-one-year-old Fagin with shoulder-length hair, had come to New York in 1966 and found the city so hostile that he vowed to help other young refugees by creating a haven for homeless hippies. He and his friend Groovy raised enough money to rent several apartments and offer free shelter to anyone who needed it. "People need a place to stay," said Galahad. "They can't walk the streets." On weeknights, as many as seventy-five kids might be found sprawled on wall-to-wall mattresses, while on weekends there were often more than a hundred. "Everybody here just loves each other," said an eighteen-year-old named Sally who wore bells around her neck. "There's no hate. It's just like brothers and sisters."[33] (Galahad's pad was featured on CBS News and in the pages of the *New York Times, Time,* and *Look.*)

But crash pads weren't always as low rent as Galahad's. "When he acquires a permanent pad, either shared or all his own, the hippie takes a giant step upward in status," noted reporter Kelly, who took pains to explain the distinction between the common street hippie as opposed to "householder hippies," who might have jobs and rent their own places, muffling them with goatskin rugs and Indian-print bedspreads.[34]

"Everything in a womb room should be soft," wrote Thad Ashby in an underground guide to crash-pad decor.[35] A surplus parachute could be hung from the ceiling to create a grotto effect. An electric fan could be used to make the walls undulate with air, advised Ashby. "If you have a stroboscopic light you can create the effect of the walls flowing, consisting of liquid."[36]

What started in the mattressed intimacy of urban crash pads spilled outside and embraced an expanding matrix of urban geography. On the streets and parks, in the head shops, bookstores, and free food centers, a crudely wavering notion of place and community, however nomadic and temporary, displaced—at least for a moment—the hard-edged ligaments of the city itself.

4 SOFT CITY

"CHANGE YOUR SURROUNDINGS AND CHANGE YOURSELF."

–SIM VAN DER RYN[1]

A wave of young design rebels abandoned conventional practice and set out to translate their experiences into spatial versions of psychedelic flux, what one critic called "LSDesign."[2] They wanted to liberate architectural space the way musicians like Jimi Hendrix were liberating rock music, to create scenarios in which interiors, even whole buildings, would appear as cellular entities, detached from conventional engineering, floating, almost nonexistent. "The new design ambiguity corresponds to current spaced-out highs by aiming at expanded consciousness through expanded spaciousness," wrote design critic C. Ray Smith. "It is the architectural nirvana of the drug culture."[3]

Even a mainstream journal like *Progressive Architecture* acknowledged LSD's potential as a design tool when it published interviews with several architects who had tried the drug.[4] "Cobwebs, blocks, and binds just disappeared," said Henrik Bull, who solved problems that had been plaguing him for months. "Anything was possible," he said. "The designs were much more free."[5] Eric Clough had a similarly liberating experience when he found himself turning into protoplasmic jelly and merging with the immediate environment. During the next hour he drew plans for a mandala-shaped building as rapidly as he could.[6] All architects reported a heightened awareness of spatial relations and the dissolution of territorial boundaries. "My ability to flow easily with life was enhanced, and therefore my creativity," said Clough, but no one seemed quite sure where all of this might lead. How would the new hallucinogens change the built environment? What would a psychedelic house or city look like?

The idea was to turn everyday architecture into spectacle, to alter scale and break down the tyranny of conventional, right-angled spaces. Lines of sight were skewed. Disorienting illusions were created with mirrors, converging panels, ramps, and staircases that led nowhere. Wall surfaces were penetrated with circular openings, oddly shaped cutouts, setbacks, and boxlike protrusions. Floors were landscaped into mounds and valleys of thick, fuzzy carpeting, ideal for crawling, tripping, making love, or otherwise recapturing an infantile relationship to the ground plane.

"We are gradually moving away from a possession-oriented mentality toward a possession-less, psychic, mind-oriented mentality," proclaimed Norma Skurka, design editor of the *New York Times*.[7] The crash-pad aesthetic—with its sense of primitive shelter, shared space, and lowness to the ground—filtered *up* into mainstream culture (minus the funk and vermin), influencing everything from college dorms and suburban dens to the habitats of prosperous bohemians. Home design was no longer about upward mobility or keeping up with the Joneses, but was seen as an agent of personal transformation. "Change your surroundings and change yourself," wrote architect/activist Sim Van Der Ryn.

A person no longer inhabited a room, apartment, or house, but rather, an *environment.* "Uptight thinking and seriousness are nonexistent in today's underground environments," noted Skurka. Apartments were equipped with noise-reduction insulation and muffled zones of introspection. Ted Hallman wove one hundred pounds of fuzzy yarn into a cavelike "Centering Environment" for meditation. Ralph Hawkins created a soundproof booth lined with fresh moss in which participants could sit in solitude and cast the *I-Ching* electronically: "Formulate, or call into being,

Envirom

ENVIROM is a soft ring of lightweight inflatable pillows designed to bring people together in play, seminars, grou Used by free schools, experimental colleges, encounter a sensitivity groups. ENVIROM offers a relaxing and inex pensive alternative to institutional furniture. Constructe heavy duty 20 gauge vinyl it withstands the toughest use Folds to blanket size, weighs 20 lbs. Seats twenty in co fort.

[Suggested and reviewed (designed) by Sim Van der

Envirom

$60.00 each
plus postage
(20 lbs. parcel post)

from:
ENVIROM
731 Virginia Street
Berkeley, CA 94710

The trend in all-enveloping furniture went beyond mere relaxation.

ABOVE: *Neke Carson,* Man-Moon Fountain, *1968.*

OPPOSITE
UPPER LEFT: *Ted Hallman, "Centering Environment," 1969;* UPPER RIGHT: *"Envirom," Sim Van der Ryn's inflatable ring of transparent vinyl;* LOWER: *John Storyk, "Relaxation Well," 1968.*

PREVIOUS PAGE
Aleksandra Kasuba, The Spectral Passage, *M.H. De Young Memorial Museum, San Francisco, California, 1975.*

your question or state of uncertainty while meditating in the chamber."[8]

If there was furniture it tended to be built in, hidden, or clustered together in multiuse islands or foldaway devices. Conventional seating gave way to soft and amorphously shaped blobs that conformed to the human body. "Sofas are already soft, limp forms that you gather around you and hug," wrote Skurka.[9] Contoured seating was submerged beneath floor level in conversation pits and sunken living rooms. Van Der Ryn created "Envirom," an inflatable ring of transparent vinyl that accommodated as many as twenty in a healing circle, group grope, or sensitivity session. (Envirom could be purchased through the *Whole Earth Catalog* for $60.)[10] Charles Hall, a design student at San Francisco State University, invented a new sleeping concept called the "Pleasure Pit," a vinyl bag filled with water and held in place by a wooden frame. His friends tried it out and raved about their sexy, sloshing encounters, so Hall went into production and patented what came to be known as the waterbed.[11] In Neke Carson's "Man-Moon Fountain," plastic bubbles were filled with gurgling water to mimic the sound of a mother's amniotic fluid.[12] John Storyk, designer of Cerebrum, created a private version of his downtown sensorium by filling a "relaxation well" with cubes of foam rubber that enveloped the sitter in a state of spongy suspension. French designer Gérard Torrens produced similar effects with "Relaxiare," a hollow chaise longue filled with polyurethane balls.[13] The trend in all-enveloping furniture went beyond mere relaxation, however.

Wendell Castle's "Enclosed Reclining Environment for One" was a blob-shaped chamber carved from laminated oak that was entered through a little Hobbit doorway. The interior was a snug, carpeted space with just enough room to enfold a single person in soul-searching solitude.[14] "When you get inside, it's almost like being in your mother's womb," said one visitor, while another compared it to a "free-form coffin."[15] This was the desired response: to feel one extreme or the other: birth or death.

KODAK SAFETY FILM

Environments for Contemplation.

ABOVE: *Ugo La Pietra,* Plastic Environment for Experiencing Optical Phenomenon, *1969.*

OPPOSITE
Wendell Castle, Enclosed Reclining Environment for One, *1969.*

FOLLOWING PAGES
P. 92: *ALEPH,* Stroboscopic Crystal Waterfall Environment, *1969.* P. 93: UPPER LEFT: *Malitte Seating, Roberto Sebastian Matta, 1966;* UPPER RIGHT: *Verner Panton,* Phantasy Landscape, *1970;* LOWER LEFT & RIGHT: *ALEPH,* Stroboscopic Waterfall *and* Egg Environment, *1969.*

P. 94: *Tom Luckey,* Rotating Barrel Room, *Warren, Vermont, 1967;* P. 95: *Aleksandra Kasuba, mirrored floor of* Sensorium, Walk-In Environment, *1971.*

As a child in Denmark, Verner Panton had a recurring dream about a womb room filled with colorful cushions. His padded environments of the sixties were, in a sense, an attempt to recapture a similar feeling of prenatal bliss. "The soft, warm protective cave evokes impressions of the mother's belly, of intra-uterine contentedness," wrote a visitor to Panton's "Phantasy Landscape," in which floor, walls, and ceiling merged with undulating bands of psychedelic color illuminated from within.[16] "Hot" colors glowed from the center, while deep blues and violets cooled the extremities.

The all-white environment—"whiter than ever before"—was another kind of birth/death statement that signified new beginnings.[17] (Procol Harem sang about "a whiter shade of pale" and the Beatles packaged their ninth album in a plain, all-white sleeve.) Whiteness dissolved the architectural envelope while creating a theatrical foil for shadows. "People take on a hypnotic air in the almost weightlessness of the all-white orbit," observed C. Ray Smith.[18]

Billboard-sized "supergraphics" were painted onto walls and ceilings with exaggerated numerals, arrows, and chevron patterns intended to abolish boxlike space through optical distortion and trick perspective. "Supergraphics ultimately blast the inhabitant into an outer space," reported *Progressive Architecture* in 1967.[19] Mylar, a shiny polyester film introduced by DuPont in 1952, became especially popular for its shimmering effects. Peter Hoppner turned his own studio into a "silver happening" with Mylar scales dangling from every surface.[20]

Many of the same effects that had been introduced at multimedia happenings and discotheques were now adapted for domestic use. Projectors and kinetic light sculptures splattered interiors with "electric wallpaper." "Painting with light is a kind of housing-without-walls," wrote Marshall McLuhan, who envisioned an architecture of pure multimedia.[21] C. Ray Smith transformed his own apartment with projected slides. One day the Sistine Chapel, the next day a sunset seen from beneath fall foliage, "when guests come, the lambent light of a lingering meteor."[22]

mirrored surface
water
This is a sectioned view from the side
11-0
4-0
6-0
water

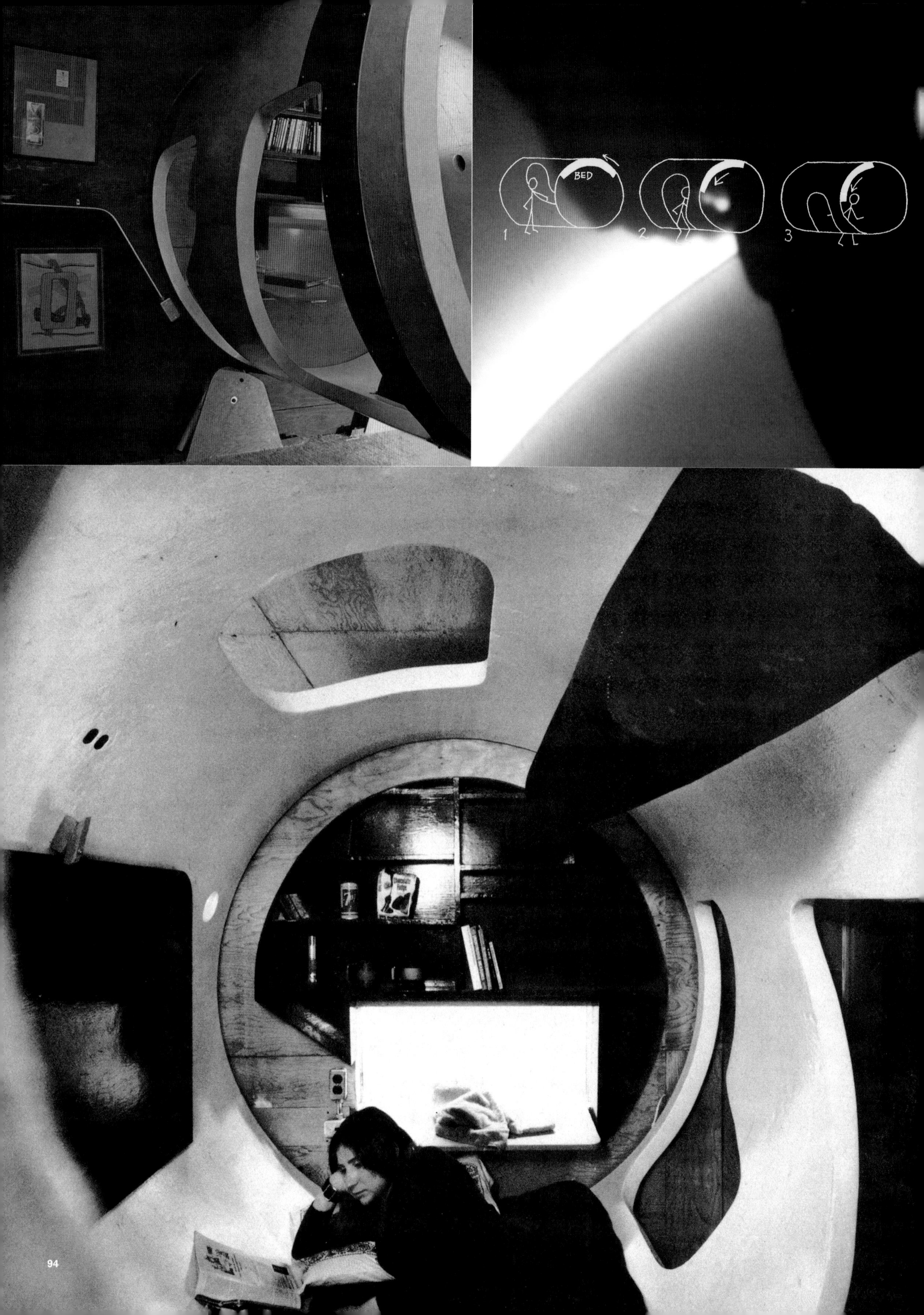
BED
1
2
3

David Sellers and Tom Luckey, former architecture students at Yale, transformed a house in Vermont into a "spooky space landscape" with randomly placed steps, ramps, and narrow terraces that ascended to the ceiling. All surfaces were covered with a sheath of wooly orange carpeting.[23] Quasar Khanh did away with all furniture and turned his own apartment into a "carpeted funhouse," with shocking-pink shag and sunken recesses.[24]

Space could be made to twist and torque with scrims of stretched fabric, as with the "Live-in-Environment" of Alexandra Kasuba, a Lithuanian-born artist who turned a New York brownstone into seven cocoonlike chambers she called "Space Shelters."[25] "The intent was to abolish the 90-degree angle," said Kasuba, who stretched a continuous membrane of translucent white nylon between floor and ceiling and shaped it into softly flowing partitions. "Not a single curve was willed," said Kasuba, who relied on a completely intuitive process of design and fabrication. "Each shape acquired its volumetric expression as if on its own volition."[26] One space, called the "Greenery," was covered with beds of real moss. Another, called the "Sensory," was a spiraling tube of fabric with a mirrored floor that reflected light from above. Here, one or two people could sit in contemplation and experience the changing spectrum of "color odors" that wafted up from a concealed nozzle.[27] At the far end of Kasuba's fallopian maze stood the "Sleeping Bower," a domelike chamber made from yak hair knitted into a cellular pattern that one visitor compared to the hive of an "exotic, heavenly insect."[28]

There was a widespread fascination with "microenvironments," rooms within rooms, and toylike contraptions that promised to turn the routines of daily life into total theater. Lester Walker's "Supercube" (1967) was a multicolored, kinetic sculpture with a bed at its center and walls that swung out to

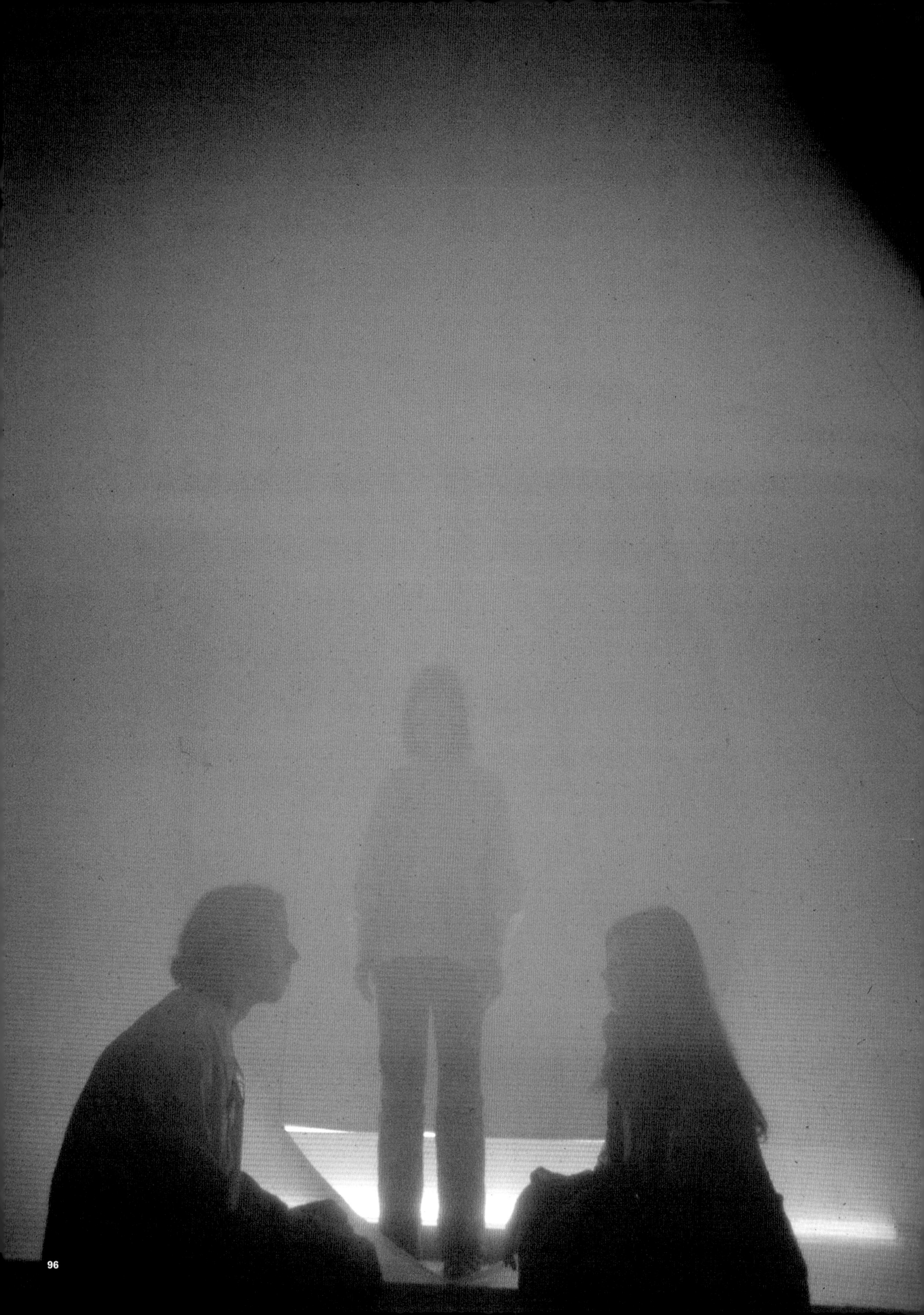

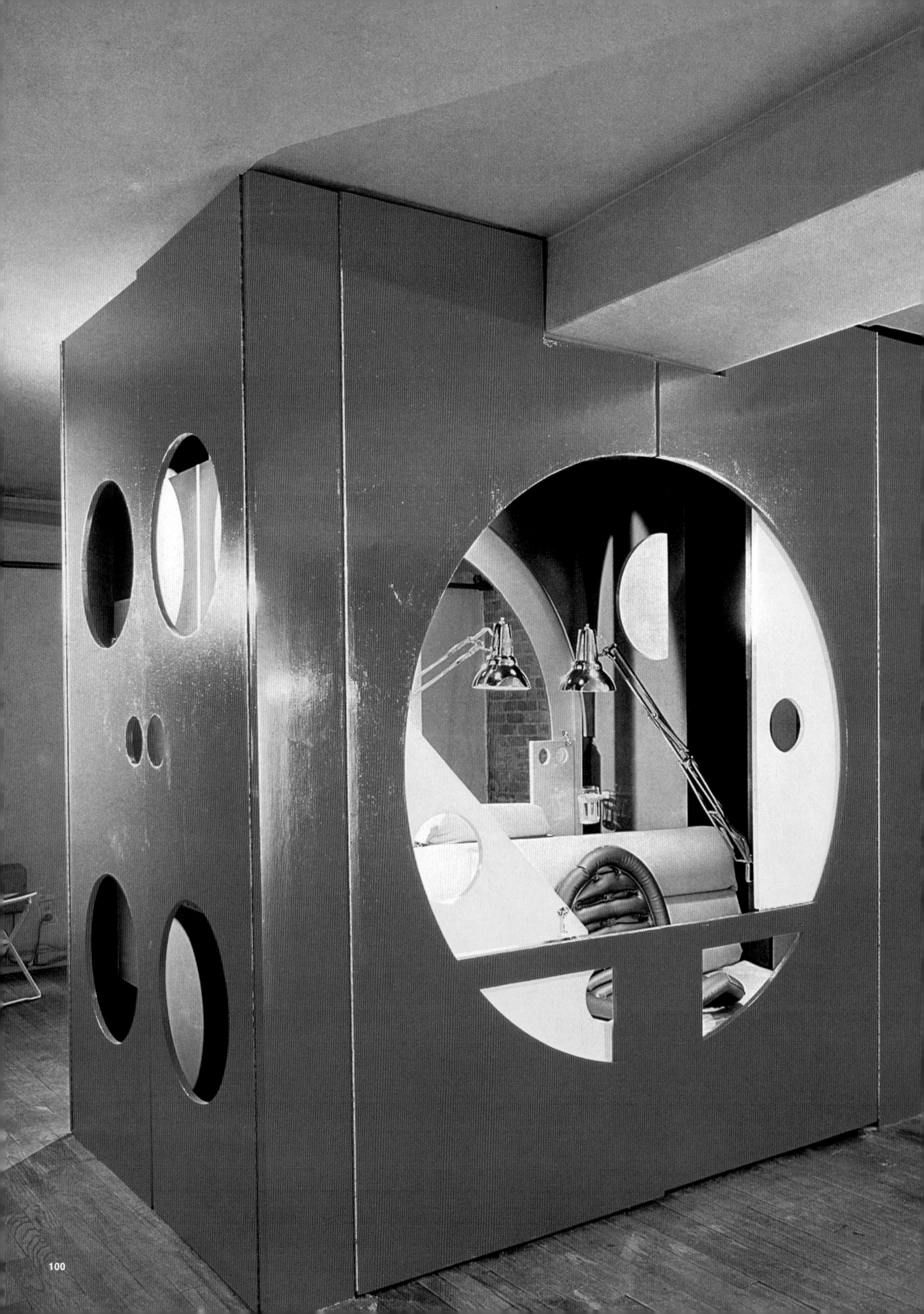

create a trippy range of spatial effects. Michael Hollander designed multilevel "living trays" that ran in and out on ball-bearing tracks and could be arranged in different positions for sleeping or entertaining. Egyptian-born Gamal El Zoghby created a multilevel environment in New York without doors or furniture, just platforms, padded alcoves, and carpeted niches.[29] "I was influenced by Kiesler's endless house and the way its floor, walls, and ceiling all became one," explained El Zoghby.[30] Tom Luckey created a "rotating room" that came close to replicating the spatial transmutations of LSD. The six-foot-diameter cylinder rotated on rubber casters. As it turned, a bed became the back of a sofa, a table morphed into a seating platform, and then a desk, and so on. For weightless sensations, the cylinder could be spun at higher speeds.

WIND-BAGS

The bubble was one of the operative metaphors of the sixties, from bubble gum and bubble furniture to bubble fashion, bubble architecture, and bubble economics. Bubbles were transparent, lighter than air, and hovered with graceful symmetry. They moved and merged in unpredictably skittish ways. Hippies delighted in their swirling surface colors.[31] Thoughts were suspended in comic-book bubbles and, according to Edward Hall's theory of "proxemics," people existed in their own self-contained bubble zones. (When the proxemic bubble was ruptured it could lead to alienation and conflict.[32])

The bubble's soft and cellular structure suggested a division of space that was somehow innocent yet generous in its complexity. Buckminster Fuller was intrigued by the beauty of the bubble's "sphericity." It was lightweight and highly adaptable as either a single cell or in clusters. "It is ephemeral—elegantly conceived, beautifully manufactured, and readily broken," wrote Fuller, whose admiration resulted in a patent for the geodesic dome, a structure that came as close to the bubble's elegant sphericity as modern engineering allowed.[33] Architect Peter Stevens saw the bubble as a model for new communities and an antidote to all that was oppressive in traditional architecture. Within the froth of common dish soap, he saw "miniature rooms," each one different from its neighbors yet perfectly interlocked with those neighbors.[34]

The vinyl inflatable, a more durable version of the soap bubble, became ubiquitous at Be-Ins, rock concerts, and antiwar demonstrations. Inflatables fit the spatial needs of the new consciousness. (*When in doubt, blow something up... with air.*) They were lightweight, inexpensive, sexy, and utopian. They personified the trend toward mobility and expendability. All you needed was a roll of vinyl sheeting, a pair of scissors, and strong tape. Add an electric fan and a naked hippie, and you had an instant happening. "Dogs bark, kids gather, old ladies get uptight, cops drift by, youths take off their clothes," noted Stewart Brand.[35]

"You name it, someone is blowing it up right now," wrote the British critic Reyner Banham, who understood the confluence of forces at play when he proposed the "Environment-Bubble" or "un-house," in which Fuller's theory of "ephemeralization" (doing more with less) and McLuhan's retribalization were cross-pollinated.[36] The astronaut sits across from the caveman, trading stories within a transparent igloo. In place of an open fire stands a high-tech service core for climate control and communication.[37]

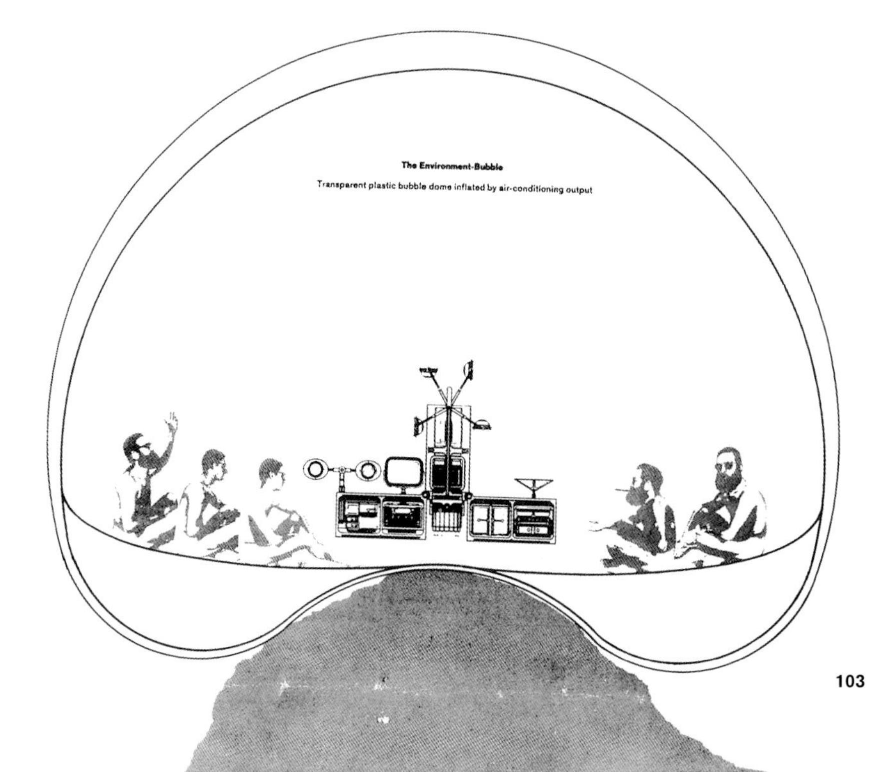

The Environment-Bubble
Transparent plastic bubble dome inflated by air-conditioning output

Bubble architecture.

ABOVE: *Jersey Devil, inflatable environment, 1970;* RIGHT: *Reyner Banham & Francois Dallegret,* The Environment Bubble, *1965.*

PREVIOUS PAGES
P. 96: *Kasuba,* Color Structure *(blue), Potsdam, NY, 1973;* P. 97: UPPER: *Kasuba,* Stretched Fabric Environment for Teresa Sevilla, *1970;* LOWER: *Kasuba,* Walk-In Environment, *1971;* LINE ART: *Kasuba,* The Spectral Passage.

P. 98: *Kasuba/Silvia Heyden,* Sleeping Bower, Walk-In Environment; P. 99: *Kasuba,* Walk-In Environment.

P. 100: *Les Walter,* Super Cube, *1967;* P. 101: *Gamal El Zoghby,* Multi-Level Living Environment, *1969.*

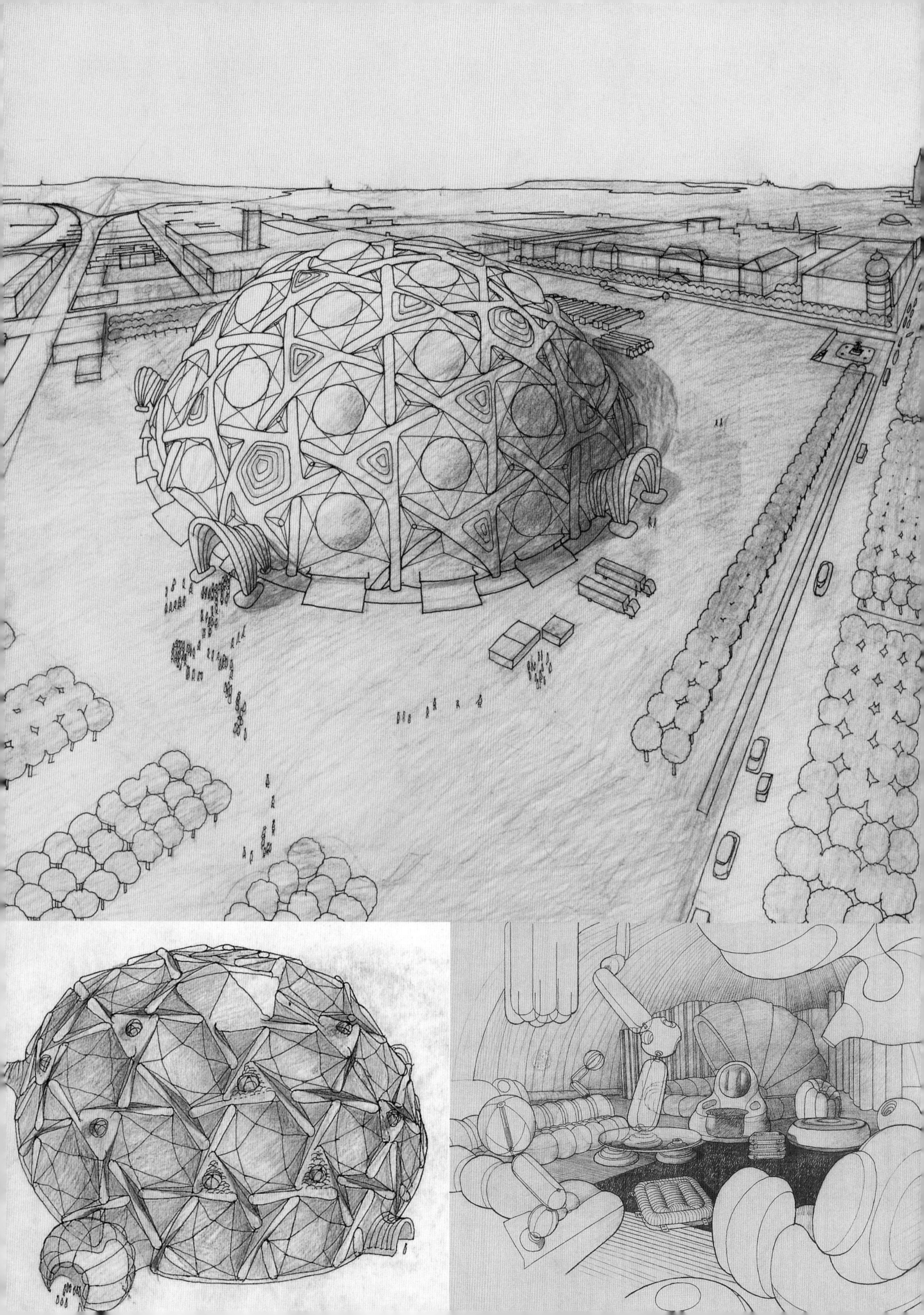

ABOVE: *Quasar (Nguyen Manh Khanh),* Pneumatic Apartment, *Paris, 1968.*

OPPOSITE
UPPER: *Jean Aubert,* Travelling Theater for 5,000 Spectators, *1967;* LOWER: *Aubert,* Pneumatic House, *1967.*

FOLLOWING PAGES
P. 106: *Ant Farm,* Enviromints, *1970;* P. 107: UPPER: *Ant Farm,* The World's Largest Snake, Inflatocookbook, *1970.*

P. 108: *Ant Farm,* 100' x 100' Pillow, *San Francisco, 1969;* P. 109: UPPER & LOWER: *Ant Farm,* Dream Cloud, *tie-dyed parachute on beach, "AstroDaze," Freeport, Texas, 1969.*

The Utopie group in Paris proposed a whole world of inflatable structures, from housing units to vast traveling theaters. Archigram's Peter Cook offered plans for a "Blow-Out Village" that deployed itself like the ribs of a giant umbrella spreading beneath a bubble of clear plastic. Mike Webb's "Cushicle" was a nomadic-dwelling bubble that could be worn like a suit and inflated whenever needed. "It enables an explorer, wanderer, or other itinerant to have a high standard of comfort with a minimum effort."[38]

More in the realm of event than architecture, these bubble buildings were symbolic of the untethered urgency of the times. "All that is solid melts into air," wrote Karl Marx, and in post-Beatles consciousness, everything seemed transitory and floating, literally filled with air.

The baggy membranes groaned and fluctuated, catching reflections and flickering light, blurring the lines between inside and outside. With a seeming life of their own, they bobbed lazily in the sun or shuddered from sudden gusts of wind. Shadows of a passing cloud, or shifts in temperature or humidity, could make their skins shrink or bloat like a jellyfish. "Every slight change—even a heated conversation—brought compensating movement in the skin," reported Banham after visiting one such inflatable in 1967.[39]

Quasar Khanh took the bubble aesthetic to the extreme with his "Pneumatic Apartment" of 1968, in which walls, floor, ceiling, even furnishings were made from inflatable vinyl. Haus-Rucker-Co. created transparent bubble environments that combined space-age mythology with a kinky sense of humor in projects like *Mind-Expander I*, a plastic pod with insectlike markings designed for intimate introspection. "You and she get into the time of the rythmometer [and] follow the red and blue lines on the dome."[40] In the summer of 1970, Haus-Rucker-Co. erected a giant air mattress in Manhattan that blocked traffic and created an instant spectacle (and front-page news) as hundreds of passersby climbed on

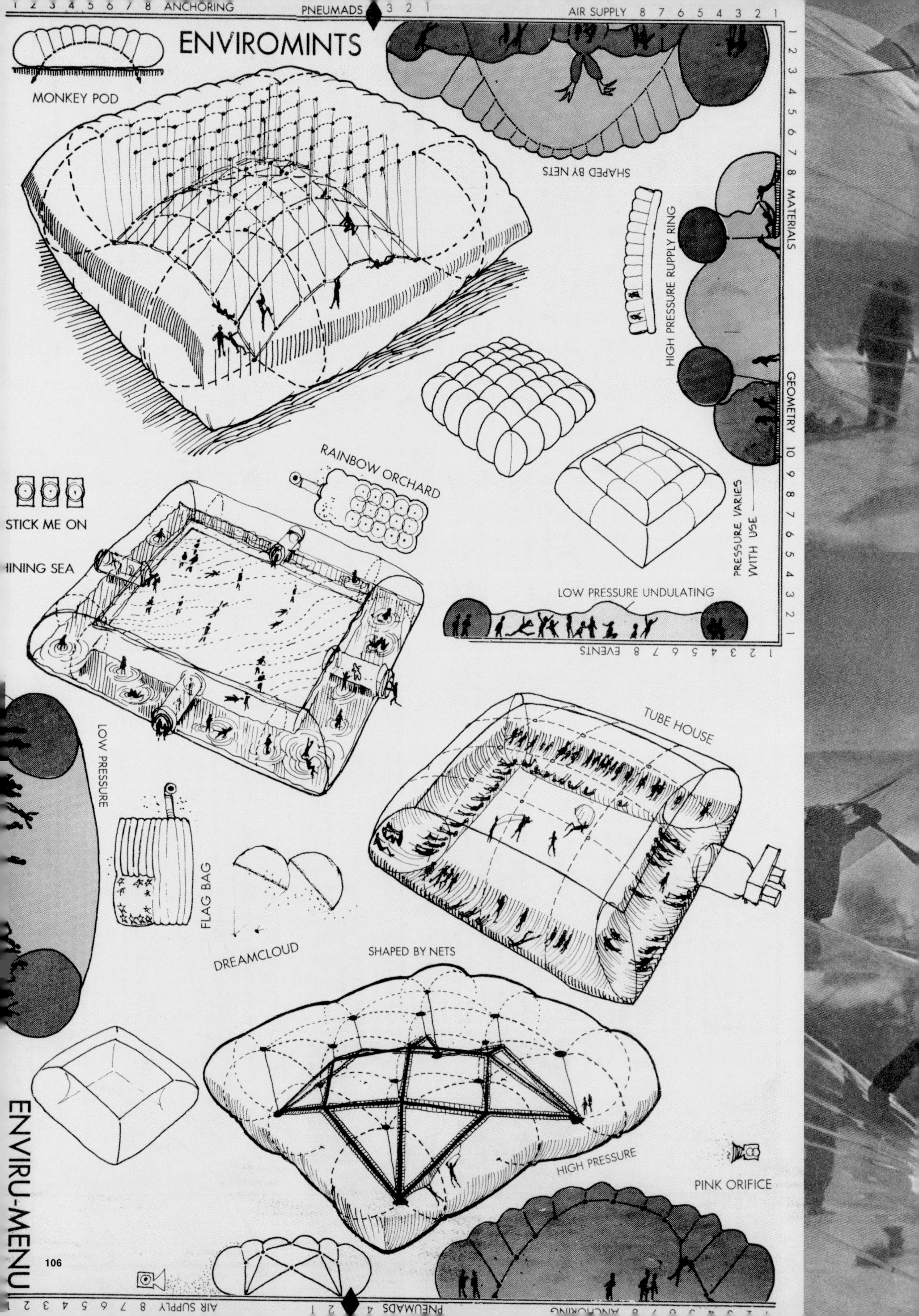
1 2 3 4 5 6 7 8 ANCHORING
PNEUMADS 4 3 2 1
AIR SUPPLY 8 7 6 5 4 3 2 1
ENVIROMINTS
MONKEY POD
SHAPED BY NETS
MATERIALS
HIGH PRESSURE RUPPLY RING
GEOMETRY
RAINBOW ORCHARD
STICK ME ON
HINING SEA
PRESSURE VARIES WITH USE
LOW PRESSURE UNDULATING
1 2 3 4 5 6 7 8 EVENTS
TUBE HOUSE
LOW PRESSURE
FLAG BAG
DREAMCLOUD
SHAPED BY NETS
HIGH PRESSURE
PINK ORIFICE
ENVIRU-MENU
106
1 2 3 4 5 6 7 8 AIR SUPPLY
PNEUMADS 4 3 2 1
ANCHORING

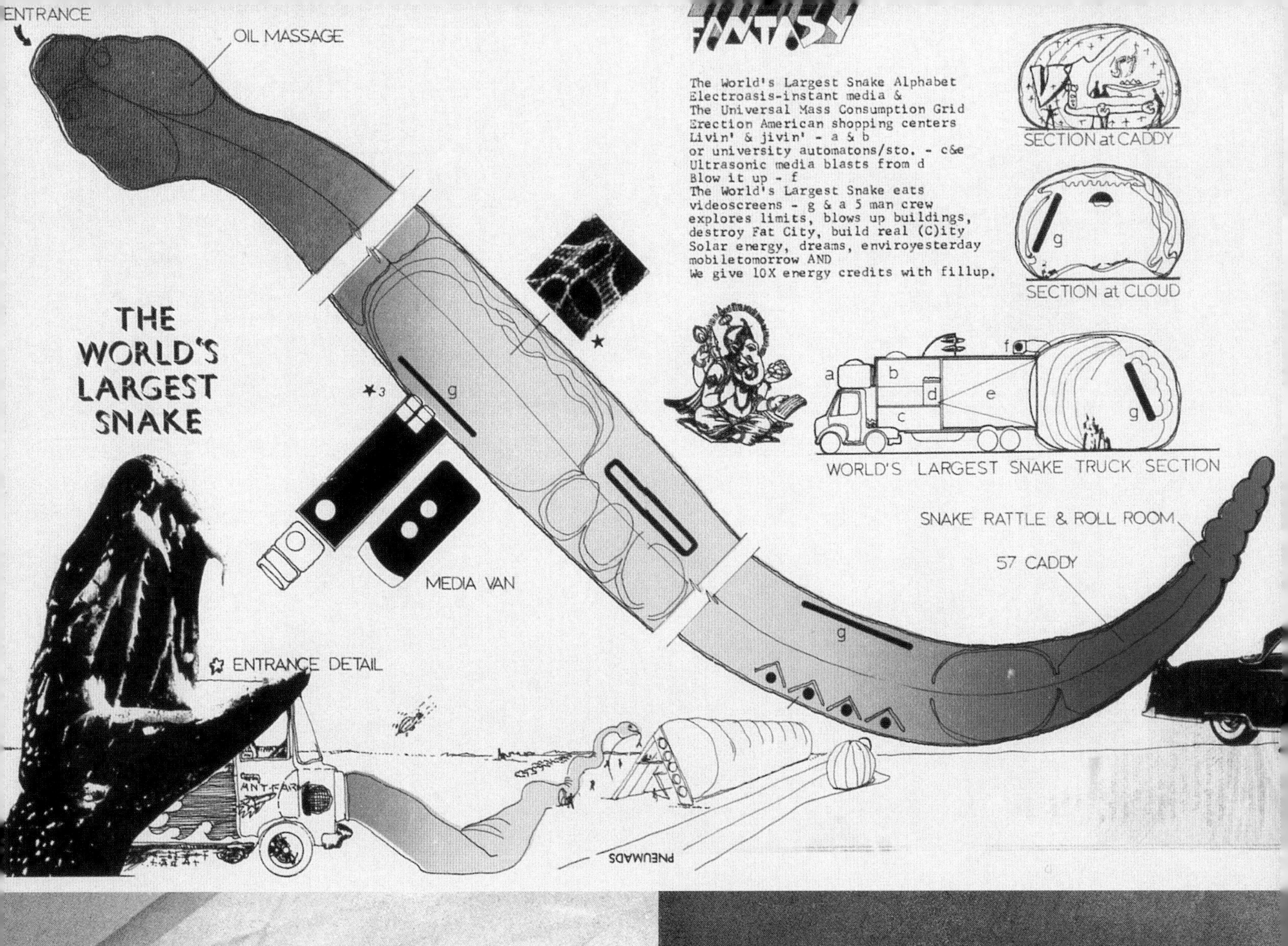
ENTRANCE
OIL MASSAGE
FANTASY
The World's Largest Snake Alphabet
Electroasis-instant media &
The Universal Mass Consumption Grid
Erection American shopping centers
Livin' & jivin' - a & b
or university automatons/sto. - c&e
Ultrasonic media blasts from d
Blow it up - f
The World's Largest Snake eats
videoscreens - g & a 5 man crew
explores limits, blows up buildings,
destroy Fat City, build real (C)ity
Solar energy, dreams, enviroyesterday
mobiletomorrow AND
We give 10X energy credits with fillup.
SECTION at CADDY
SECTION at CLOUD
THE WORLD'S LARGEST SNAKE
WORLD'S LARGEST SNAKE TRUCK SECTION
SNAKE RATTLE & ROLL ROOM
57 CADDY
MEDIA VAN
ENTRANCE DETAIL
ANT FARM
PNEUMADS

board and rolled around like infants.[41] Eventstructure Research Group (ERG) of the Netherlands designed similar "pneumatic media devices" that interacted with the natural environment, such as an air-inflated "tunnel-bridge" across a river in Germany or PVC tetrahedrons made for "waterwalking" across a lake.[42]

While wary of the craze—he referred to inflatables as "Monumental Wind-bags"—Banham did admire their friendly, floppy sense of reciprocity: "Quite unlike the relationship with the static shell of a traditional building where you can beat your fists on the walls and scream and get no more than an echo for response."[43] Stewart Brand described them enthusiastically as "person-flinging giddiness makers."[44] Others reveled in their unpredictable movements, recognizing something akin to the *mouches volants* and flowing boundaries of early acid narratives. "Their walls are constantly becoming the ceilings and the ceiling the floor and the door is rolling around the ceiling," wrote one admirer.[45]

"The inflatable responds to the vibrations of the people, amplifying their existence instead of repressing it," proclaimed the pneumatic pioneers of Ant Farm, a guerilla cadre that traveled across the United States. putting on antiwar performances, using walk-in bubbles as props.[46] Their mission, as they saw it, was to stimulate a shift in psychic orientation: "Searching out a means, a spatial expression of alternatives to the rigid architectural paths we were led down as children."[47] Their standard event structure was a fifty-foot-by-fifty-foot vinyl pillow inflated with a fan and tethered to the ground with ropes and nets. It could be packed in the back of a truck and reassembled whenever needed.

Ant Farm's book-length manifesto, *Inflatocookbook* (1970), was bound in a floppy vinyl cover and filled with visionary projects like a giant inflated snake and the Truckin'

I USE
F-310

A moment of pneumatic suspension.

ABOVE: *Ant Farm's inflatable* 50′ x 50′ Pillow, *Freestone, California, 1969.*

OPPOSITE
All Ant Farm. UPPER: Clean Air Pod, *Berkeley, 1970;* LOWER LEFT: ICE 9, *1971;* MIDDLE RIGHT: Spare Tire Inflatable, *Freestone, 1970;* LOWER RIGHT: 50′ x 50′ Pillow, *temporary offices for the* Whole Earth Catalog, *Saline Valley, California, 1969.*

University, a "friendly, self-help, mobile, truck environmental-event setup for turning on friends and faraway people."[48] Truckin' University was never built, but students at Antioch College realized a similar concept called the "Nomadic/Pneumatic Campus" that was designed as an alternative to the typically oppressive classroom setting. Open-air "micro-environments" floated freely beneath a translucent mountain of white and yellow polyvinyl. (Partially sponsored by Goodyear, the forty-foot-high bubble could accommodate as many as three hundred students.)[49]

In their ghostly temporality, the plastic inflatables suggested an idealized kind of equilibrium between inward and outward pressures, a moment of pneumatic suspension, as well as the promise of softer things to come.[50] But the bubble *bubble* was bound to burst. "Not everyone wants to live in a balloon," noted architect Nicholas Negroponte.[51] The inherent vulnerability of their thin membranes made the windbags impractical for long-term habitation. "When the sun goes behind a cloud you cease cooking and immediately start freezing," wrote Brand.[52] A malfunctioning vent, poor anchorage, a simple pinprick, or the malicious stab of a pocketknife could reduce them to pathetic heaps. In addition, a maturing environmental consciousness no longer tolerated toxic, smelly plastics or the wasteful notion of "disposable architecture." Antioch's Nomadic/Pneumatic Campus blew away during a storm and punctured itself ignominiously on a traffic sign. Ant Farm's one-hundred-foot inflatable ended its days as the bad trips pavilion at the Altamont rock concert in 1969 and was thereafter slit open with a sixty-foot gash. The pneumatic moment was over before it fully began.

PLUG-IN CITIES

American cities were literally burning to the ground. Six days of race riots in Watts left thirty-five dead and hundreds of buildings in ruin. The long, hot summer of 1967 saw forty-three killed in Detroit alone and $100 million in damages. As a concept, the city seemed obsolete, beyond hope. A problem of such magnitude called for epic, sweeping solutions. Architects and urban planners responded with highly imaginative ways to retrofit the old urban nodes and build totally new ones. Scale exploded and "mega" became the radical prefix of the day. Paul and Percival Goodman prescribed a concentrated city for two and a half million people housed inside an immense cylinder, one mile in diameter.[53] The Japanese Metabolists proposed a Godzilla-sized megastructure straddling Tokyo Bay and providing housing for ten million. (On a comparatively restrained scale, Bucky Fuller envisioned an air-conditioned bubble over midtown Manhattan.) Mike Mitchell and Dave Boutwell proposed a linear city for one billion people to stretch all the way from New York to San Francisco, while the Italian collaborative, Super Studio, designed a continuous structure that would encircle the entire globe.

Paolo Soleri filled his notebooks with fantastical urban forms called "Arcologies" that combined architecture and ecology in an attempt to redefine the human condition. "Arcology becomes the cleavage of the human in the body of matter and life, probing for the ever-changing condition of the present," wrote Soleri in characteristically cryptic prose. He drew his cities like musculature, stretched and twisted into biomorphic sinews. "Novanoah," a buoyant city for 2.4 million inhabitants, would float on the sea, while "Arcanyon" spanned the walls of a desert canyon.

Architecture journals of the late sixties were filled with similar proposals that expanded and contracted with fluctuating populations: tender cities of human potential; cities that hung suspended in midair; cities that breathed; cities that nurtured creativity. French artist Yves Klein proposed a city made from fire and smoke, and why not? The possibilities seemed limitless. "Perhaps we shall reach a point where there is a means of making a new, more free-forming *soft* city which is really circumstantial and not tied to hierarchic notions," wrote Archigram's Peter Cook, while others speculated about "alternative scenarios" for a younger, nomadic generation.[54] "Everything is constantly changing," wrote Dutch visionary Constant Nieuwenhuys, who worked out elaborate plans for "New-Babylon," a weblike city designed for both material and psychic flexibility.[55] French urbanist Yona Friedman proposed a space framework that would modulate itself daily, allowing individuals to personalize their living environments by "typing" in their preferred choice of variables.

Moshe Safdie dreamt of a magic housing machine while early cyber nerds at MIT were speculating about artificial ecosystems that responded automatically to emotional and biological needs: "Buildings that open up like flowers in fine weather and clamp down before the storm, that seek to delight as well as serve you."[56] Mind-altering drugs would be unnecessary in these kinds of intimately interactive settings. "If the heartbeat accelerates, the room becomes redder (for example); if his breathing deepens, the room takes on a richer hue... producing a profound experience without brain damage."[57]

Haus-Rucker-Co. hoped to restimulate the urban wasteland with podlike dwellings called "pneumacosms" that would sprout like alien spores from the shells of old infrastructure. "Plug them into the socket of existing city armatures and enjoy living three-dimensionally."[58] William Katavolos, founder of the Guild for Organic Design, predicted the

novanoah-1
ht. 3300 ft.
dia. 17,300 ft.
cov. 6800 acres
dens. 60 per acre
pop. 400,000
buffalo
honolulu
jacksonville

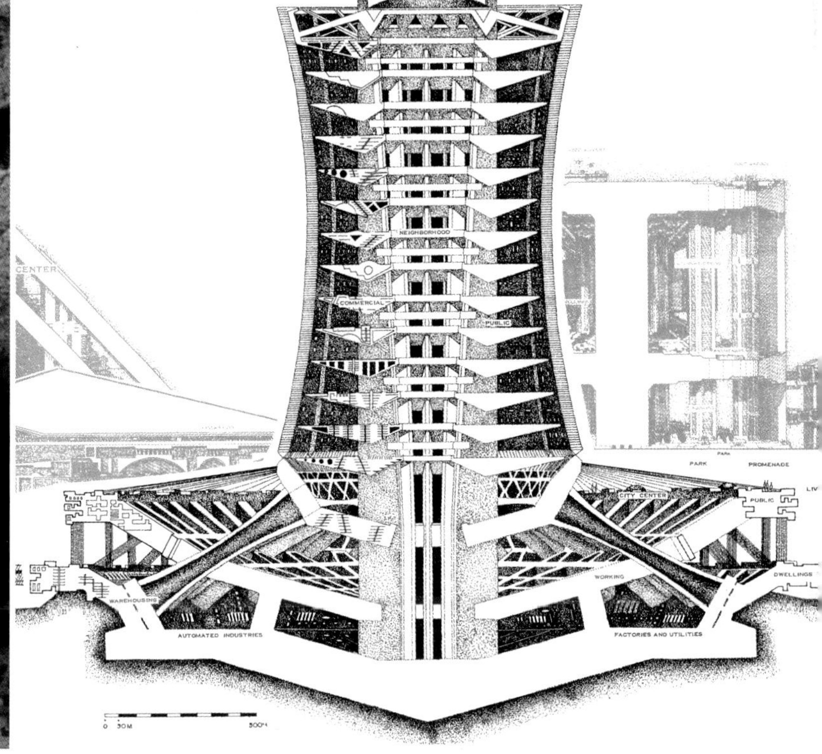

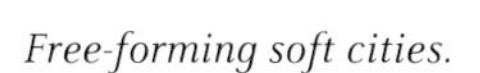

Free-forming soft cities.

ABOVE: *Paolo Soleri,* Visionary Cities, *1970.*

OPPOSITE
Kenzo Tange, Tokyo Bay Project, *1960.*

FOLLOWING PAGES
PP. 114–117: *All Soleri,* Arcologies, *1964–1970.*

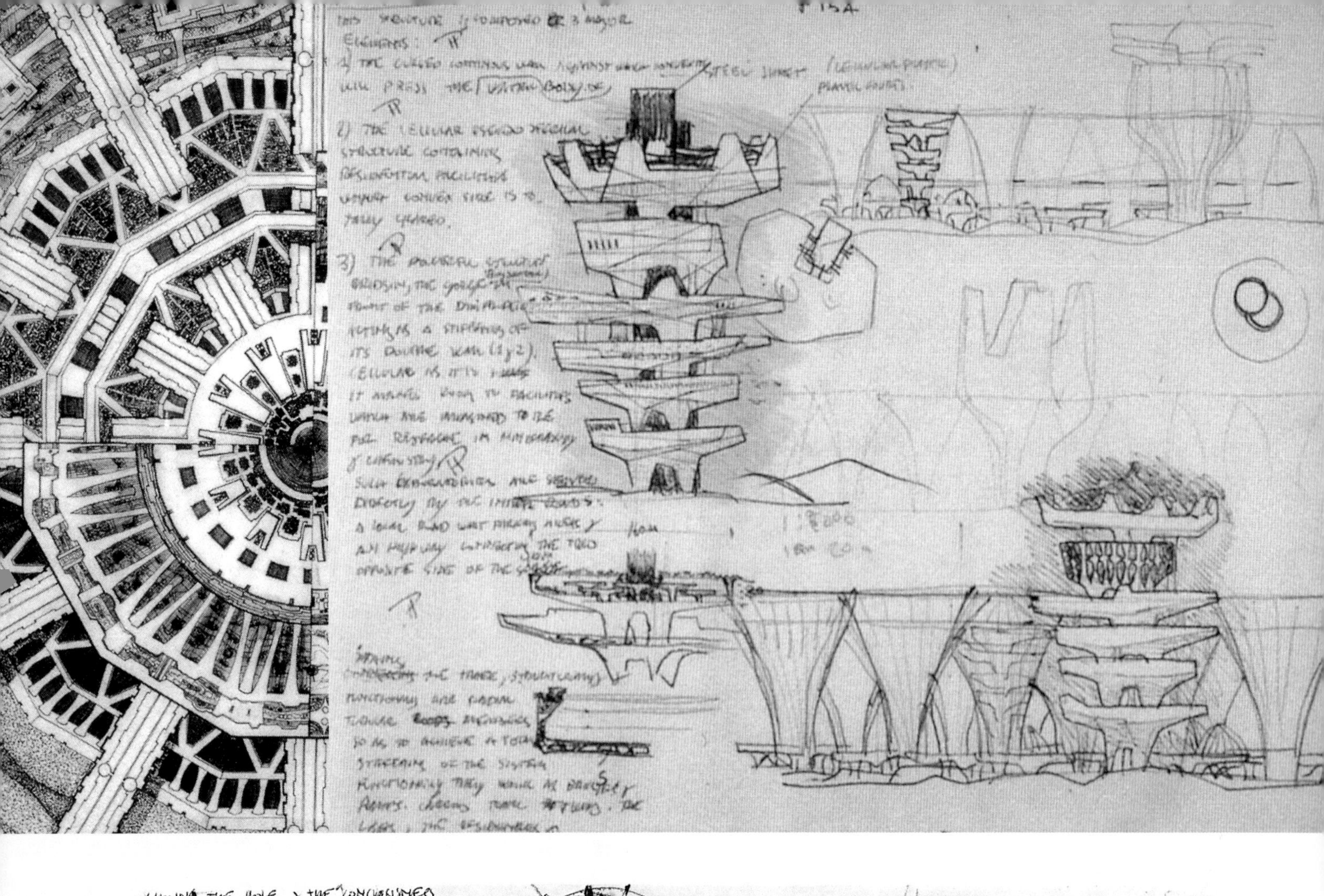

THIS STRUCTURE IS COMPOSED OF 3 MAJOR ELEMENTS:

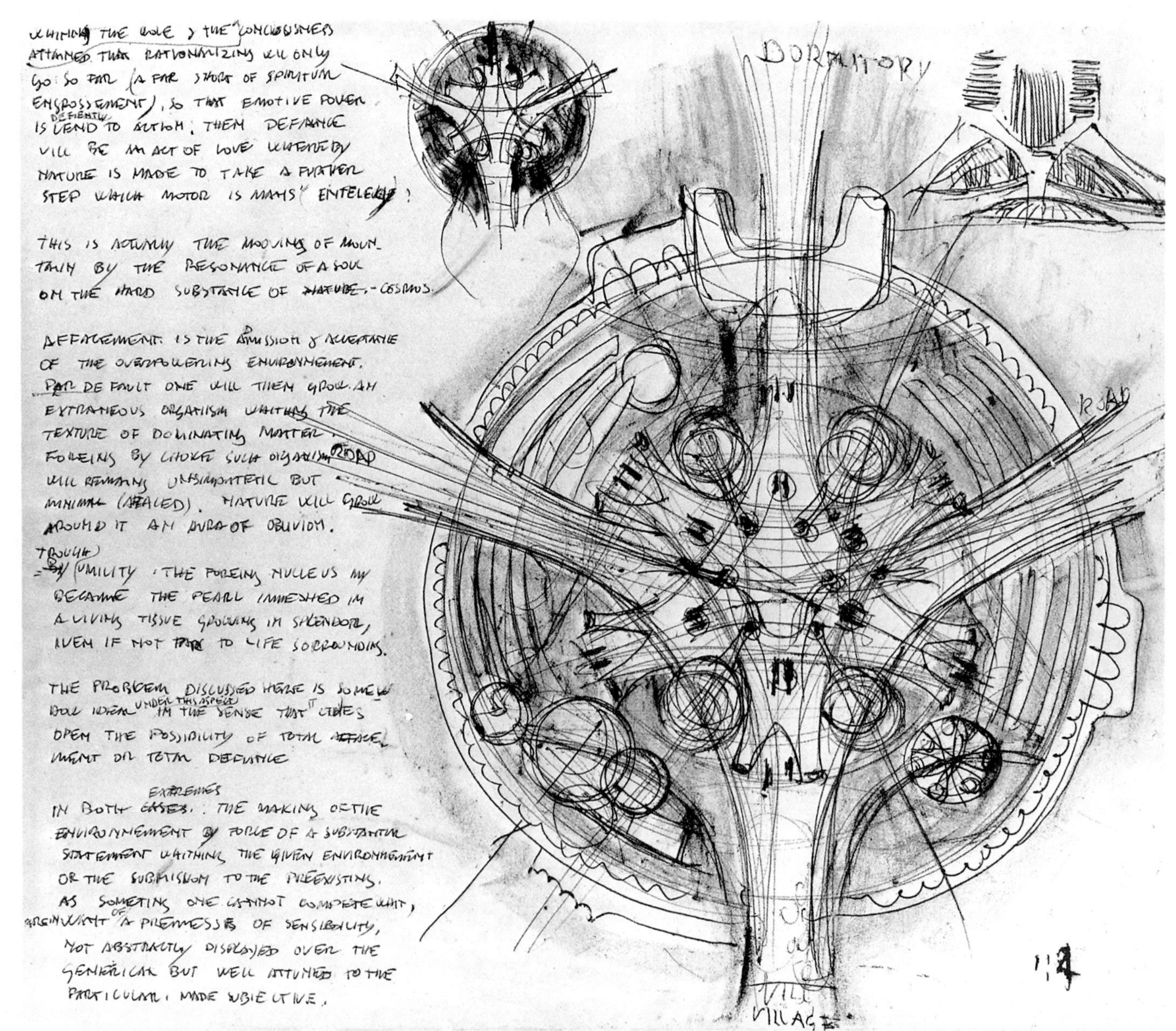

WITHING THE WOLE OF THE CONCIOUSNESS
ATTAINED THAT RATIONALIZING WILL ONLY
GO SO FAR (A FAR SHORT OF SPIRITUAL
ENGROSSEMENT), SO THAT EMOTIVE POWER
IS DEFINITELY LEND TO ACTION, THEN DEFIANCE
WILL BE AN ACT OF LOVE WHEREBY
NATURE IS MADE TO TAKE A FURTHER
STEP WHICH MOTOR IS MANS' ENTELECHY.
THIS IS ACTUALLY THE MOOVING OF MOUNTAIN BY THE RESONANCE OF A SOUL
ON THE HARD SUBSTANCE OF COSMOS.
EFFACEMENT IS THE ADMISSION OF ACCEPTANCE
OF THE OVERPOWERING ENVIRONEMENT.
PAR DEFAULT ONE WILL THEN GROW AN
EXTRANEOUS ORGANISM WITHIN THE
TEXTURE OF DOMINATING MATTER.
FOREING BY CHOICE SUCH ORGANISM
WILL REMAINS UNSIMPATETIC BUT
MINIMAL (REALIZED). NATURE WILL GROW
AROUND IT AN AURA OF OBLIVION.
THROUGH HUMILITY THE FOREING NUCLEUS MY
BECAME THE PEARL IMMESHED IN
A LIVING TISSUE GROWING IN SPLENDOR,
EVEN IF NOT TO LIFE SORROUNDING.
THE PROBLEM DISCUSSED HERE IS SOMEWHOW IDEAL UNDER THIS ASPECT IN THE SENSE THAT IT LEAVES
OPEN THE POSSIBILITY OF TOTAL EFFACEMENT OR TOTAL DEFIANCE
IN BOTH EXTREMES CASES: THE MAKING OF THE
ENVIRONMENT BY FORCE OF A SUBSTANTIAL
STATEMENT WITHING THE GIVEN ENVIRONMENT
OR THE SUBMISSION TO THE PREEXISTING.
AS SOMETING ONE CANNOT COMPETE WITH,
OF A PREMESSES OF SENSIBILITY,
NOT ABSTRACTLY DISPLAYED OVER THE
GENERICAL BUT WELL ATTUNED TO THE
PARTICULAR, MADE SUBJECTIVE.
DORMITORY
ROAD
ROAD
VILLAGE
114

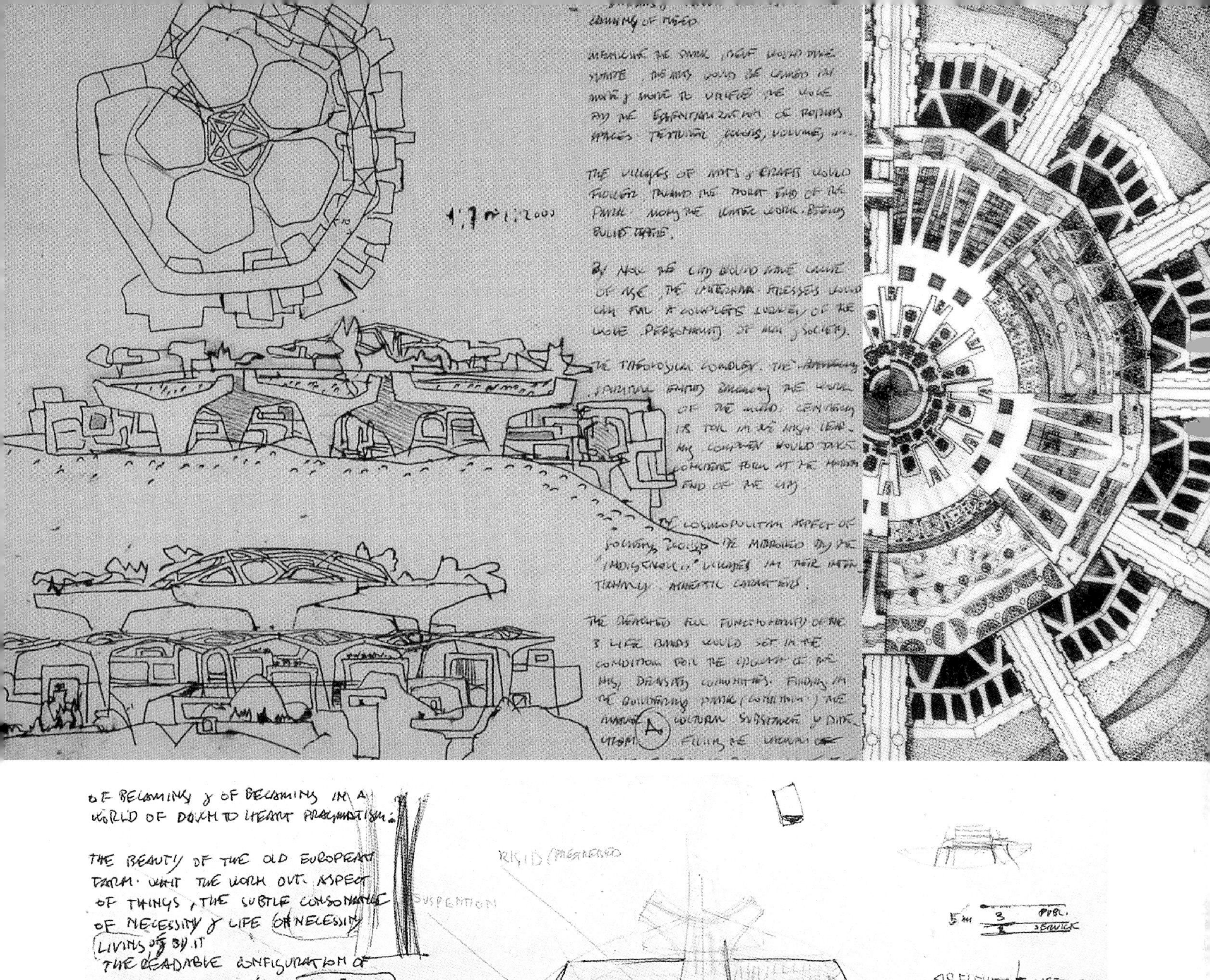
THE VILLAGES OF ARTS & CRAFTS WOULD
BY NOW THE CITY WOULD HAVE COME
OF AGE
THE THEOLOGICAL COMPLEX.
OF THE MIND.
WOULD TAKE
END OF THE CITY.
COSMOPOLITAN ASPECT OF
SOCIETY WOULD BE MIRRORED BY THE
"INDIGENOUS" VILLAGES IN THEIR
THE DETACHED FULL FUNCTIONALITY OF THE
3 LIFE BANDS WOULD SET IN THE
CONDITION FOR THE GROWTH OF THE
CULTURAL SUBSTANCE
A

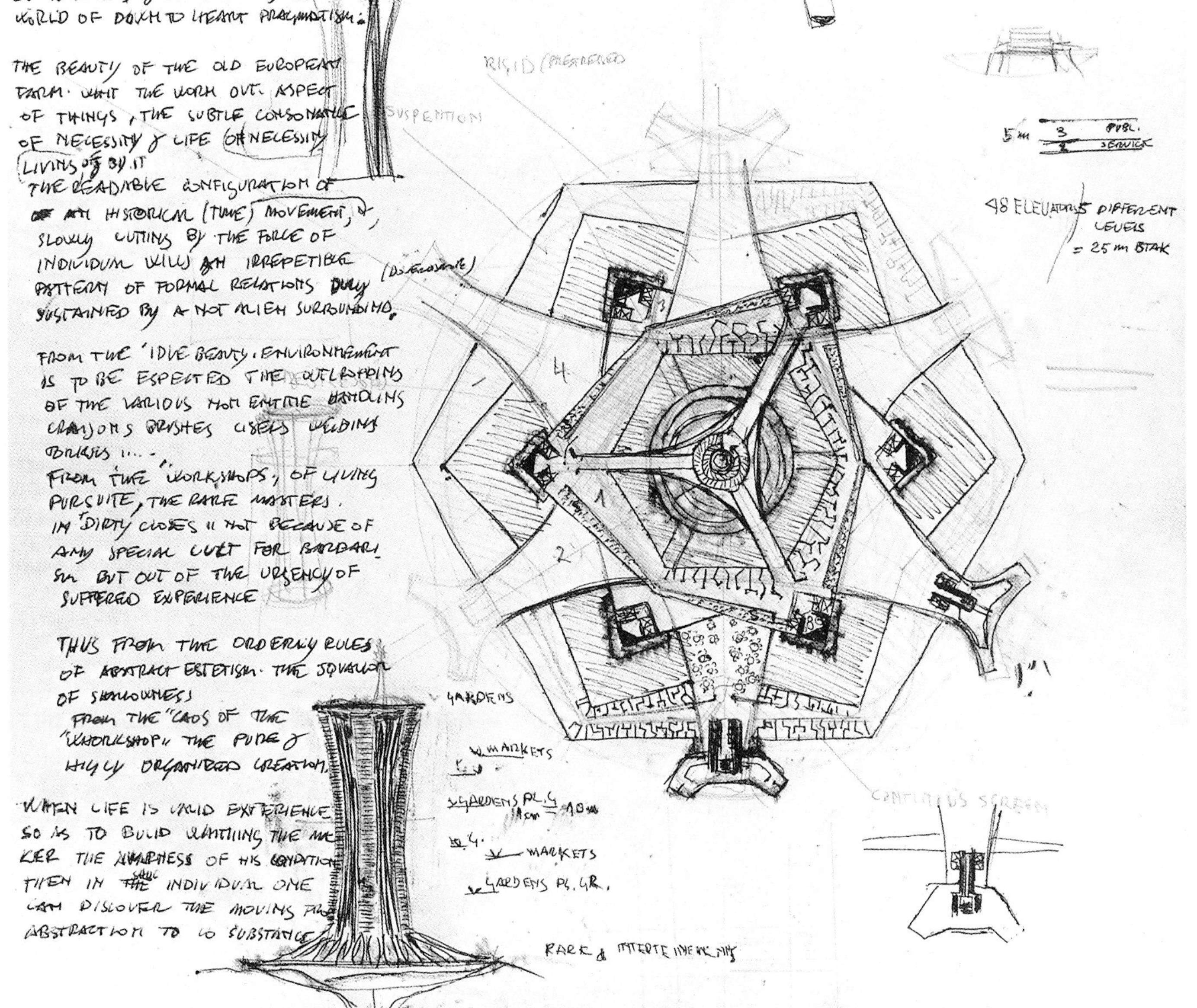
OF BECOMING & OF BECOMING IN A
WORLD OF DOWN TO HEART PRAGMATISM.
THE BEAUTY OF THE OLD EUROPEAN
FARM. WHIT THE WORN OUT. ASPECT
OF THINGS, THE SUBTLE CONSONANCE
OF NECESSITY & LIFE OF NECESSITY
LIVING BY IT
THE READABLE CONFIGURATION OF
AN HISTORICAL (TIME) MOVEMENT,
SLOWLY CUTTING BY THE FORCE OF
INDIVIDUAL WILL AN IRREPETIBLE
PATTERN OF FORMAL RELATIONS
SUSTAINED BY A NOT ALIEN SURROUNDING.
FROM THE IDLE BEAUTY. ENVIRONMENT
IS TO BE ESPECTED THE
OF THE VARIOUS
FROM THE "WORKSHOPS" OF LIVING
PURSUITE, THE RARE MASTERS.
IN "DIRTY CLOSES" NOT BECAUSE OF
ANY SPECIAL CULT FOR BARBARI-
SM BUT OUT OF THE URGENCY OF
SUFFERED EXPERIENCE
THUS FROM THE ORDERLY RULES
OF ABSTRACT ESTETISM. THE SQUALOR
OF SHALLOWNESS
FROM THE "CAOS OF THE
"WORKSHOP" THE PURE &
HIGHLY ORGANIZED CREATION.
WHEN LIFE IS VALID EXPERIENCE
SO AS TO BUILD WITHIN THE MA-
KER THE AWARNESS OF HIS CONDITION
THEN IN THE SAME INDIVIDUAL ONE
CAN DISCOVER THE MOVING
ABSTRACTION TO SUBSTANCE
RIGID (PRESTRESSED
SUSPENTION
5 m
3
PUBL.
SERVICE
48 ELEVATORS 5 DIFFERENT
LEVELS
= 25 m BTAK
4
1
2
3
8
GARDENS
MARKETS
GARDENS PL. 4
MARKETS
GARDENS PL. GR.
PARK & ENTERTAINMENTS

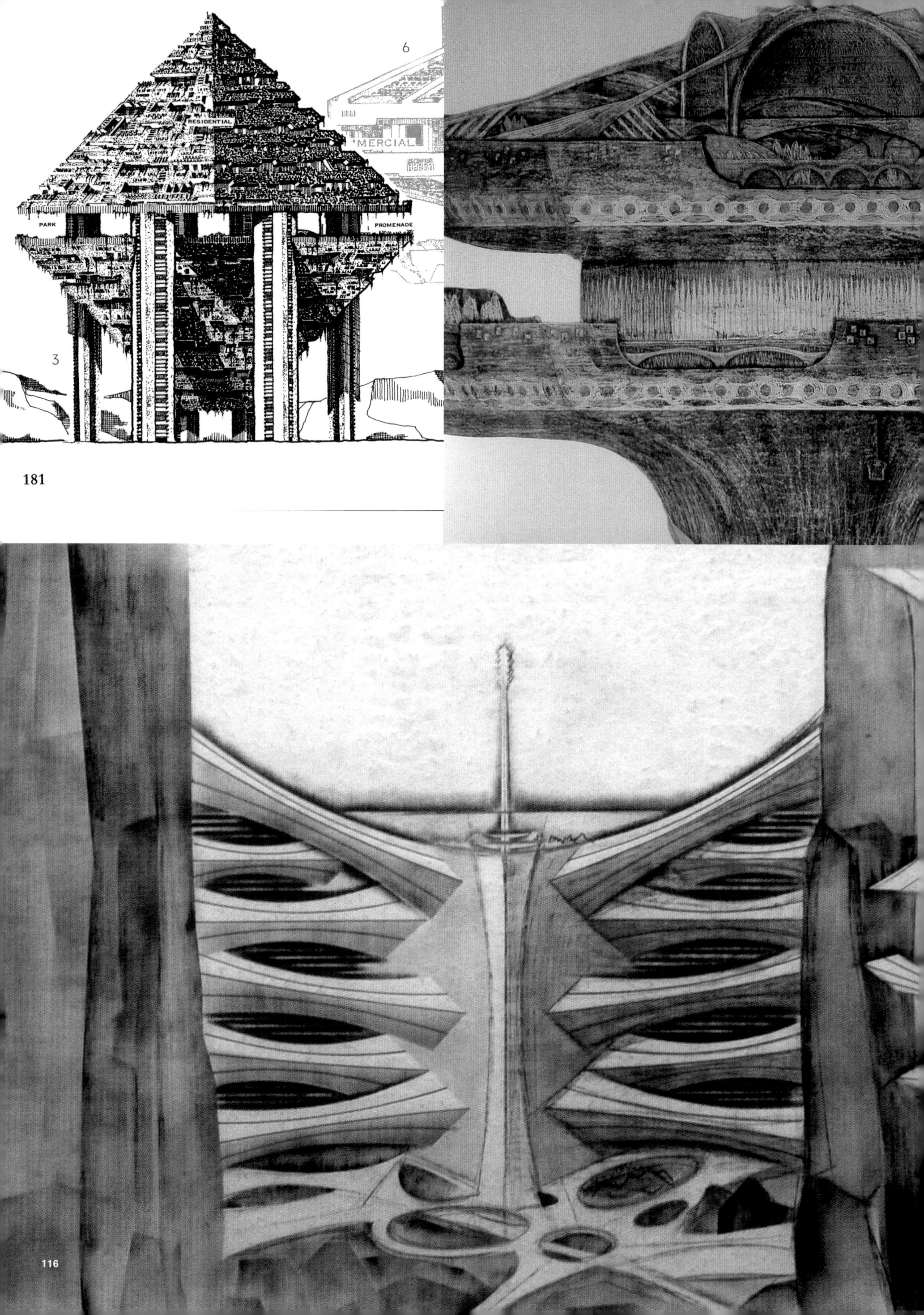
6
RESIDENTIAL
MERCIAL
PARK
PROMENADE
3
181

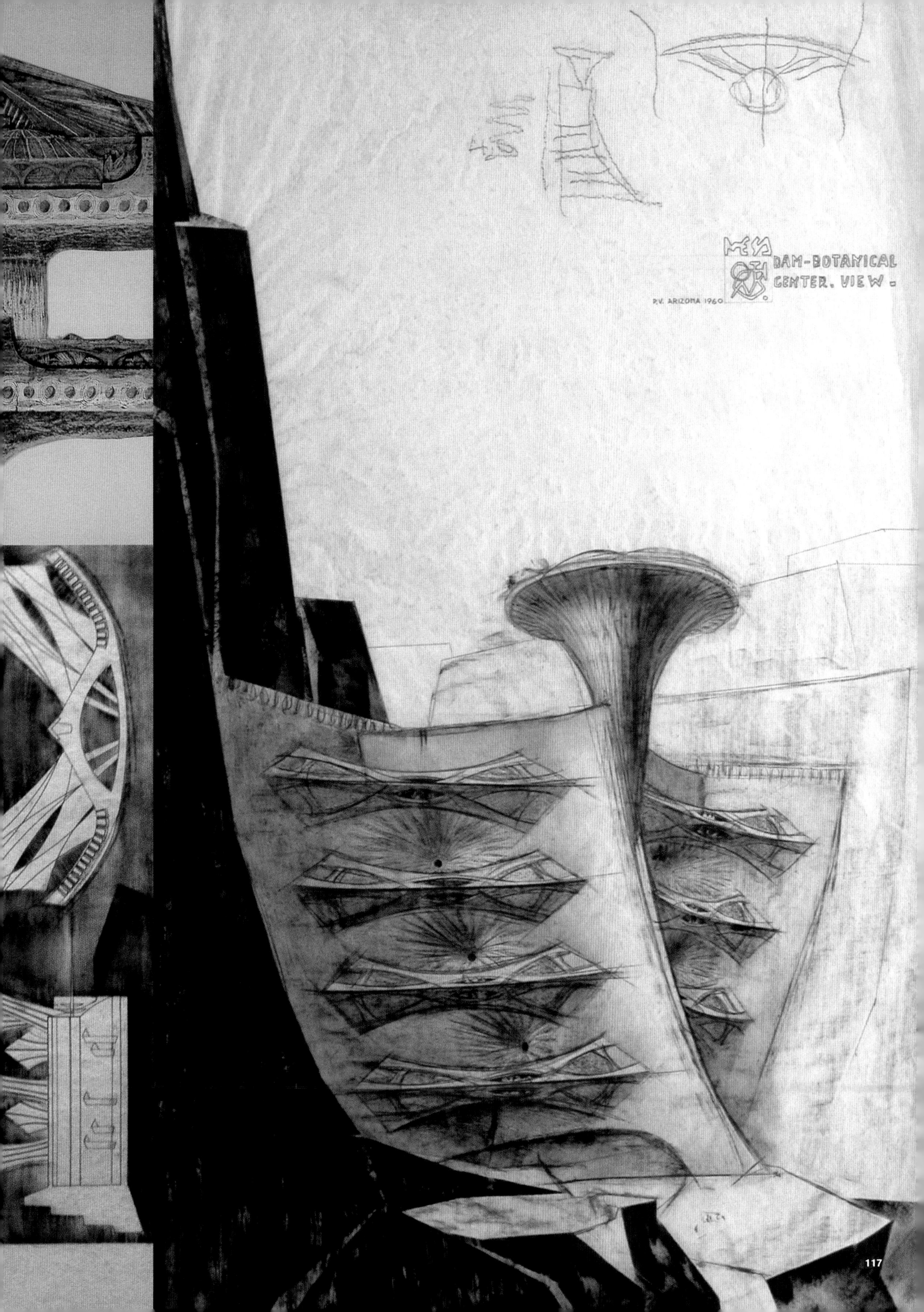
DAM-BOTANICAL
CENTER. VIEW -
P.V. ARIZONA 1960

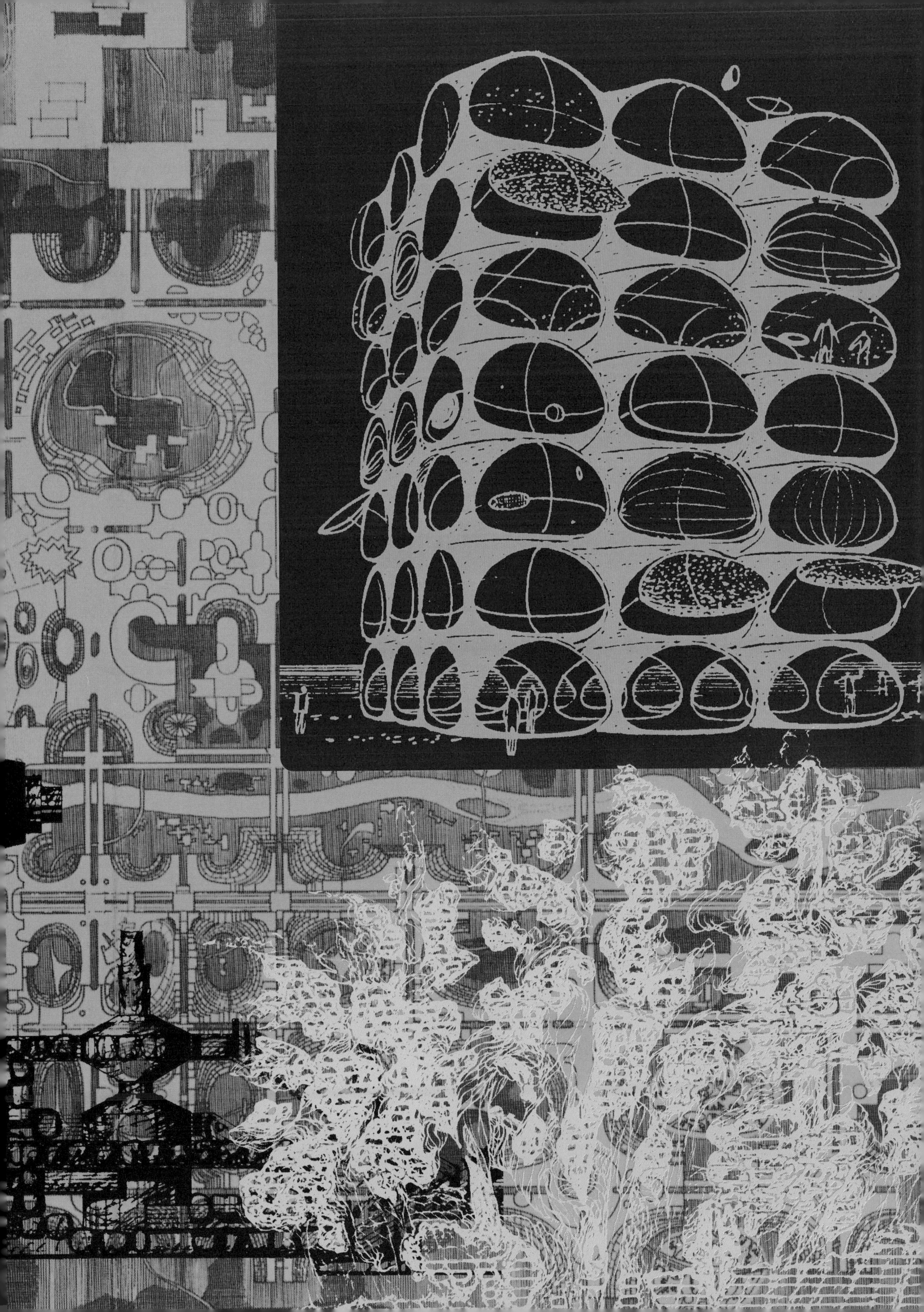

ABOVE: *Haus-Rucker Co.,* Yellow Heart, *1968;* BACKGROUND: *Yona Friedman,* Osaka Board, *1970.*

OPPOSITE
Haus-Rucker Co. (Klaus Pinter), Downtown Megastructures, *1971.*

PREVIOUS PAGES
P. 118: UPPER: *Günther Feuerstein,* Urban Utopia for Salzburg, *1969;* LOWER: *Yona Friedman,* Ville Spatiale, *c. 1964;* P. 119: UPPER: *Chanéac,* Crater City, *site plan, 1968;* LOWER LEFT: *John Osajimas,* Congress Center, *Vienna, c. 1968;* LOWER RIGHT: *Chanéac,* Cellules Polyvalentes, *1960.*

FOLLOWING PAGES
P. 122: Yellow Heart; P. 123: *All Haus-Rucker Co.,* LOWER: Pneumacosm, *1967.*

development of intelligent, self-generating organisms that would be able to shape themselves into new cities and "exploding patterns."[59] Rudolph Doernach, father of "hydrogenetic biotecture," proposed artificial icebergs as habitable cities and "edible towns" shaped by microorganisms. Walls and windows containing genetic information would adapt, like human skin, to both meteorological and social changes.[60]

Members of the English collaborative Archigram produced cheeky cut-and-paste proposals that collaged pop iconography with high technology.[61] Peter Cook's "Plug-In City" featured podlike units that could be attached or removed according to individual whim. "You turn the switches and choose the conditions."[62] Plug-In City expressed its perpetually expanding character with naked service cores, protruding nozzles, Erector-Set components, cranes, and rapid modes of integrated transport (monorail and hovercraft) as a delirious work in progress, programmed for continual change.

Riffing further on the frenetic mobility of modern times, Ron Herron's *Walking City* took the form of robotic insects moving around the world on telescoping legs. Herron's cartoon-like renderings were, at once, terrifying and ridiculous. Archigram's *Instant City*, another nomadic entity, could be moved from location to location like a demountable circus, programmed to reshape itself with nets, cables, canopies suspended from airships, robotic armatures, and inflatable domes, all animated with audio-visual displays.[63]

The work of radical urbanists like Archigram was, for the most part, speculative architecture intended to lubricate the imagination. On the rare occasion when their utopian

schemes were realized, it tended to be for fairs or temporary expositions like Montreal's Expo '67 or Osaka's Expo '70, where projects such as Moshe Safdie's "Habitat," Bucky Fuller's 250-foot dome, Otto Frei's suspended roof, and Kenzo Tange's theme pavilion were confined safely to the realm of family entertainment.

To many, the whole idea of a city, any kind of concentrated urban node, was anathema. McLuhan believed that the city would disintegrate altogether and be replaced by small tribal clusters. "As electrically contracted, the globe is no more than a village," he wrote.[11] "We actually live mythically and integrally, as it were, but we continue to think in the old, fragmented space and time patterns of the pre-electric age."[12] While it was fine to dream about new kinds of human communities, there was a frantic desire among the younger generation to stop talking about the future and actually make it happen: no more speculation, no more paper utopias.

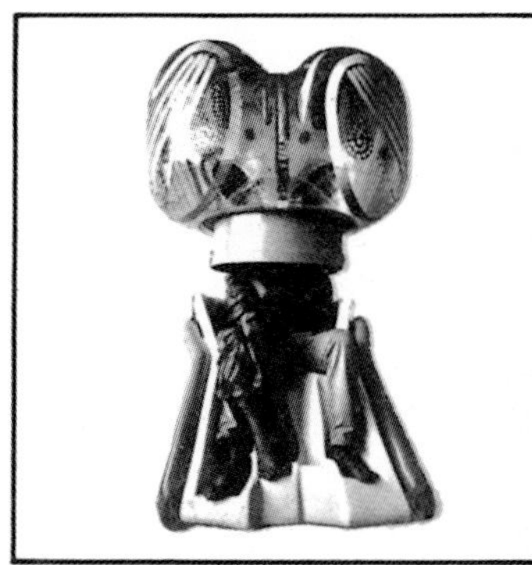
Mind-Expander 1

Pneumacosm

Balloon for Two

Connexion-Skin

Yellow Heart (Model)

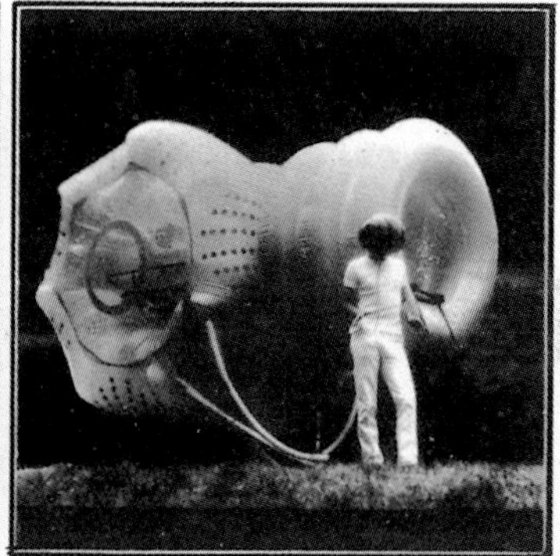
Yellow Heart

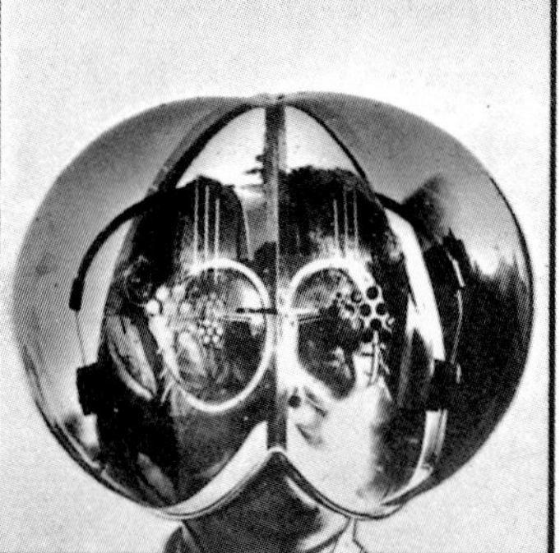
Flyhead

Electric Skin

Mind-Expander 2

HRC – TV-Show

Mooncake

Information-Stand

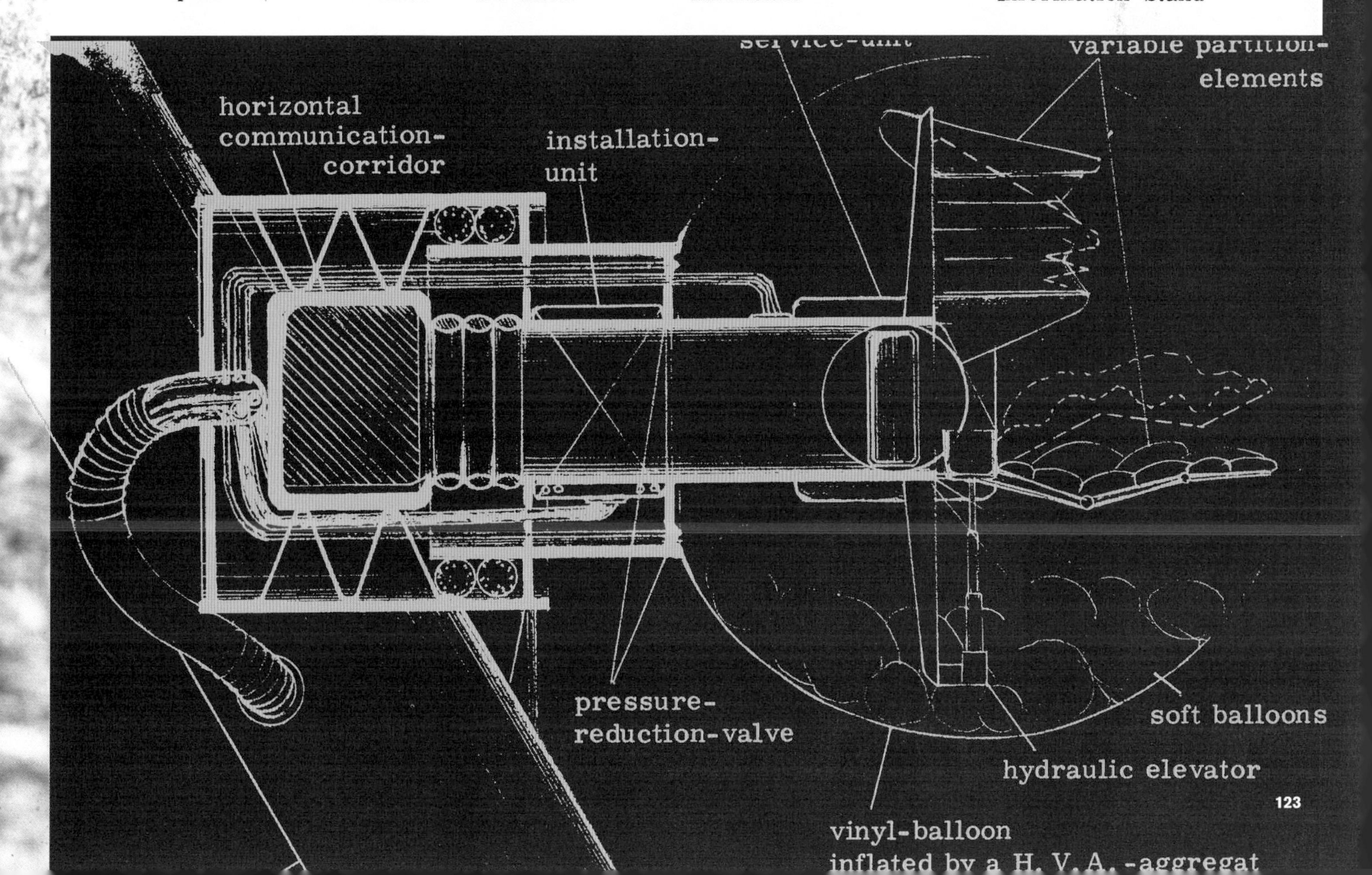

5 UNSETTLERS

"WE ARE IMMIGRANTS ON OUR OWN NATIVE SOIL."

—BILL VOYD[1]

Thousands of individual revolutions make up a greater revolution that appears to be happening everywhere, or nowhere, at the same time. (There is no central committee, no barricade, no Boston Tea Party.) It's both centrifugal and centripetal, pulling inward and pushing outward at the same time, a molecular parity that acid allows one to grasp. In other words, you don't have to be in the same place to be connected. "No matter where you are, you're at the center of the universe," says one long-haired mystic.[2] No cities are necessary, no tightly structured enclaves. Webs are spun through ether and extended through contact high, extrasensory perception, dreams, astral travel. Communication is casual, left to chance, on sheets stapled to phone poles, personal notes printed in underground papers, pinned to head-shop walls, or messages passed along by starry-eyed nomads following the migratory routes east to west, sharing joints and news of the far-flung revolution.

Everyone spreads out in a kind of freak diaspora, moving farther away from concentrated urban nodes. There is the prevailing sense of a quest, a furtive search for the *right place*, the *other place*, for Kesey's *cool place*, as personified by the cross-country pilgrimages of so many who abandon the cities and seek some ideal matrix of nature and culture, a place that lies somewhere over the hills and through the woods, a place that hippie chronicler Robert Houriet called "infinite sky."[3]

By the summer of 1967—the so-called "Summer of Love"—the cities already seemed desperate, like doomed ships. Things were looking grim in both the East Village and the Haight. "We face great holocausts, terrible catastrophes, all American cities burned from within, and without," proclaimed a Digger broadsheet in San Francisco.[4] There were more busts, police crackdowns, increasing incidents of overdose, and bad drugs circulating. The sense of common purpose and communality that had flourished for a brief moment between, say, the Trips Festival and the Human Be-In, was spent. Ken Kesey had been busted and was on the lam in Mexico. The cosmic oneness of LSD was being replaced by the jagged alienation of heroin and crystal meth. Thousands of runaway teenagers were swarming into the neighborhoods. Spooky cultists and psychotic loners were mingling with the fresh-faced arrivals. Paranoia was running at fever pitch.

Add to this the relentless exploitation and misrepresentation by the press. "There were so many observers on Haight Street from *Life* and *Look* and CBS that they were largely observing one another," noted Joan Didion, reporting for the *Saturday Evening Post*.[5] This wasn't an exaggeration. When *Look* reporter William Hedgepeth was working the Haight in hippie disguise, another writer approached him and requested an interview. Hedgepeth stayed in character and agreed to talk. "I 'confessed' to everything," he said, "except that I was with *Look*."[6]

Nasty rumors were spreading through the hip underground that the Mafia was moving in on the drug scene, or that the CIA was lacing LSD with elephant tranquilizer. Police started to forcibly evict some of the more notorious crash pads. "These people are creating the slums they live in," said Dr. Ellis D. Sox, San Francisco's director of public health, who ordered a sanitation crackdown. "I am concerned about rats out there," said Sox, who was known in the Haight as "LSD Socks." "I don't want to be an alarmist, but rats can cause bubonic plague." The story made

LIFE
THE YOUTH COMMUNES
New Way of Living Confronts the U.S.
JULY 1
COOPERATIVE COMMUNITIES
HOW TO START THEM, AND WHY
KRIYANANDA
GETTING BACK TOGETHER
ROBERT HOURIET
The first full account of revolutionary life styles radically altering American society.
"A trip you can't take without being touched . . . he makes you want to try it too." The New York Times
WITH PHOTOGRAPHS
AVON / V-317 / $1.25
WOODSTOCK NATION
Abbie Hoffman
A TALK-ROCK ALBUM
TOWER T-095-19
The Youth Communes
An articulate analysis of the movement of American youth toward communal living.
Roy Ald

headlines on the front page of the *San Francisco Examiner* (March 24, 1967): "HIPPIE CLEAN-UP ORDERED."

Venereal disease was out of control, and there was an alarming increase in incidents of rape and racial violence between white hippies and ethnic minorities. "Rape is as common as bullshit on Haight Street," wrote Chester Anderson in a Communication Company broadside, comparing the situation on the street to the villages of South Vietnam.[7] "Cities have too many sharp edges," said a wandering love child named Sonny who knew what he was talking about.[8] "Shob" Carter, a friendly acid dealer, was stabbed to death in San Francisco. One of his hands was amputated as a warning to others. A few days later, Superspade, another local dealer, was also murdered. Back in New York, there was more bloodshed. Twenty-one-year-old Groovy (James Hutchinson) was brutally beaten to death, his face crushed in by a brick. His girlfriend, eighteen-year-old Linda Fitzpatrick, was also killed. Groovy was a cofounder of Galahad's crash pad and had appeared in many press accounts of hippie street life. Linda was the daughter of a wealthy businessman, a fact that propelled the story onto the front pages. Apparent victims of another drug deal gone bad, their bodies were found in a dingy East Village basement. As *Time* reported: "The deaths of Groovy and Linda . . . sent a chill through all of hippiedom."[9]

"There must be some way out of here," sang Bob Dylan in the opening lyrics of *All Along the Watchtower*, a song that was released late in 1967 and captured the darkening mood on the streets. ("There's too much confusion. I can't get no relief.") Hippie elders like Allen Ginsberg, Tim Leary, Gary Snyder, and Allen Watts were preaching exodus, encouraging the young and disenchanted to retribalize as soon as possible. "The whole [city] scene is going to fold into tribes that live out in the country and grow their own food," said Chuck, a New York hippie who was already making plans to leave.[10] "Workers of the world, disperse," said another.[11] Underground papers like the *East Village Other* and the *San Francisco Oracle* were publishing back-to-the-land manifestos and reports from the rural front about organic farming, solar energy, and the healing virtues of open land. "As the cities teeter on ruin, many young minds are thinking of what it was that Moses did when he took his people into the wilderness for forty years," ran an editorial in the *Other*.[12] "We've got to get back to small subsistence villages and tribes," said Jake Guest, a member of a fledgling commune in Vermont. "Instead of huge sewage plants, we need thousands more outhouses and compost piles."[13]

The "Free City" spirit that had made the Bay Area such a mecca for the subculture was eroding. On May 15, 1969, there was a violent confrontation at People's Park, Berkeley, between the police and a crowd of six thousand students, street hippies and free-city activists. It was the ultimate showdown between flower power and the straight establishment, and the establishment appeared to win, at least in terms of force. Governor Ronald Reagan ordered police and National Guardsmen to evacuate the liberated area. Hundreds were arrested and hundreds wounded, with at least one fatality, during the ensuing street battles. Even urban radicals who had so often dismissed the back-to-nature movement as a cop-out were losing faith and calling for a move to the wilds. "Stake out a retreat," read one of the Digger broadsheets. "Learn berries and nuts and fruits and small animals and all the plants. Learn water."[14]

Some believed that the final apocalypse was already at hand. As the Piscean age moved into the Aquarian, there would be catastrophic kinds of reckoning. Cities would be

OPPOSITE
The idea of a separate, "dropped-out" nation was promoted in the popular press and various back-to-the-land publications.

PREVIOUS PAGES
P. 124: *A gathering at Strawberry Lake, Colorado, 1972 (photo: Paul Dembski).*

FOLLOWING PAGES
PP. 128–129: *Paradise Now, leaving the city (photo: Paul Dembski).*

PP. 130–131: *mobile dwellings, converted trucks and busses (photos and drawings: Jane Pincus Lidz).*

PARADISE
NOW

of LIVING

PATCHS
H926644
STOP
H905638
MOTOR HOME
USA

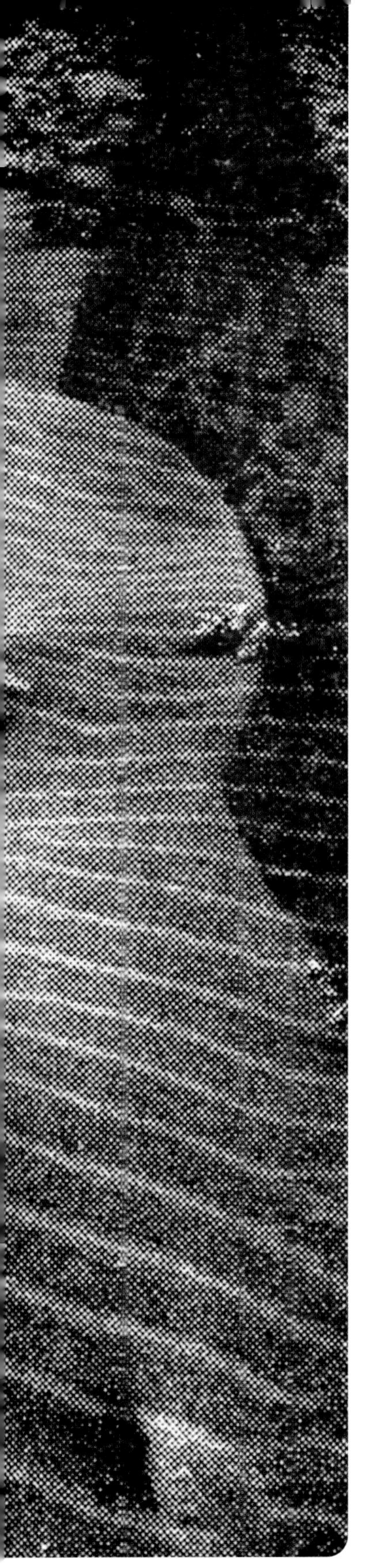

Back to the land.

ABOVE: *Mother Earth illustration from the* San Francisco Oracle; LOWER: *Naked farming and yoga at Morning Star commune, Sebastopol, California.*

leveled by tidal waves and earthquakes (not that hard to imagine in a city like San Francisco, which sat on a major fault line). "We believed that California was going to fall into the ocean," said Minor Van Arsdale, a Berkeley dropout who left for higher ground and moved to Taos.[15]

The August 1967 issue of the *Oracle* chronicled the growing dangers of street life, and prescribed a general move to safe, rural outposts where extended families, communes, and small tribes were being formed. "Backpacks, sleeping bags, rifles, and a knowledge of edible plants and animals found in the wilderness is the next logical step." Appearing in the same issue was the seductive image of a naked earth goddess. Superimposed over her breasts and stomach were the rippling contours of a desert landscape. Lichen and wild grasses appeared to be growing from the crevices of her body in a sexually suggestive way, but the message was clear. It was time to simplify, time to get intimate with Mother Earth.

Acid encouraged people to escape the city's artificial environments, to go outside and feel the pulsating rhythm of the planets. There was a good deal of tree hugging—literal tree hugging—going on at the time as so many sensory awareness groups left the session room and ventured into the wilds to stimulate environmental awareness and group consciousness. Nice college kids suddenly found themselves standing naked on a beach with twenty other people building primitive structures. "On a wind- and wave-swept beach, a driftwood community is created, destroyed, recreated, and invested with ritual," read the "score" for one of the Experiments in Environment that Ann and Lawrence Halprin organized during the summer of 1968.[16]

They led people blindfolded up a winding trail of eucalyptus trees on Mount Tamalpais. They moved, as if in slow motion, through the shallows of a tidal pool near Carmel, communing with the water and crustaceous sea life. In another encounter, thirty young participants removed their clothes, oiled and massaged each other's bodies—"stroke, mash, push, pull, pet, caress"—then bathed each other and moved together as a single organism through the mountain passes. They felt wind on their skin, touched leaves, rolled over one another in high grass. What were they learning, what were they thinking? After a moment of initial embarrassment, there was a rush of oneness as the group rediscovered "long-buried and half-forgotten selves" and a sense of kinship with nature.[17]

For most, the back-to-the-land revolution started with a similar kind of outing, a day trip to the desert or a weekend in the woods to drop acid, commune with nature, meditate under the stars. Hippies immersed themselves in streams and waterfalls or clung lovingly to the trunk of a redwood. There were healing circles in Vermont, moonlit rituals in Oregon, solstice gatherings in Colorado, and pagan weddings on the mesas of New Mexico.

Ex-urban forays took on Biblical overtones as old skins were shed and new identities assumed. Ramon Sender, composer and organizer of the Trips Festival, went into the desert with forty tabs of acid and found himself face to face with God. A few months later, he abandoned his career in experimental music and helped to establish one of the first open-land communes in America. In the spring of 1967, Emmett Grogan, cofounder of the Diggers, left San Francisco for a soul-searching trek with a Pueblo Indian named Little Bird and returned a changed man.[18]

About the time that Grogan was drifting across the desert of New Mexico, psychedelic guru Stephen Gaskin was having his own wilderness epiphany. He and a group of friends drove across the Golden Gate Bridge and hiked up Mount Tamalpais, past a creek bed and up into a high meadow where they dropped acid. "I was laying down on the ground, tripped out into dirt, letting myself flow with the mountain," recalled Gaskin. He felt himself connect with every living thing on the mountain. He blew his cow horn and listened to the crickets and birds reply: "Not loud, but a giant, huge sound, coming up from acres and acres and acres at once.... We were one with them and we were one with the hill. We were all really One."[19] To Gaskin, this moment marked an auspicious shift in consciousness. *Leave the city. Get back to the earth*. On his way down the hill, Gaskin stopped by a stream, took a handful of water, and sprinkled it over his head, "like a baptism from the earth."[20] Some time later, he and a flock of two hundred psychedelic pilgrims left California on a cross-country odyssey and eventually established a commune in backwoods Tennessee.

These kinds of revelations and acid pastorals became a part of hippie mythology, representing an initiation into the next phase of the Aquarian journey. Thousands would experience similar kinds of burning-bush moments. Stephen Diamond, a graduate of Columbia University, dropped mescaline in rural Massachusetts and communicated with the spirit of a maple tree, which told him to close his eyes and raise his hands. He felt a jolt of energy surging through his body and a sudden release from the burdens of his past. "There was no question that the tree and I were one and the same," he wrote.[21] Roberta Price, an honors graduate from Vassar College, abandoned her life in the straight world after communing with a boulder in Colorado. "[The rock was] about fourteen feet high—striated granite, spotted with chartreuse and orange lichen," wrote Price, who dropped acid, lay naked on the boulder, and made love to her boyfriend, becoming one with the rock. "My blood surged, and my heart pulsated with the mountains," she wrote. "I was on the edge of a new and profound understanding of the life force seeping through the lichen and me."[22]

Hoards of young people followed suit, longing for immersion in the Tao of natural living. They came as refugees from the cities, from Haight-Ashbury and the East Village. They squatted, appropriated, and liberated ground in the hinterlands. "In short, we are learning how to be alive again," wrote one urban refugee, who dropped out of college and headed west with nothing more than his knapsack and a dog-eared copy of the *I-Ching*.[23] These were the children of both Dr. Spock *and* Dr. Seuss who, like Peter Pan, refused to grow up. "For us, everything is possible," wrote Raymond Mungo, after abandoning a life of radical activism and retreating to a commune in Vermont. "If the heart is willing, what ecstatic adventure is too risky?"[24]

Once the multitudes had left the cities, how would they survive? No one was quite sure, but the answer was sure to come in a spontaneous rush of effervescence. Again, it was the group mind, the Oneness, springing outward and seeding a whole new trip, the wilderness trip. What everyone shared in common was boundless faith mixed with a willingness to relearn everything, to embrace poverty and live as voluntary peasants. Inspired by Thoreau, they made little encampments with tents and tepees or in temporary sheds made from boughs and leaves. They weren't afraid. Some lived in converted trucks or vans. By the late 1960s there were thousands of rural communes sprouting up around the world, as many as eight thousand in North America alone.[25]

Reasons cited for abandoning civilization were usually the same vaguely articulated motives: getting it together, reconnecting with the earth, finding a center. But it didn't matter. This was all part of a great awakening: open land, open homes, open hearts. The new pioneers were escaping the hassles of the city, col-

OPPOSITE
Roberta Price bringing in the harvest at Libré commune, Colorado (photo: David Perkins).

UPPER: *Basic shelter at Wheeler's Ranch (photos: Bill Wheeler);*
LOWER: *Simple bath, Morning Star East, New Mexico.*

OPPOSITE
UPPER: *Shacks at Lorien and Wheeler's Ranch;*
LOWER: *Peñasco, New Mexico (photo: Roberta Price).*

US ARMY RECRUITING STATION
2235 W HICKORY ST.
DENTON 387-5400

lege, parents, suburban mediocrity. They just wanted a quiet place to write poetry, meditate, find themselves, convene with God, or otherwise escape the shadow of their childhoods—the duck-and-cover paranoia of the Cold War, JFK's assassination—and enter a world in which time itself slowed to a barely perceptible crawl. "Find a little bit of land somewhere and plant a carrot seed," advised Stephen Gaskin. "Now sit down and watch it grow. When it is fully grown pull it up and eat it."[26]

Among the thousands who hit the road during the summer of 1968 was Paul Steiner, an eighteen-year-old radical expelled from his New York high school for publishing an underground newspaper. He consulted the *I-Ching*, tossed coins, and got Hexagram #49 about revolution and furthering through perseverance: "The great man changes like a tiger," read the oracle, and at that moment, Steiner decided to change like a tiger and start a new life. He and his girlfriend left the next morning for New Mexico and never looked back. "We wanted a base. We wanted a place to sit and watch it all happen from," wrote Steiner.[27]

There were enclaves of long-haired gypsies gathering in the woods north of San Francisco, in Marin County, in the hamlet of Canyon. There were hundreds camping in the redwood groves of Mount Tamalpais or farther down the peninsula toward Santa Cruz. They drove south in psychedelic buses to Big Sur with its bohemian legacy and foggy coastline.[28] There were also reports of naked flute players colonizing the canyons of Limekiln Creek, fifty miles south of Carmel.

Some made their way up to the Esalen Institute and experienced the *nowness* of Gestalt with Abraham Maslow and Fritz Perls, bathing in the natural hot springs, and feeling the moss and the texture of rough bark on their naked buttocks.[29] Others drifted without clear purpose along the beaches or up into the craggy outcroppings of Gorda Mountain, where a transient commune of sorts was starting to seed itself on the property of Amelia Newell, a silver-haired priestess who played auto-harp and wore floor-length gowns painted with mystic symbols. Artists, runaways, aging beats, and homeless hippies from the Haight gathered around the campfire eating brown rice and onions. "I could see about eighty people moving around in the strange foggy mist that hung over the mountain top," wrote a sociologist who visited Gorda for research purposes. "It was either a scene from Man in the Beginning or a small troupe of human stragglers who had survived the desolation of the earth by atomic destruction."[30]

There was no guiding vision or purpose behind Gorda, just an open-door acceptance of everyone and anyone, no matter how eccentric—or in some cases, criminally insane—they happened to be. But for many, it proved to be a first stop, a way station of sorts, that prepared them for full immersion in the art of ecstatic living. There was an old stone house and a few moss-covered shacks, but most of Gorda's population slept in tents or in caves. There was a rain-soaked couch lying beneath a silver oak and an old church organ painted with flowers. A community bathtub sat out in the open, but the water supply had been cut by disgruntled neighbors.

OUTLAW NATION

In 1967 the Hudson Institute predicted that by the year 2000 the United States would have an entire "dropped-out nation" existing within its borders. But there were others who knew that such a nation was already forming itself as a fluctuating free space in the deserts, mountains, and forests, wherever long-haired tribes were gathering, creating communal settlements, and learning to live off the land. "[There is] enough dissatisfaction with life in America to build parallel, exemplary

OPPOSITE
Hippie farmer, Lorien Commune, Questa, New Mexico, 1969 (photo: Dennis Stock/Magnum).

demi-societies of our own," wrote Richard Honigman in the *San Francisco Oracle*,[31] or as the Motherfuckers, a radical East Village collective, put it: "Blown minds of screaming-singing-beaded-stoned-armed-feathered Future-People are only the sparks of a revolutionary explosion and evolutionary planetary regeneration."[32] The feathered Future-People were beginning to venture off the map into uncharted territory.

This idea of a wholly separate dropped-out nation evolved in the popular imagination as if there were an actual place, a true entity with its own laws and borders that would somehow coexist within the outlines of an older American space, reclaiming it, transforming it.[33] This was a concept that started with the media's perception of Haight-Ashbury as being a kind of self-contained gulag. The Gray Line bus company ran "Hippie Hop" tours through the Haight, calling it "the only foreign tour within the continental United States" so tourists could gawk at the flower children from the safety of an air-conditioned bus: "We are now entering the largest hippie colony in the world and the very heart and fountainhead of the hippie subculture. We are now passing through the 'Bearded Curtain'..."[34]

Walter Bowart, editor of the *East Village Other*, called it a psychedelic free-American community.[35] "There are no more frontiers," he wrote. "All terms have become inverted. The west has become east, giving birth to the Underground States of America,"[36] a wildly romantic twist to Frederick Jackson Turner's frontier thesis. As Turner had written seventy years earlier, the American frontier served as a gate of escape from the bondage of the past.[37] Now a young, rebellious generation was rediscovering that frontier. "We must be the pioneers, all over again," said one of the new homesteaders. "We are immigrants on our own native soil," declared another.[38]

Tim Leary had been talking about a "new age frontier" since the mid-sixties, while Alan Watts imagined a fringe society existing far outside the mainstream that would be *organically*, not politically, organized.[39] "It has no boss," said Watts, "yet all parts recognize each other in the same way as the cells of a body all cooperate together."[40] When Kesey set out on his cross-country bus trip, he described himself and his band of Pranksters as *unsettlers* moving west to east, backward across the Great Plains, hoping to "locate a better reality."[41] (In his way, Kesey was building an updated version of the Puritan's "City upon a Hill," even if it did take the form of a wildly painted bus, lubed by acid, moving ever further away from reason.[42]) "As navigator of this venture I try as much as possible to set out in a direction that, in the first place, is practically impossible to achieve," said Kesey, whose language was oblique but whose mission was clear: to seek a better reality and fully merge the outer world with the inner.[43]

Jefferson Airplane sang of a "new continent of earth and fire."[44] Others spoke of the "New Atlantis." Gary Snyder (Beat poet and hippie elder) spoke of a "magic geography" that was hidden beneath the corrupt geography of modern civilization, just waiting to be

New settlers in the Outlaw Area.

ABOVE: *Toothbrushes, Lama Foundation, New Mexico.*

OPPOSITE
Group chanting at Gila National Forest, New Mexico.

FOLLOWING PAGES
PP. 144–145: *Talking Stick, Strawberry Lake, Colorado (photo: Paul Dembski).*

rediscovered.[45] Stewart Brand, founder and editor of the *Whole Earth Catalog*, wrote about an "Outlaw Area," far removed from mainstream civilization, where freaks and new utopians would act out McLuhan's call for retribalization and reinvent the human community. While he made vague allusions to space stations and Huxley's utopian *Island*, Brand left the rest to the imagination.[46] "Any design fantasy is just loose talk until it happens," he wrote, explaining how the Outlaw Area would be an Aquarian haven, "bending reality off into unimaginable directions with no restrictions save the harsh ones of nature."[47] It would stand in opposition to the death-and-money cult of corporate greed, consumerism, the military-industrial machinery of death, and the soul-withering lassitude of suburbia. It would develop its own kind of tribal governance and noncapitalist currency. (Ant Farm even printed counterfeit money inscribed with the motto "Outlaw Area Energy Credit" and a marijuana plant in place of the dollar's Great Seal.[48])

The Outlaw Area would be inspiring and youthful, filled with vibrant color and unexpected contradictions. It would be free flowing, globular, trippy, all-inclusive. "For evolution it's an open end, a place for other stuff to happen," wrote Brand, stressing the need to embrace all levels of society, especially the outcasts, otherwise it would be just another bourgeois utopia. (Kesey said "I prefer the troublemaker," while the Jefferson Airplane sang "We are all outlaws."[49])

"High energy, minimum prior form, violent range of constant inputs; it should be wild," wrote Brand—citing Thoreau's *In wildness is the preservation of the world*—bringing together both the cream and the dregs of society, the drifters, the crazies, the kind of social misfits that Lou Gottlieb referred to as "impossibles." (Indeed, the closeness to madness, darkness, and violence—the very proximity that gave the movement its edge and vibrancy—would also be a root cause of its downfall.) But here in Brand's loosely knit manifesto were the guiding principles for a new order:

1) "high energy"
2) "minimum prior form"
3) "violent range of constant inputs"
4) "wildness"

While acknowledging that it was, in part, an imaginary place, Brand insisted that the Outlaw Area was also a place that existed in real space and listed, in the way of examples, the oceans, mountains, desert, north woods, tundra, jungle and other "state-of-the-art frontiers whose languages are still foreign to lawmakers."[50] In fact, something like Brand's Outlaw Area had been seeding itself in the hinterlands for several years. When Leary traveled through the southwest in 1967 he was surprised to find so many tribal outposts already thriving. He visited Drop City in Trinidad, Colorado, and other start-up communes near Taos, New Mexico, referring to them collectively as "drop cities." (A Denver newspaper reported that Leary was planning to establish his own psychedelic ashram near Paradise, Arizona, but he denied the rumor.[51])

What form would the outlaw communities take? In *Walden*, prime document of hippie self-sufficiency, Thoreau built himself the most rudimentary shack but dreamt of what he called a "larger and more populous house, standing in a golden age."[52] This imaginary shelter would consist of a single, all-embracing space, a "vast, rude, substantial primitive hall" with its interior as open and manifest as a bird's nest, presaging the domes of the communal scene by a hundred years.[53] In *Walden II* (1948), behavioral psychologist B. F. Skinner described a twentieth-century version of Thoreau's vision with buildings set in a verdant

landscape of hills and orchards. The main building was made from rammed earth and followed the rise of the land with a series of communal spaces connected by a gracefully ascending passageway adorned with hanging flowers. This elongated structure, called the "Ladder," provided a thematic armature and a sense of common purpose. While *Walden II* was a fictional allegory, the founding members of Twin Oaks commune would interpret it as a how-to manual and in 1967 set about re-creating Skinner's utopia in rural Virginia, complete with rammed-earth buildings.[54]

Ken Kesey envisioned what he called the "New Planet," a softly enveloping orb in which his acid tribe would be able to gather and blow their collective mind. It would take the form of a great geodesic dome perched on top of a cylindrical shaft, looking something like an oversized toadstool. The dome would have a foam-rubber floor so that people could lie down and experience an all-consuming, multimedia apocalypse. "[They] would take LSD or speed or smoke grass and lie back and experience what they would, enclosed and submerged in a planet of lights and sounds such as the universe never knew.... The sounds roiling around in the globe like a typhoon."[55]

Following his own advice, Stewart Brand decided to leave the city and relocate to the Outlaw Area. He packed up the *Whole Earth Catalog* production offices and moved them from Menlo Park to a remote area of the Mojave Desert, where his publishing team would be housed in one of Ant Farm's fifty-foot inflatables. (A small geodesic dome was erected inside the transparent bag and served as a darkroom while Brand himself stayed in an Airstream trailer parked nearby.) Editors and layout artists tried as best they could to adapt to the situation, staring out at the wild saline landscape that surrounded them. But even Brand and his radically hip staff found it challenging. The editor admired the "trippy" effects of the great bubble but found it impossible to concentrate. "The blazing redundant surfaces disorient; one wallows in space," noted Brand.[56] After a week on-site, a desert storm swept through the valley and ripped away some of the mooring cables. One corner of the inflatable sprang loose, throwing a secretary and her typewriter through the air. No one was injured, but Brand decided to deflate his desert outpost and move back to Menlo Park.[57]

SOLUX

In 1966 Steve Durkee and his wife Barbara—representing the spiritual wing of the USCO collaborative—abandoned the East Coast and went in search of land to build an Aquarian community called Solux. "What we conceive, finally, is a return to the wilderness," said Durkee, "going away from high-energy centers like New York or L.A. or San Francisco or London and getting out in the middle—because *everything is connected now* or will be in a short period of time."[58] Solux, an offshoot of McLuhan's global village, would be built in the desert, in a place with lots of psychic space and no police, explained Barbara Durkee, describing it as a "spiritual dude ranch."[59] As with Kesey's New Planet, a giant geodesic dome would stand at the center of the complex, surrounded by a ring of smaller domes designed to house the twelve "tribes" of the revolution. The Durkees weren't sure how to accommodate so many wildly divergent temperaments so they decided to separate them and give each one a piece of the pie, such as the macrobiotics or those wanting sexual freedom. "If some people want to live nude and want everybody to ball everybody else, why they will have one dome," said Steve Durkee.[60]

The architecture of the central building was designed to symbolize the re-creation of the universe. It would rest on a twenty-four-

OPPOSITE
A tribe of happy hippies pose for Life *magazine, 1969.*

FOLLOWING PAGES
PP. 148–149: *Rough-hewn cabins on the new frontier.*

How to split a log, chop a log, flatten a log, and trim a tree.

SOLUX IS A SPIRITUAL CENTER PLANNED FOR CONSTRUCTION IN A REMOTE AREA IN THE SOUTH-WEST US. ITS LOCATION IN A REMOTE AREA, FREE FROM THE INTENSE PSYCHIC VIBRATIONS OF LARGE ENERGY-CENTERS IS MEANT TO ACCELERATE/FACILITATE REINTEGRATION PROCESSES BY TUNING IN TO ELEMENTAL REALITIES
IT IS DESIGNED TO BE A MAGNETIC GENERATOR & ENERGY TRANSMISSION STATION TO RESTORE THE CURRENT OF SPIRITUAL IMPRESSIONS TO THE DIVINE CIRCULATORY SYSTEM, SO THAT LOVE, LIGHT & PEACE MAY FLOW FREELY FROM THE POINT OF LIGHT WHICH IS INFINITE CONCIOUSNESS, INTO THE HEARTS OF ALL.

IT WILL BE EVIDENT FROM A STUDY OF THESE PLANS, THAT SOLUX ANTICIPATES A RADICAL CHANGE IN CURRENT SOCIAL STRUCTURES, ENVISIONING A CO-OP-ERATING SELF SUPPORTIVE, MULTI-FAMILY TRIBAL UNION, CREATED THROUGH THE RELEASE OF LOVE BY SPIRITUAL AWAKENING.
CONSTRUCTION OF THIS GROUP SHELTER LIVING SYSTEM IS A SOCIAL MEDIUM. GIVEN THE EXPERIMENTAL NATURE OF THIS PROJECT, WE HOPE TO ATTRACT TO THE WORK OF CONSTRUCTION, ESPECIALLY DURING SUMMER, THE HELP OF ARCHITECTURAL STUDENTS, ENGINEERS, ARTISTS-BUILDERS AND THOSE ON THE PATH.

THOSE WHO INQUIRE CONCERNING PARTICIPATION IN THE SOLUX PROJ. WILL BE SCREENED ON THE BASIS OF SKILLS, EXPERIENCE AND PERSONAL INTERVIEW. PLEASE SEND BIRTHDATE/HR. OF BIRTH/PLACE OF BIRTH W. APPL.

THE FUNCTIONING OF SUCH A SOCIAL ORGANISM, AVOWEDLY EXPERIMENTAL, MUST RISE FROM A SPIRITUALLY SOUND & ECONOMICALLY VALID BASE, BOTH IN TERMS OF ITS OWN INTRESTS & THOSE OF THE LARGER COMMUNITY. SINCE THE INITIATORS OF THIS PROJECT ARE INVOLVED IN EXPLORING NEW MEDIA, IT IS EXPECTED THAT THE COMMUNITY WILL BASE SOME PART OF ITS ECONOMIC STRUCTURE ON THE HARDWARE & SOFTWARE OF CURRENT TECHNOLOGY IN THE LIGHT OF ITS SPIRITUAL, EDUCATIONAL & CREATIVE POTENTIALS.
AGRICULTURAL & EDUCATIONAL FUNCTIONS ARE FORSEEN AS DIRECT PRODUCTS OF THE ENVIRONMENT. IN CLOSE PROXIMITY TO SOLUX WILL BE FACILITIES DESIGNED FOR THOSE WHO WISH TO VISIT & EXPERIENCE THE LIFEWAYS OF THIS COMMUNITY IN TERMS OF THEIR OWN PSYCHIC & PHYSICAL REINTEGRATION.

THE SPIRITUAL JOURNEY CALLS FOR A MERGING OF THE LIMITED SELF IN UNIVERSAL LIFE WHICH INVOLVES THE SURRENDER OF SEPARATIVE EXISTENCE. MANIFESTING THE ART OF CO-OPERATIVE & HARMONIOUS LIFE & BECOMING ESTABLISHED IN THE SPHERE OF DIVINE LOVE & TRUTH IS NOT A MATTER OF FORMS, RITUALS & CEREMONIES, BUT OF ACQUIRED DISCIPLINE, DEVELOPING THE SENSE OF PERSPECTIVE AND FOCUSING AWARENESS IN REAL TIME.

TO FIND GOD IS TO COME TO ONE'S OWN SELF

INQUIRIES MAY BE ADDRESSED TO: THE TABERNACLE • 21 CHURCH ST. GARNERVILLE N.Y.

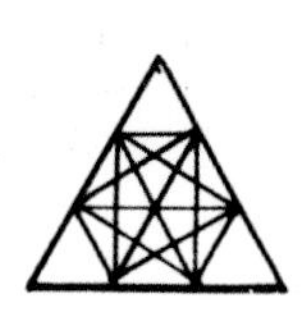

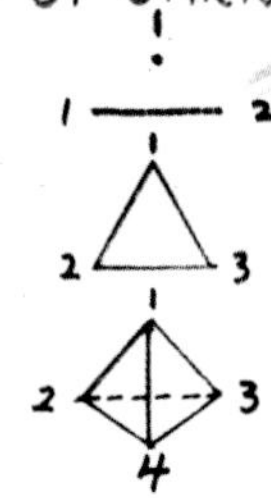

OPPOSITE
Solux Manifesto, written by the "spiritual wing" of USCO, 1966.

sided base, and the interior would consist of a vast meditation space built like an upside-down kiva entered from below. This cosmic orb would remain empty like Thoreau's primitive hall and be furnished with only a matted floor and translucent walls. As if to emphasize the airy, you-can't-get-there-from-here nature of the place, Durkee explained that there wouldn't be any roads leading into Solux. "The only way will be through the air," he said. "We are living in the twentieth century; and once you get into the air, you begin to understand that all roads go nowhere."[61]

The time for dreaming was over. A widely dispersed band of do-it-yourself builders and outlaw architects would dedicate themselves to translating the vague and fluctuating space harmonies of the revolution into something tangible. Working with their own hands and limited means, they would begin to build the New Atlantis.

DROP CITY

"The Revolution is not only feasible, but inevitable," proclaimed the founders of Drop City. "All power to the imagination."[62] In the spring of 1965, well before the term "hippie" had even come into usage, three art students from the University of Kansas—Clark Richert, and Gene and Joann Bronowski—bought six acres of a windswept goat pasture in the tiny burg of El Moro in southern Colorado. Their goal was to build a completely open, anarchistic society—a place to reinvent oneself. Initially, the Drop City group had been influenced by the multimedia happenings of the New York avant-garde, in particular the work of Allen Kaprow.

"We really saw ourselves as artists and we saw Drop City as an ongoing work of art," said Richert who, along with the Bronowskis, coined the term "Drop Art" to describe their activities.[63] (It rhymed with Pop Art and Op Art, two major trends in the contemporary art scene.) While still art students in Kansas City, they put on a series of "Droppings" in which various objects—furniture, painted rocks, water balloons—were pushed out of windows or off the roofs of buildings. Drop City was a continuation, an expansion of those early pieces. "We regarded Drop City as Drop Art," explained Richert, but unlike the Kaprow-style happenings that had been loosely scripted and staged for a certain time and place, Drop City would be a nonstop, round-the-clock happening or *dropping* that kept going, 365 days a year.[64]

"We thought that a great leap in human consciousness was imminent, about to reshape the planet," wrote Dropper John Curl.[65] The past would be obliterated. Old attitudes, opinions, ego-driven ambitions were cast off. "You had the sense that anything was possible, that the potential was unlimited," said Jo Ann Bernofsky. "We knew that we wanted to do something outrageous."[66] The Droppers adopted new ideas in communal living, making it up as they went along. Money and possessions were shared. Lovers and everyday chores were shared. Members of the community would take part in an ongoing collaborative performance by living spontaneously and intuitively. Art, life, and politics would merge into an all-for-one web of synergy. Everyone adopted a new name, happily discarding former identities: Curly Benson, Drop Lady, Clard Svenson, Larry Lard, Suzy Spotless, Oleo Margarine, and so on.

They believed in living off of the spoils of America. In the beginning, they slept in their cars. Then they set up tents and started to build the most rudimentary kinds of shelters. "We didn't know how to build anything when we got there," said Richert. "At first we considered building A-frames, because they seemed like the cheapest thing to do."[67] While some attempts were made to grow vegetables and raise goats, the unsettlers of Drop City learned

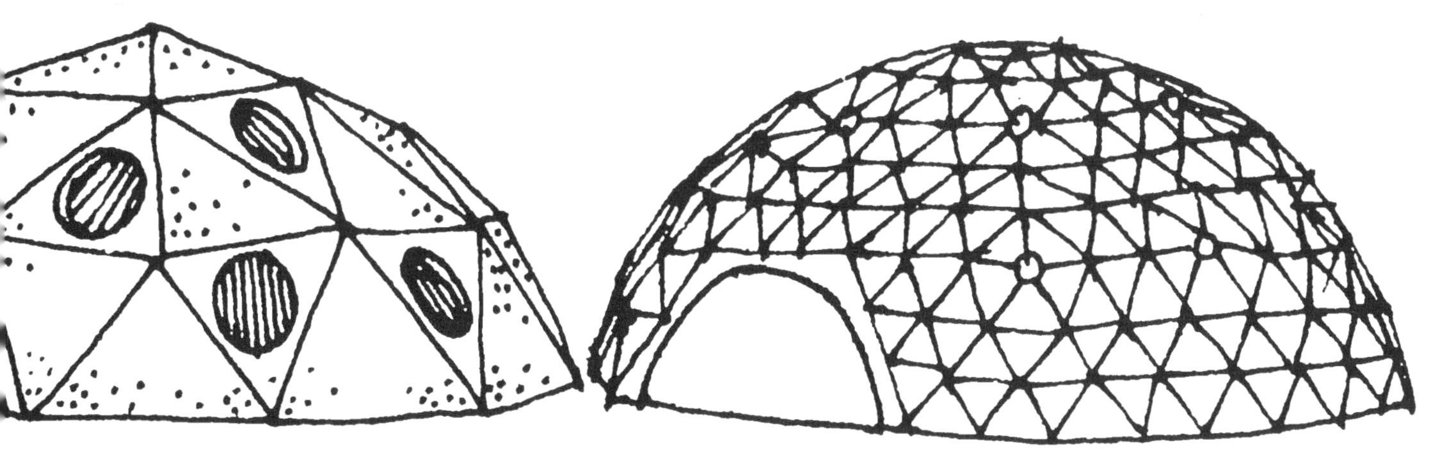

OPPOSITE
UPPER: *The patchwork domes of Drop City;* LOWER: *"a mobile hallucination," Hog Farm's portable performance dome in Sunland-Tujunga, California, 1968 (photo: Lisa Law).*

to scrounge most of their food from the supermarket in nearby Trinidad, where bruised fruit and vegetables were discarded on a daily basis. "Trapped inside a waste-economy man finds an identity as a consumer," wrote Dropper Bill Voyd. "Once outside the trap he finds enormous resources at his disposal-free."[68] Droppers worked together on multimedia performances, dance, group chanting, and a variety of public happenings or "Mind-Blows" held in and around Drop City. (Hundreds of sympathetic freaks turned out to participate in one such event that took place in June 1966 and went on, nonstop, for ninety-six hours.) "Life forms and art forms begin to interact," explained one Dropper. "The identity of the artist becomes irrelevant in relation to the scale of values employed, because the communal context of the work of art removes it from the marketplace."[69]

One of the commune's signature projects was the *Ultimate Painting*, created by four Droppers working in collaboration over a six-month period. It took the form of a circular painting, an "infinite sphere loaded with spatial paradox," that measured five feet in diameter and could be spun at various speeds.[70] Brightly colored shapes produced hallucinatory effects on the viewer when the great painting was rotated beneath a flashing strobe. "If you look at it for twenty minutes the stuff begins to come out and fill the whole room."[71] But by far the most significant collaborative effort at Drop City was the architecture. More than the spin art, more than the droppings or multimedia razzle-dazzle, it was the globular domes—what one visitor described as "candy-colored toad-stools"— that made Drop City the first capital of the outlaw nation.[72]

Farther west, another open-door commune was taking root about the same time. The Hog Farm was a direct offshoot of the Kesey Prankster group. Founders Hugh Romney (AKA Wavy Gravy) and Paul Foster had both been "on the bus," and with a motley crew of friends, they took over a thirty-acre pig farm in Sunland, California. In exchange for free rent, they agreed to feed the farmers' hogs, hence the name.[73] Like the Droppers, they were devoted to an ongoing experiment in free-form cohabitation. "[We are] an expanded family, a mobile hallucination, a sociological experiment, an army of clowns." They too believed in living free off the spoils of society and could feed thirty people on three dollars a day and a garbage run to the local supermarket.

MORNING STAR

Alternative forces were also moving northward into Sonoma County and the little burg of Sebastopol, where the old Morning Star Ranch was turned into a liberated settlement zone. The thirty-acre property belonged to open-land patriarch Lou Gottlieb, former member of the Limeliters folk trio who, through LSD, had experienced a sudden spiritual awakening and announced that his land was open to anyone who wished to come. Compared to the streets of Haight-Ashbury, the place seemed like a paradise with its own apple orchard, rolling hills, and soaring redwood trees. There were picturesque old farm buildings, two wells, and a stream running through the middle of the property.

At first it was only a quiet group of Gottlieb's friends and a few back-to-nature hermits who hoped to create a psychedelic ashram for the practice of "sun yoga" and deep immersion in nature. Ramon Sender, after his forty days in the desert, moved to Morning Star with his dog, Katy. So did other Trips Festival alumni like Ben Jacopetti and his wife, Rain.[74] Gottlieb left his job as music critic for the *San Francisco Chronicle* and moved into the old egg-storage building, which he remodeled into

OM CHANTI PEACE OM

OPPOSITE
UPPER LEFT: *Lou Gottlieb, open-land patriarch and founder of Morning Star commune;*
LOWER: *Morning yoga practice.*

a music studio for his grand piano. Bruce Baille, Justin, Mama Dog, Marjorie, Victoria, and Don and Sandy King were also among the early settlers. Near-vana, Gottlieb's dark-haired lover, arrived a little later and assumed her role as Morning Star's "sacred weapon." Tim Leary showed up and gave the group his blessings. The first of the Haight-Ashbury fugitives arrived in November 1966 along with several Diggers who came to harvest the apple orchard for their free-food program.

How does one begin to shape an environment that encourages constant change and all forms of extreme behavior? Gottlieb made plans for a large assembly hall, where the freaky mob could gather for meditation and yoga, as well as a series of dormitories "beautifully constructed in folk architecture."[75] In the beginning he consulted architects at Berkeley about designing some kind of experimental outpost, but this kind of self-conscious foresight didn't match the spontaneous spirit of the place. "The architects came up with some nice buildings but, you know, I used to think there was a bridge but there isn't," said Gottlieb. "If you want to build something here you just build it and see what it looks like. You don't make plans."[76] Everything was already perfect as it was. The land chose the people. The land provided sustenance and shelter. "Here is Utopia," cried Gottlieb to a group of visitors startled by the naked girls and uncollected garbage. "You thought you would never see it? Well, if you know of a better way, tell me and I'll try it."[77]

During the initial phase of its existence, from 1966 to 1967, Morning Star reached a level of group synergy. Older artists, musicians, and drop-out intellectuals were grooving in the sunshine, tripping with young street hippies and inner-city outcasts. The mix, however combustible, had all the markings of a New Jerusalem. Here, certainly, was Brand's call for "wildness" conjoined with total abandon. Circles of star-eyed gypsies held hands in the grass, practicing sun yoga, chanting. (Local police cruised Morning Star regularly just to check out the hippie girls.) Near-vana, love goddess, assumed a difficult asana, standing on her head, naked, while breast-feeding her baby, Covelo Vishnu God. She offered birthing advice to all prospective mothers: "Open land—open cervix! Tuning in to the sun with mellow acid trips and love-making kept me happy and unafraid.... Fucking is great all during pregnancy.... we even fucked when I went into labor. This made parturition an orgasm rather than a clinical affair.... I had planned to take LSD for labor but I got higher than I've ever been without it."[78] Indeed, it seemed as if every young woman at Morning Star got pregnant that year, bringing a fresh litter of babies with names like Psyche Joy Ananda, Raspberry Sundown Hummingbird, and Rainbow Canyon.

Lou Gottlieb printed up his recipe for afterbirth:

1 placenta
1 onion
½ cup ghee or melted butter

"Steam the placenta until it can be ground in a meat grinder without drippings. Sauté the onion until light brown... Form into an attractive mound and garnish with whatever you have. Serve with Ritz crackers, chapati, tortillas ..."[79]

There were tantric orgies in the moonlight, astral projection in the orchard, drums, flutes, whole orchestras of handmade instruments, nude horseback riding through the hills, natural childbirthing in the chicken coop. Spur-of-the-moment rituals were held to celebrate summer and winter solstices. Sacred mandalas were painted on rocks and trees. The group moved mysteriously as a single, multiheaded organism. "I experienced consciousness-expansion in daily living," said Haight-Ashbury exile Pam Read, who confessed to having telepathic occurrences and dreams in common with other people.[80]

Spiritual awakening evolved through a jumble of Zen, Hindu, Kabala, Christian mysticism—some of the older residents retained ties with the Aurobindo Ashram in India—together with sun worship, astrology, back-to-nature pantheism, *I-Ching*, Tarot, black magic, Ouija-board wisdom, and the karmic insights of LSD. All of it percolated in the collective brain pan and produced Morning Star's very own religion, otherwise known as "Ahimsa," or the Sacred Order of the Morning Star Faith, which was symbolized by an eight-point star combined with a cross, a circle, and a heart:

Purpose: The living of a primitive life in harmony with revealed Divine Law.

Mission: The opening of lands as sanctuaries for the One, naked, nameless, and homeless.

Earth Yoga: Live on the land in such a way so as to harmonize into invisibility.

By the summer of 1967, the situation was ripening. Followers of Ahimsa were living on the land but not necessarily harmonizing into invisibility. The Diggers posted notices in Haight-Ashbury, announcing that Morning Star was now a free-land outpost, calling it the "Digger Farm." Everyone was welcome and encouraged to donate tents, seeds, tar paper, and other homesteading supplies.[81] Some of the Diggers returned to San Francisco with wide-eyed reports of the new Eden up north. Others stayed and planted vegetable gardens and made compost heaps. The woods filled with hippie kids camping out. Weekends were particularly crowded with curiosity seekers. "Tibetan-style yogis perched on fence posts and shell-decorated goddesses walked the boundary paths tinkling like wind chimes," wrote one visitor. "'Oms' and chants floated across the starlit meadows."[82] The Upper House turned into a giant crash pad jammed to the rafters with new arrivals.

By June, there were more than sixty full-time residents, but Gottlieb and the original band of settlers found it hard to turn anyone away, devoted as they were to the principles of "LATWIDN" (Land Access To Which Is Denied No One). Instead of resisting, they embraced the newcomers and tried to go with the flow. "How could we deny anyone the opportunity of rebirth from the earth, our common mother?"[83] Some were homeless fugitives who took on comic-book identities as soon as they arrived. Fluid Floyd, Deputy Dog, Lucy Livingood, Zen Jack, and Kickapoo Bob arrived in one wave, and more were on their way. Along with sweet-natured hippies came less desirable elements: sad-eyed runaways, suicidal teenagers, winos, and ill-tempered bikers, whom Gottlieb dubbed the "Impossibles."

It was turning into a riotous evolutionary experiment, pushing beyond acceptable boundaries of human interaction, sexuality, shelter, sanitation, and religious practice. There were no rules or guidelines. "Morning Star is a divine drama with people like me who don't have anything better to do as actors," said David Pratt.[84] Apart from the Haight-Ashbury influx, there was a steady stream of rubbernecking tourists, journalists, photographers, and sociologists hoping to catch a glimpse of a genuine hippie in his or her natural setting. The commune was also starting to get hassled by the local authorities for sanitation and building-code violations. On July 7, 1967, *Time* magazine ran a cover story on the counter culture and featured Morning Star as a prime example of the new rural enclaves. "An hour's drive north of San Francisco, in apple-growing country near Sebastopol along the

OPPOSITE
Cryptic symbols and chants of AHIMSA, Sacred Order of the Morning Star Faith.

WAKE UP
I AM
AOM
EK ONG KAR SAT NAM
SIRI WA GURU
MAHA YOWI YANC
RAGO PATI RA GAVA RAGA ROM
PA TITA PAVANA SITA ROM
SITA ROM JIA SITA ROM
RAGÒ PATI RA GAVA RAGA ROM
RAMA RAMA JIA SITA ROM
RAMA RAMA JIA SITA ROM
JESU CHRISTO PARE AIE NAM
PA TIA AH IM SA TIE BAGHAVAN
(172)
CHARLIE'S

Russian River, some 30 to 50 country hippies live on a 31-acre ranch called Morning Star."[85] *Time*'s report, one of the oddities of sixties media coverage, painted a dewy-eyed picture of flower children living in a never-never land of organic bliss.

"The Morning Star experiment is perhaps the most hopeful development in the hippie philosophy to date," wrote *Time*'s editors. "Most Morning Star colonists avoid acid. [This was certainly not the case.] 'I'd rather have beautiful children than beautiful visions,' says a tanned, clear-eyed hippie girl named Joan." There were also glowing descriptions of quaintly crafted shelters and bountiful gardens—"Cabbages and turnips, lettuce and onions march in glossy green rows, neatly mulched with redwood sawdust"—while gorgeous, free-love goddesses lounged in the buffalo grass, sewing colorful dresses, "clad in nothing but beads, bells, and feather headdresses."[86] Needless to say, *Time*'s coverage brought hundreds more people who couldn't resist the urge to visit this new-age nirvana and see for themselves. By the end of summer, Gottlieb and the others found themselves scrounging food to provide dinner for more than three hundred.

First efforts at making shelter were crude and began with the most rudimentary kind of hands-on building: tepees wrapped with plastic tarp, hogans made from mud and branches, tents, lean-tos, shacks, tree houses, anything that provided a vestige of protection and kept out the rain. "You don't need money, architect, plans, permits," said Gottlieb, who encouraged these forms of spontaneous building. "How about a hobbity hole in the hill, all snug and warm and hidden from the cops?"

Coyote, a newcomer, built himself a funky tree house near the orchard. Otto erected a wooden A-frame behind the barn. Cindy and Herb lived in a "Scotch Broom Room," a primitive kind of bower woven together from branches and weeds. Joe Conti and Lucy Livingood squatted in a canvas tent, while Choctaw Ed erected a rainbow-hued tepee. Don and Sandy built a cabin out of throwaway lumber while David Pratt, an artist, built a multistory perch, high in a redwood tree. "Man has a nest-building instinct just like the other animals," said Gottlieb. "It is totally frustrated by our lock-step society whose restrictive codes on home-building make it impossible to build a home that doesn't sterilize, insulate, and rigidify the inhabitants. You haven't lived until you're living in you own home-made nest."[87]

Pam and Larry Read lived in the "Meadowboat" with their son, golden-haired Adam Siddartha. It was little more than a sleeping platform built into the side of a hill, with one end resting on a tree stump, but it had a certain structural integrity compared to the other jury-rigged shelters at Morning Star. Diagonal bracing and outrigger-style beams supported a corrugated metal roof and gave the house a profile that reminded some of a boat floating through the meadow, hence the name. It was certainly the best-known building at Morning Star after *Time* featured it in its 1967 hippie spread. There, on page 20, frolicking in front of her snug little shelter, was Pam Read, completely naked: "It's hip to unzip at Morning Star commune," read the caption.[88]

While *Time* may have reveled in the fiction of a wholesome rural utopia, local property owners were shocked to find so many stoned-out barbarians at their gates. Neighbors complained about the piles of rotting garbage, naked yoga, and conspicuous displays of free love along their property lines. But it was the excrement that offended them the most. There weren't adequate sanitation facilities for the hundreds now camping out, so woods and fields were despoiled with human shit. Half-hearted attempts were made to build a communal outhouse, but it was

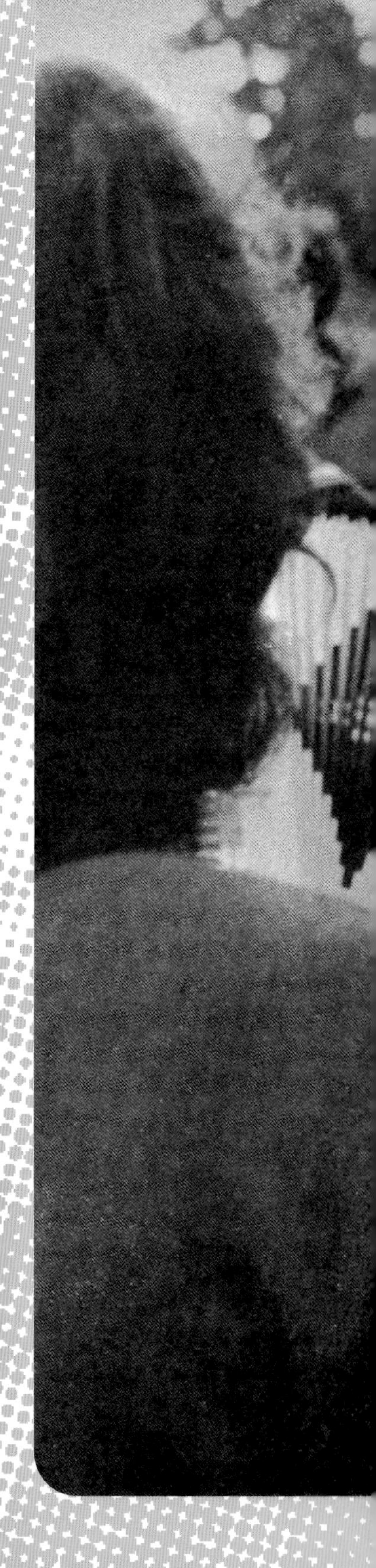

OPPOSITE
LOWER LEFT: *Pam & Larry Read's meadowboat, Morning Star, 1967;* LOWER RIGHT: *Shelters at Wheeler's Ranch, Sonoma County, California.*

JASON
JASON
DALE and Suzanne's
R.I.P. Superman
91
BUCK
Photo by Sylvia
PHOTO BY RICK BLANC
WE LOVE THE SANTA ROSA POLICE
upperhouse
Photo by Sylvia
TED
Photo by Sylvia
by Sylvia
TUCK & SANDY
APPROACHING THE ALTAR

never finished, and soon Morning Star became the target of escalating harassment by local police, county health inspectors, and building officials.

The first arrests were made in the fall of 1967, when as many as twenty Morning Star residents went to jail for contempt of court. Charges included camping without permits and running an "organized camp," to which Gottlieb responded: "If they find any evidence of organization here, I wish they would show it to me." To avoid personal liability, Gottlieb announced he had deeded the property to God, but the county judge ruled that a deity wasn't allowed to hold title in Sonoma County. After more injunctions, the county bulldozers moved in and flattened all nonconforming buildings including the Lower House, the Upper House, the garage, the old barn, David and Penny's tree house, Pam and Larry's Meadowboat—virtually everything except for Gottlieb's studio. The wrecking crew made a huge pile out of all the debris and burned it so that people wouldn't be able to salvage materials for rebuilding. The fires smoldered for weeks.

By this point, many of the Morning Star regulars were moving to nearby Wheeler's Ranch, another open-door commune, where they started, once again, to stake ground and build their own quirky shelters. Fluteplayer Tom and Naked Diane moved into a hollowed-out redwood stump. Transit Harry hung a bedspring between four trees and covered it with an Army-surplus parachute. Ramon Sender, his wife, Gina, and their dog, Katy, took shelter in the "Mouse House," a canvas-and-wood structure built beneath wild lilac bushes. "The importance of building your own nest was central to the Open Land philosophy," said Bill Wheeler, owner of the three-hundred-acre tract. "Those who did it—both men and women—found it one of the most exhilarating experiences of their lives."[89] Charlotte and Bryce fabricated a circular structure behind Hoffie's Hill, shaped around the contours of a large boulder, supported by branches and covered with a canvas tarp. One visitor described their homespun yurt as a "masterpiece of hippie architecture," an "Aquarian Haven," but it leaked badly during rainstorms.[90]

The settlers at Wheeler's Ranch wanted to shape their lives as free-form poetry: open-ended and steeped with meaning and mystery. They wanted to live like heroes, act out their own myths, and experience each day as a revelation. "We are free to be whoever we are and whoever we want to be: pan the piper, the golden goddess, the elfin dancers, laughing among the mushrooms,"[91] wrote Alicia Bay Laurel in her back-to-the-land paean, *Living on the Earth*, composed while living at Wheeler's Ranch.[92] As much as any book of the period, it captured the generational yearning for escape and simplification. (The book would become a surprise best seller.)

While Bay Laurel made occasional references to real people and real places, her story's appeal lay in the way it evoked a totally innocent and undefiled sense of place, a fairytale land where everything was reduced to essential necessities and homespun truths. "This book is for people who would rather chop wood than work behind a desk," she wrote in her hand-scrawled text beside simple line drawings of smiling, naked hippies. If you believed, if you really believed, you could go out and live as beautifully as one of Bay Laurel's drawings.

The book unfolds as a kind of allegorical journey: leaving the city, hiking into the forest, moving deeper into what the author calls the "unmapped land." Words and illustrations flow together in seamless continuity. There are no chapter breaks or divisions in the narrative. Bay Laurel offers advice on everything from herb gathering and making bread, to churning butter, digging a "proper

OPPOSITE
Morning Star Scrapbook, *1973*.

"We are free to be whoever we want to be...": hand-built shelters at Wheeler's Ranch and Morning Star.

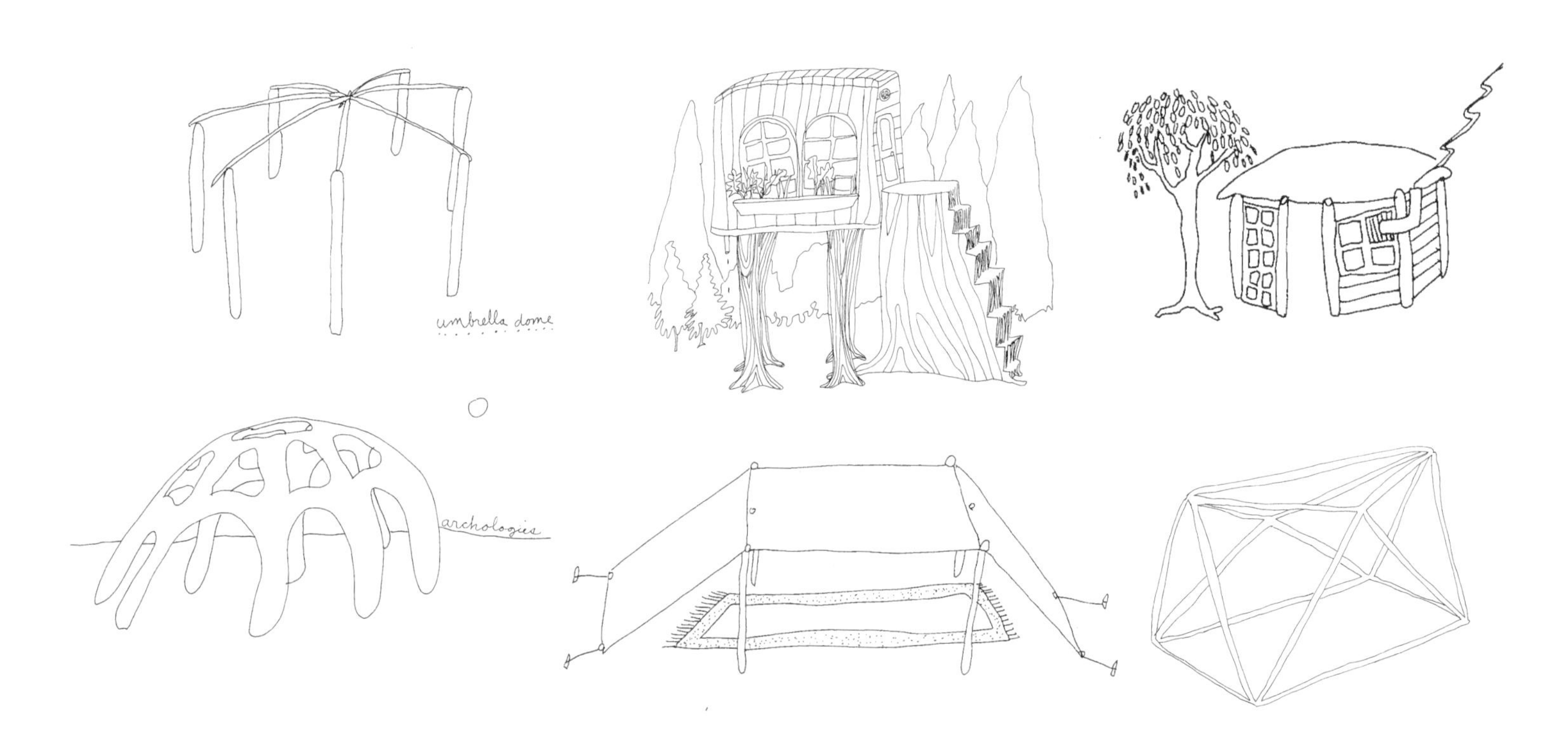

shit hole," and giving birth: "the mother should eat some of the placenta." There are even helpful tips on dealing with death: "Pour on kerosene and lots of incense. Burning bodies don't smell so good."

A good deal of attention is devoted to the making of shelter: how to fabricate a basic house, for instance, by stretching a blanket across four poles and tying the corners. For a more permanent abode Bay Laurel suggests digging holes two feet deep and inserting tall poles. "Bend poles to meet as arches. Lash them together... cover with a tarp or an old tent.... If rain is imminent: cover with plastic." While it all has the sound of a child's make-believe world, Bay Laurel herself was living in just such a hut, one that was made out of wattle and mud.

ABOVE: *Alicia Bay Laurel, basic shelter (Umbrella Dome, Tree Stump House, Hexagonal Cabin, Arcology, Tent of Three Blankets, Triangle House) illustrations from* Living on the Earth, *1971.*

OPPOSITE
Alicia Bay Laurel, "In the Morning," Being of the Sun, *1973.*

6 MAGIC CIRCLES

"WE WANTED TO CREATE A STRUCTURE THAT DIDN'T REMIND US OF ANYTHING—A NEW KIND OF SPACE IN WHICH TO CREATE NEW SELVES."

—THE RED ROCKERS[1]

I enjoy playing with bubbles very much,"[2] wrote outlaw architect Steve Baer, who built a bubble-making machine out of a bicycle pump, surgical tubing, and an inner tube so that he could study bubble mutations at close hand. He was particularly fascinated by the way a froth of bubbles would adjust to one another in a matrix of perfect 120-degree angles linking dozens of different curvatures. Here was a soft alternative to the hard-edged logic of conventional architecture. "You would suspect that anything with a form as perfect as a single bubble would be a prima donna, but bump bubbles together and they leap into cooperative forms as if they had planned it ahead of time."[3] During the mid- to late sixties, Baer began to translate his bubble experiments into a freak-funk kind of architecture that combined the cosmic mathematics of Bucky Fuller with psychedelic insights and hands-on spontaneity.

Within the expanding consciousness of a generation, there was a spatial shift from square to round, from hard-edged to soft, from static to mobile, from exclusive to all-inclusive, and it seemed to be welling up from the deepest part of the human psyche. It drifted inexorably away from the linear, from the right angle, from the grid, the box—away from the whole Euclidean dead end—moving into an imaginary place that was at once flowing, ceremonial, globular, and tribal, a place in which time and space were seamlessly interwoven. There was magic in circles, and for many of the fuzzily dispossessed, the revolution would manifest itself in the form of a brazenly free-standing pod, or dome.

Those who were coming of age in the sixties stood united in their loathing of the square and the tyranny of its myriad mutations: the soul-withering suburban subdivision, the monolithic blocks of postwar modernism, the glass-and-steel grid of the American corporation. Square was bad, round was good. "Build circular musical structures and help destroy rational box-reality," declared one hippie builder who believed that the square had contaminated every aspect of western civilization.[4] How was one expected to live freely inside a room with four walls, corners, and a ceiling that pressed down, restricting thoughts and movement? The conventional house, the conventional room, were part of the same mind-set that had created the war in Vietnam. "Today, most of the designs we carry out upon our earth resemble nothing so much as a succession of architectural bombing runs," wrote Baer.

"I want a lodge that is round like the day and the sun and the path of the stars," says a character in *When Legends Die*, Hal Borland's popular 1963 novel about tribal ways. In *Understanding Media*, Marshall McLuhan condemns the tradition of the square room as speaking the "language of the sedentary specialist," while extolling the virtues of the round hut, the igloo, and the conical wigwam as expressing the "integral nomadic ways of food-gathering communities."[5] (McLuhan's book was published in 1964 and quickly became one of the canonical texts of the period. Its unorthodox views on space, community, and communications had resonance with a generation that had come of age watching television.) There was much to learn from primitive forms of building and the virtues of tepees, hogans, yurts, igloos, and other vernacular forms of nonpedigreed architecture. "Eventually we must go forward so that we find ourselves back with the man who works with branches, reeds, and mud," wrote Baer.[6]

It was fine to dream about bubble houses, but how was one to build something practical and sustainable given the effects of weather, the cost of building materials, and the laws of gravity? By 1959 it was estimated that almost one thousand geodesic-type domes, based on Fuller's patent, had been

built around the world. But Fuller's vision would find its true legacy in the mid- to late sixties when the children of the counterculture adopted his patent as a symbol of resistance and solidarity. Fuller's influence spread rapidly through word of mouth, books, articles, and the infamously long and rambling lectures that he delivered at college campuses. Young admirers like Baer, Clark Richert, Jay Baldwin, Lloyd Kahn, and Steve Durkee would borrow Fuller's basic concepts and adapt them to the needs of the self-build communities that were now springing up in the hinterlands.

"Corners constrict the mind," wrote one outlaw. "Domes break into new dimensions."[7] Indeed, the dome could be seen as the seed for a whole new way of being—one that was communal, self-supporting, nonhierarchical. Its simple, round geometry suggested a multifaceted crystal, the eye of God, a circle of fellowship, and the mysterious oneness that so many had experienced on LSD and Psilocybin. "You merge with the dome; its skin becomes your skin . . ."[8]

THE DOMES OF DROP

"Suddenly, there are the shapes. Angular, unearthly, demented, like gawky igloos in a kaleidoscope," wrote journalist William Hedgepeth upon approaching Drop City in the summer of 1968. First impressions were all the more dreamlike for his having arrived during a summer storm, a kind of psychedelic *Sturm and Drang,* with wild rain and "stroboscopic flits" of lightning. As Hedgepeth came closer, the clouds parted to reveal a group of domes glowing preternaturally in the lambent air. "Yellow blue green red pink purple: brazen things just lying up there, coldly geodesic, looming on the little rise," he wrote, comparing the commune to a surreal hallucination.[9] Indeed, it would have the same effect on others visiting for the first time. "Drop City dropped on us like a flash," wrote Richard Fairfield, an underground journalist who came shortly after Hedgepeth and had an equally memorable arrival.[10] Pierre Lacombe, a French journalist, visited that same summer and wrote breathless descriptions of *"les coupoles géodesiques pour l'habitat hippy."*[11] But Drop City was neither a dream nor a mirage that had dropped out of thin air. It had been built with great effort and imagination over a three-year ritual of trial and error, starting as a flash of inspiration in April 1965, when Clark Richert and two of his fellow Droppers, attended a lecture by Buckminster Fuller at the University of Colorado in Boulder.[12] They became overnight converts to Fuller's way of thinking and decided to build domes in place of conventional structures. A cluster of geodesic domes—like so many bubbles in the wilderness—would convey the desired message. "Houses in our society are walls, blocking man from man, man from the universe, man from himself," wrote Bill Voyd, a founding member of Drop City. "The works of art we envisage are total, vast."[13]

But at that point Fuller's formula wasn't readily available so the Droppers had to figure it out for themselves.[15] One took measurements from a playground jungle gym that looked something like a geodesic dome. Another made a scale model from drinking straws and pipe cleaners. "I thought I understood the geometry of the dome," said Richert, who worked on the model but soon learned that it wasn't as

A dome culture blossoms.

BELOW: *Buckminster Fuller's* Spherical Truss for Ford Motor Company, *1953.*

OPPOSITE
Dome information in The Whole Earth Catalog, *1969.*

PREVIOUS PAGES
P. 168 UPPER: *Paolo Soleri, Ceramic Apse, Arcosanti, Arizona (photo: Terrence Moore);* LOWER: *Soleri & Mark Mills, Dome House, Cave Creek, Arizona, 1949;* P. 169: *Soleri, Ceramics Studio, Cosanti.*

FOLLOWING PAGE
P. 172 LEFT: *How to build a triacontahedron,* Dome Book Two.

·na Domes

ere are about a dozen Dyna Domes on the outskirts of ·enix. Each new one built gets a little closer to the city ·its, and it's the hope of domebuilder Bill Woods to have city fathers wake up one morning, find themselves ·rounded by domes, and admit the new creatures under wings of the building codes.

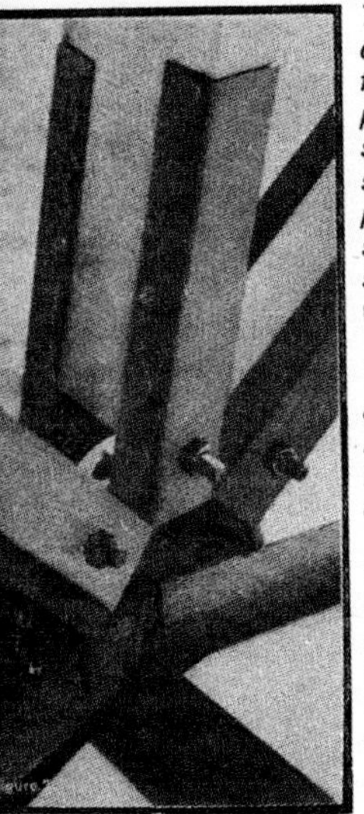

These are good quality, low cost plywood domes, with fiberglass exterior, and polyurethane foam insulation sprayed on the inside. Wood struts are put together with patented metal connectors, seams are filled with high-strength caulk, then taped with fiberglass.

You have the choice of having a dome erected (within 500 miles of Phoenix), buying a kit, or purchasing just the connectors with plans.

Woods has been experimenting for some time with foam-fiber-glass buildings, has built a machine that produces the sandwich panels, and is about to market a foam dome.

Complete dome, erected on concrete floor within 500 miles of Phoenix: approx. $4.00 per sq. ft. floor space.

Complete kit with instructions for erection: approx. $2.00 per sq. ft. floor space.

Hub connectors, with plans for building it yourself: $2.00 per strut.

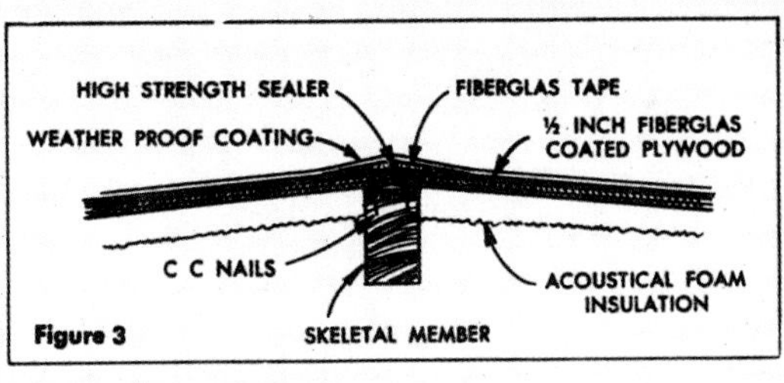

Brochure **free** from:
Dyna Dome
22226 North 23rd Avenue
Phoenix, Arizona 85027

·meworks

·meworks builds structure systems, structures, solar energy ·lectors and systems, and glamour. From their desert base ·r Albuquerque they are shortly blossoming into an industry. ·nething I'm considering at present is whether to personally ·est in that growth.
—S. B.

·r design, fabrication, consulting, lectures, write:

stretch
section of an ennea.
stretched through one zone

·turo

·s interesting that Finland, with its extensive forests and ·ely-crafted wooden structures, should present the first ·ll-detailed commerically available foam-fiberglass ·elling. Called Futuro, this gleaming elliptical pod with ·ractable stairs, looks like it just landed. Now in ·oduction in Philadelphia and slated for west-coast ·oduction in San Jose, the lightweight home can be ·licopter-dropped, and requires no site preparation. ·ructural strength and insulation are outstanding ·tures. The interior furnishings (optional) look ·stic and shiny—perhaps the direction that future ·using will take.

The Futuro House is now on display at 20th and Parkway, Philadelphia.

Futuro House

$10,000 for shell
$14,000 for completely equipped house
F. O. B. Philadelphia

from:
Futuro Corporation
1900 Rittenhouse Square
Philadelphia, PA 19103

·JTURO FACTS

100% insulated 2" polyurethane foam—heats from -22 to 72 F. in 30 minutes.
Positive pressure ventilation system—air conditioning available.
Complete kitchen facilities.
Bathroom facilities with shower and either chemical or standard water closet.
Internal partitions can be modified to sleep up to eight people in one unit or can be divided into two double bed motel units, or supplied bare, except for water closet. Furnishings include 6 convertible chaise/beds, lighted arm rests, center table, barbecue, fireplace, carpets, partitions, shelves, etc.
Interior and exterior are made of fiberglas, including furnishing (except for carpeting). Estimated life span in excess of 30 years.
Almost completely maintenance free for life of unit.
Exterior colors available: Pale blue, pine forest green, pale pink, lemon yellow. Interior decor complements exterior.
Snow load in excess of 10 feet; wind load over 100 miles per hour, sealed against all water, dust or air infiltration.
Gross weight about 8000 pounds; diameter 26 feet; internal height at center—11 feet; effective area at window height—500 square feet; volume—5000 cubic feet; supporting structure—steel tubing with legs proportioned for 0 to 20 site slope.

11. No site preparation whatsoever, except for concrete piers to bolt down legs (plus utilities to site). Special independently operated utilities for more remote areas.
12. Designed for maximum security when stairs are retracted.
13. Twenty double acrylic windows—optionally operable. Viewable windows can be placed in either lower or upper hemisphere.
14. Portable (assembled) by helicopter or barge.
15. Portable (disassembled) by truck or rail.

ZONING AND BUILDING CODES—Futuro is available for Class I or II Fire Ratings and will be suitable for sparsely developed areas, or those conforming to National Building Codes.

TYPICAL SHIPPING COSTS—(f.o.b. Philadelphia)—Helicopter assembled about $1000 per 100 miles. Car or Truckload disassembled varies. West Indies—Barge and Helicopter at Island $3,000 assembled.

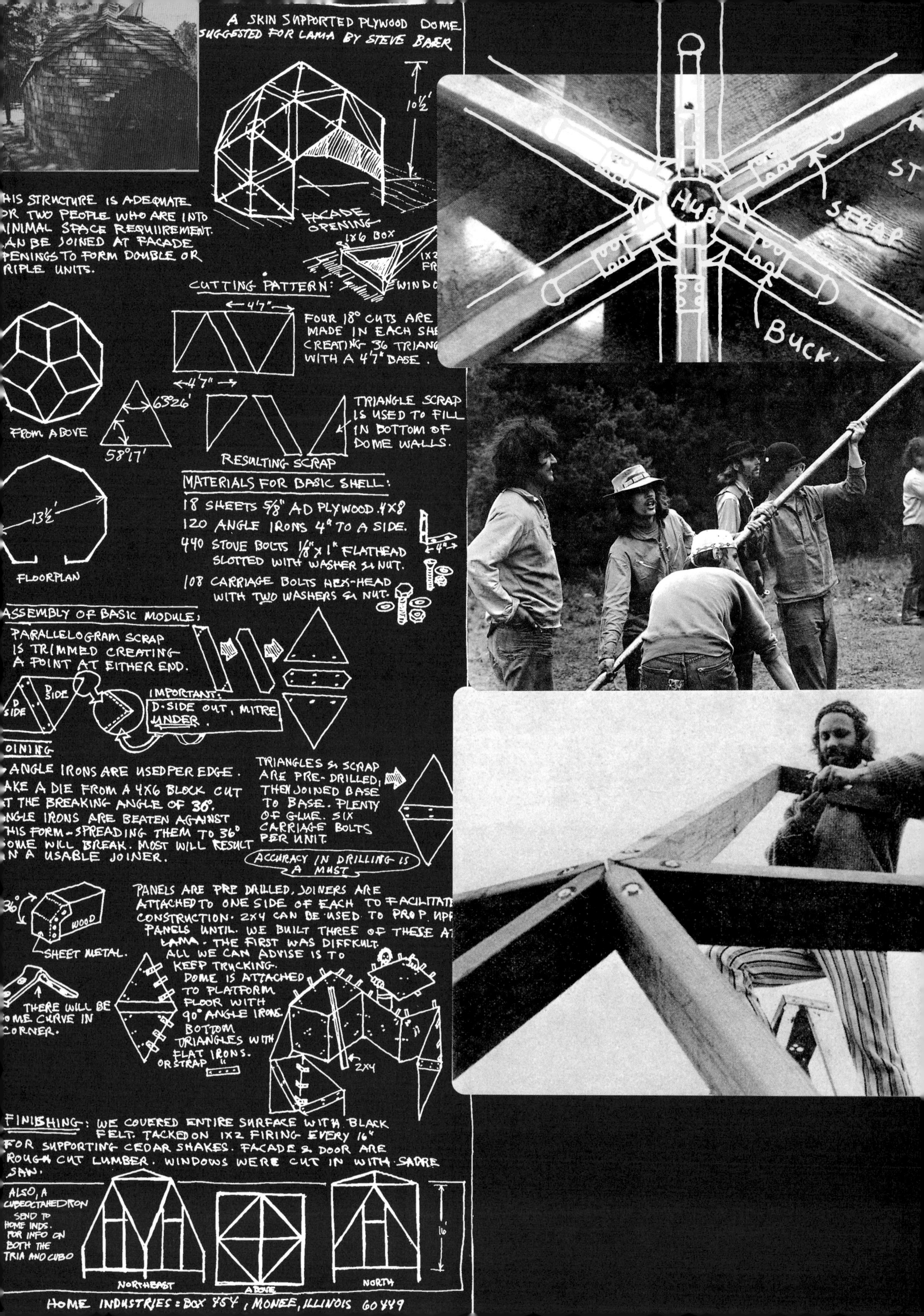

A SKIN SUPPORTED PLYWOOD DOME
SUGGESTED FOR LAMA BY STEVE BAER
10½'
HIS STRUCTURE IS ADEQUATE
OR TWO PEOPLE WHO ARE INTO
INIMAL SPACE REQUIREMENT.
AN BE JOINED AT FACADE
PENINGS TO FORM DOUBLE OR
RIPLE UNITS.
FACADE OPENING
1X6 BOX
WINDO
CUTTING PATTERN:
4'7"
FOUR 18° CUTS ARE
MADE IN EACH SHE
CREATING 36 TRIANG
WITH A 4'7" BASE.
4'7"
63°26'
58°17'
FROM ABOVE
TRIANGLE SCRAP
IS USED TO FILL
IN BOTTOM OF
DOME WALLS.
RESULTING SCRAP
MATERIALS FOR BASIC SHELL:
18 SHEETS 5/8" AD PLYWOOD 4X8
120 ANGLE IRONS 4" TO A SIDE.
440 STOVE BOLTS 1/8" x 1" FLATHEAD
SLOTTED WITH WASHER & NUT.
108 CARRIAGE BOLTS HEX-HEAD
WITH TWO WASHERS & NUT.
13½'
FLOORPLAN
4"
ASSEMBLY OF BASIC MODULE:
PARALLELOGRAM SCRAP
IS TRIMMED CREATING
A POINT AT EITHER END.
D SIDE
D SIDE
IMPORTANT:
D-SIDE OUT, MITRE
UNDER.
OINING
ANGLE IRONS ARE USED PER EDGE.
AKE A DIE FROM A 4X6 BLOCK CUT
T THE BREAKING ANGLE OF 36°.
NGLE IRONS ARE BEATEN AGAINST
HIS FORM - SPREADING THEM TO 36°
OME WILL BREAK. MOST WILL RESULT
N A USABLE JOINER.
TRIANGLES & SCRAP
ARE PRE-DRILLED,
THEN JOINED BASE
TO BASE. PLENTY
OF GLUE. SIX
CARRIAGE BOLTS
PER UNIT.
ACCURACY IN DRILLING IS
A MUST
36°
WOOD
SHEET METAL.
THERE WILL BE
OME CURVE IN
CORNER.
PANELS ARE PRE DRILLED, JOINERS ARE
ATTACHED TO ONE SIDE OF EACH TO FACILITATE
CONSTRUCTION. 2X4 CAN BE USED TO PROP UPP
PANELS UNTIL WE BUILT THREE OF THESE AT
LAMA. THE FIRST WAS DIFFICULT.
ALL WE CAN ADVISE IS TO
KEEP TRUCKING.
DOME IS ATTACHED
TO PLATFORM
FLOOR WITH
90° ANGLE IRONS.
BOTTOM
TRIANGLES WITH
FLAT IRONS.
OR STRAP
2X4
FINISHING: WE COVERED ENTIRE SURFACE WITH BLACK
FELT. TACKED ON 1X2 FIRING EVERY 16"
FOR SUPPORTING CEDAR SHAKES. FACADE & DOOR ARE
ROUGH CUT LUMBER. WINDOWS WERE CUT IN WITH SABRE
SAW.
ALSO, A
CUBEOCTAHEDRON
SEND TO
HOME INDS.
FOR INFO ON
BOTH THE
TRIA AND CUBO
16'
NORTHEAST
ABOVE
NORTH
HOME INDUSTRIES: BOX 454, MONEE, ILLINOIS 60449
HUB
ST
SCRAP
BUCK

D H
I I C C
D H
E C I
B B B H B
B D C B I
B E C I
D H
C E G
F D E F G H
C F F E F F
D G H
G E E
G D H

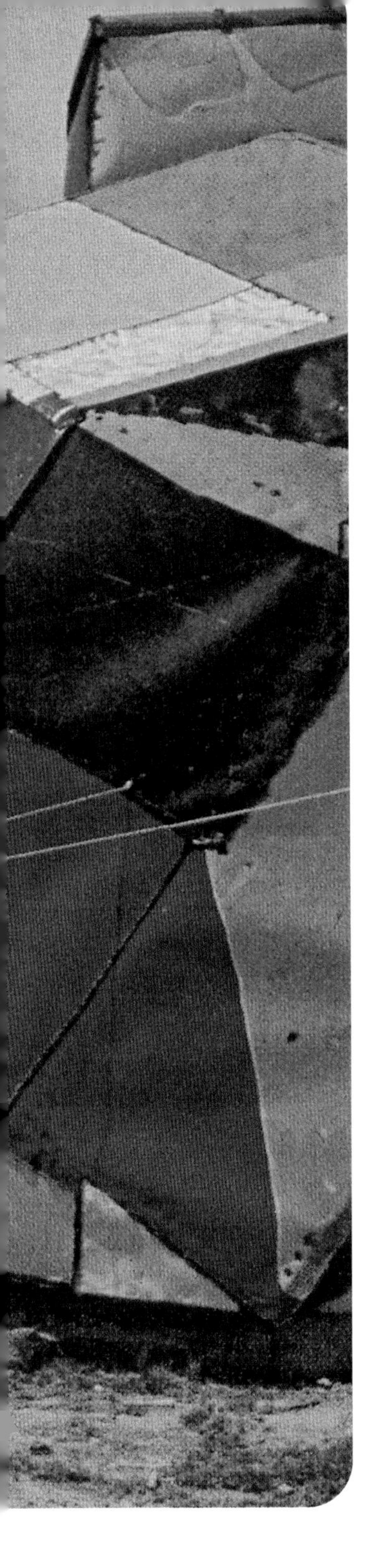

Drop City commune, Colorado.

ABOVE: *Kitchen complex.*

OPPOSITE
Coating the first dome with tar.

FOLLOWING PAGES
PP. 176–177: *"Like gawky igloos in a kaleidoscope . . ." the domes of Drop City;*
LOWER LEFT: *Theater dome under construction.*

easy as he had anticipated.[15] In fact, the first dome actually built at Drop City was not a true geodesic but a duo-dodecahedron, a polyhedron with twelve pentagonal faces.

Since there were no funds, the Droppers resorted to scrounging. "Our buildings were always made from free junk," said Richert. They borrowed, stole, and appropriated material from construction sites and derelict buildings. Late at night they disassembled abandoned railroad bridges and carried the timbers back to Drop City. They gathered scrap ends of culled wood, damaged insulation, and factory-reject plywood from local lumberyards. For the first dome they used short pieces of two-by-fours joined with plywood plates. Tar paper was stapled over the frame and then covered with chicken wire, bottle caps, and stucco. (The bottle caps separated the chicken wire from the tar paper and helped to create a better support for the stucco. The Droppers learned this technique from studying the buildings of a neighboring farm.) The outside of the dome was painted with tar-impregnated aluminum paint to help prevent leaks. Five-sided porthole windows were improvised from old automobile windows. These, along with the silver paint, made the first dome look like a space pod built for aboriginal astronauts, an impression that was reinforced by the spindly antenna that stuck up from its roof. Their next structure, a twenty-foot-diameter Icosadod dome, was designed as a communal kitchen. The frame was built with three-inch pipes covered with sheets of plywood and coated with tar. After the relative success of these first two experiments, however crude, the Droppers felt confident enough to try something more ambitious.

With its forty-foot-diameter base, the Theater Dome was twice as big as the duo-dodecahedron and Icosadod domes. It was also the first true geodesic and was designed to serve as a communal performing space.

The frame was built with two-by-four-inch scraps that were screwed to metal hubs made from sections of sewer pipe. Despite the fact that the scrap lumber had to be spliced together the frame was surprisingly sturdy.

It was at about this time, April 1966, that Steve Baer, a twenty-eight-year-old hippie architect/builder, arrived at Drop City and brought his own unique contribution. "Who were these people?" wondered Baer, who drove up from Albuquerque one weekend to see what was going on.[16] He was stunned by what he saw. Baer had dropped out of Amherst College in 1957 and turned from English literature to a passion for complex geometries. He became a convert to Fuller's thinking in 1963 after reading *Untitled Epic Poem on the History of Industrialization.* "As I read it I felt as if my mind were learning to swim," said Baer, who would immerse himself in the arcane world of chord lengths and octet trusses, becoming one of the leading lights of the alternative building movement.

The Droppers were just finishing the framing of the Theater Dome when Baer got there. "I climbed up on Clard's huge geodesic dome. Richard was digging a cellar. The radio was on," recalled Baer.[17] (The cellar in question was for a projection system, similar to Stan Vanderbeek's Movie-Drome, to project multimedia imagery onto the dome's interior walls.) Baer was impressed by the Droppers exuberance and confidence, how they were building such a complex structure without fussing over details. They followed the path of least resistance and managed to accept mistakes along the way, even incorporating them into the overall design. One of the structural members on the Theater Dome was a few inches short and wouldn't reach the central hub, so they just bolted it in place as it was and it still seemed to do the job. Baer, who was accustomed to a certain degree of mathematical accuracy, was astonished.

The theater's framework was complete but the Droppers still weren't sure what to use for exterior cladding. (Tar paper and stucco seemed inappropriate for such a large dome.) Baer suggested using metal taken from old automobiles. The going rate for most car tops was only twenty-five cents and at some salvage yards they could be taken for free. You just had to know what you were doing. Baer and the Droppers figured out a way to stand on the roof of a junked car and swing the head of a double-edged axe in a smooth pendulum motion, cutting out a section of metal as if with a giant can opener. "Chop along the sides first then the front and back," advised Baer. "Don't swing the axe hard once you have a slot going. If you hit flat, as you would a log, you'll only smash the metal in."[18] An experienced chopper could cut as many as five or six roofs in an hour. The next step was to shape the rough-edged metal into a triangular panel and for this they made a flexible plywood template to mark and cut each plate before fitting it to the frame.

The Droppers were making it up as they went along, trusting their instincts and going with the flow. Baer was witness to the mysteries of their organic process. "The growth of a dome panel by panel is a marvel, watching it take its shape and strength is something at once very strange and very familiar, as if you were watching the growth of a life form from another planet, unusual because of its foreignness, familiar because it seems alive."[19]

After the Theater Dome was finished, Baer returned to his home in Corrales, New Mexico, inspired. The relaxed attitude at Drop City had come as an epiphany: "You don't need to know that much," he wrote. "You just need to go ahead and try it out." This, in a sense, became the credo for his own work and the entire self-build revolution: *Don't worry, just do it.* "Seeing Drop City, especially the mistakes and weak materials, gave me great confidence," wrote Baer, who was dreaming about structures and new kinds of architecture. While acknowledging the importance of the geodesic dome as a symbolic entity, he was looking for a looser, less symmetrical version of Fuller's formula, one that would be more adaptable to the ad-hoc spontaneity of the outlaw communities. Fuller's patented formula required accurate measurements, uniform parts, and a good deal of planning.

Baer went to work with his bubble machine and paper models. He laid out nets of rubber bands tacked and stretched across the floor of his house. He studied the theories of Evgraf S. Fedorov, eminent Russian crystallographer, and read the non-Euclydian ideas of English mathematician, H. S. M. Coxeter. It was through Coxeter that Baer became aware of the zonagon, a polygon whose sides are in equal and parallel pairs. Unlike most polyhedrons, the zonagon can be stretched or compressed without altering its angles. An asymmetrical dome could be built from multi-shaped panels, not just triangular ones. The structures could be expanded and combined to create less rigid, more flexible kinds of spaces, a significant breakthrough for free-form builders. Baer made small models of zonahedra with sheets of folded cardboard and returned to Drop City to test his theories.

The first true zome was the Cartop Dome an eccentrically shaped structure—measuring approximately twenty-seven by fourteen feet—that was finished in 1966. It was made entirely from car-top panels without any underlying structural supports, as if it had been folded and glued out of cardboard. The whole thing cost only about fifteen dollars and that was mainly to buy sheet-metal screws for fastening the panels. "After we built the cartop dome we realized that everyone in the world can have a beautiful, comfortable dwelling unit for less than $1,000," said one Dropper.[20]

By mid-1966 there were more than twenty full-time residents at Drop City as well

THE WORD ZOME.
Steve Durkee invented this word. We were talking about these structures and agreed that they really were not domes because they are not symetrical. Stretching the zones of a zonahedra makes it asymetrical. Durkee said "they are zomes" I was very excited by this word - it sounds right. The word doesn't change any buildings but I kept waking up that night with the word going through my head. The next day at work Durkee and I kept saying things like - "well almost time to go zome"

OPPOSITE
Duo-dodecahedron dome with TV antenna, Drop City, 1966.

ABOVE: *Steve Baer, cutting car tops & the origins of the word "Zome."*

FOLLOWING PAGES
PP. 180–181: *Pages from Baer's* Dome Cookbook, *1968.*

In the past the hard part of using cartops has been cutting out the panels. The tops are heavy and have sharp edges so every time you load or unload them or even just turn one around on a table you have work to do. I first marked out triangular panels using a flexible steel tape. The tops are compound curves(curved two ways at once like a sphere) so I measured the sides of the triangles along the curves. When they were cut out they weren't flat but when the flanges were bent in on a sheet metal brake all the measured distances straightened out and I did in fact then have plane triangles whos sides were the lenghts I'd measured across the curves. Since then we have succesfuly used patterns made of strips of flexible ¼" plywood. After the panel is marked it can be cut out with any tin cutting tool. None that I have used is ideal, the easiest cutting I have done is with a pneumatic chisel when the top was still anchored to the car.

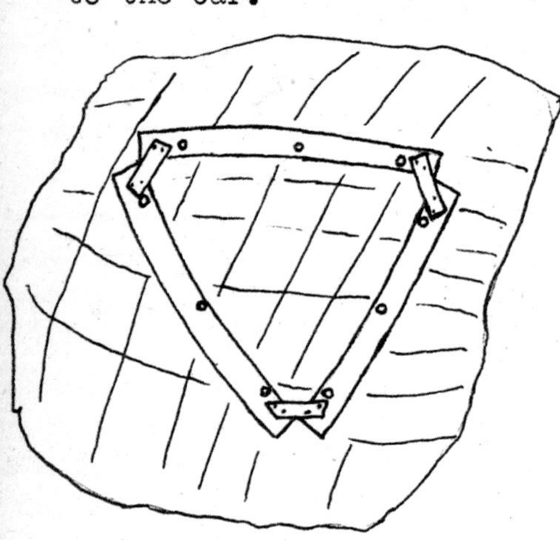

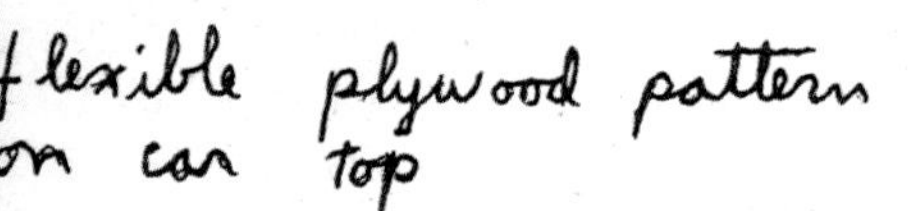

flexible plywood pattern on car top

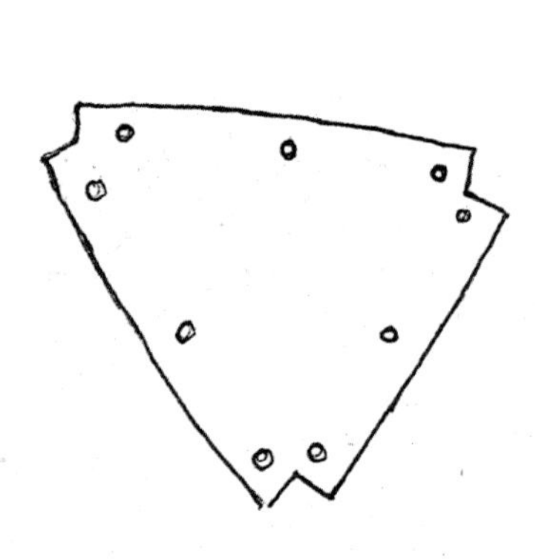

panel cut and drilled

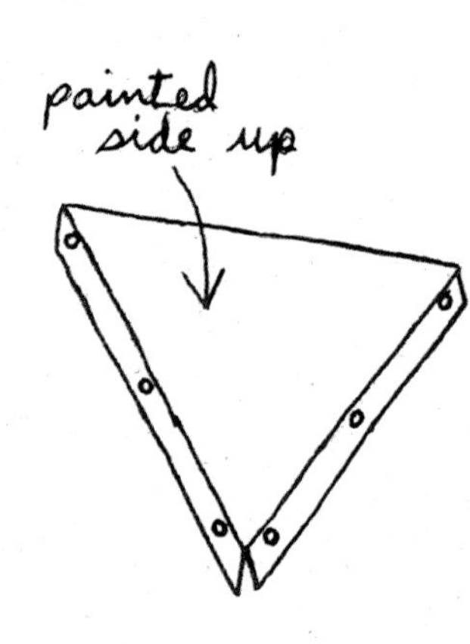

panel, cut, drilled and broken

An enneacontahedron is the zonahedron produced by the star formed of the 10 diameters (vertex to vertex) of a regular dodecahedron but cubes can be inscribed in a dodecahedron - corner to corner. The rhombic dodecahedron is formed from the star made of the diameters of a cube - so many of the faces of an enneacontahedron are [illegible]

In making a structural cartop panel a great deal of care has to be given to accuracy, particularly to getting the crotches between the flanges the correct distances apart, these points become the tips of the sructural panel and thus determine the edges. The holes are also important, the end holes shoul be as close to the corners as possible bring them back just far enough so the connecting bolts can be fitted through. They should also be as close to the fold as possible the farther down they are on the flange the more flexing the seam can do.

So far we have divided all the dome faces into triangular panels but I am not sure that the strength or accuracy of the dome require it. We are about to attempt some structures made with four sided cartop panels.

this worked on all 4 sided panels. Haven't tried big ones yet.

I still haven't tried welding the panels together and the best method of connecting them so far has been to drill holes in the flanges and bolt them together with ¼" bolts. Even after this is done the dome may be springy to walk on . Circular cartop plates put over every vertice and screwed or bolted to the tip of each panel will take out theis springyness. This idea was given to me by two hot rodders who stopped by the dome when they were out testing a beutifuly constructed dune buggy they had just finished.

welding with a continuous bead along the edges didn't work. You burn holes - set the tar backing on fire and it's slow.

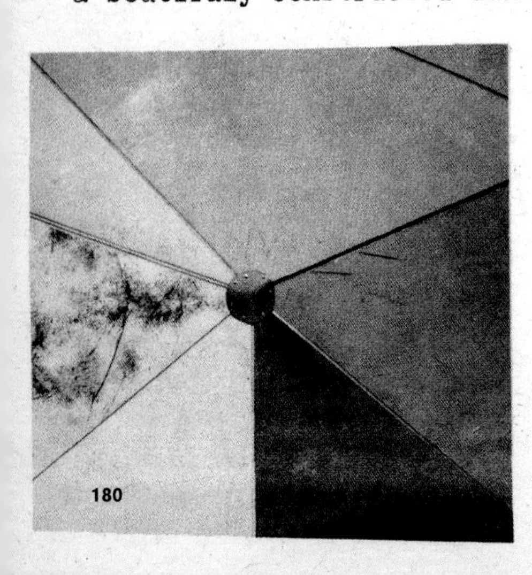

Zome made only with car tops. stretched enneacontahedron.

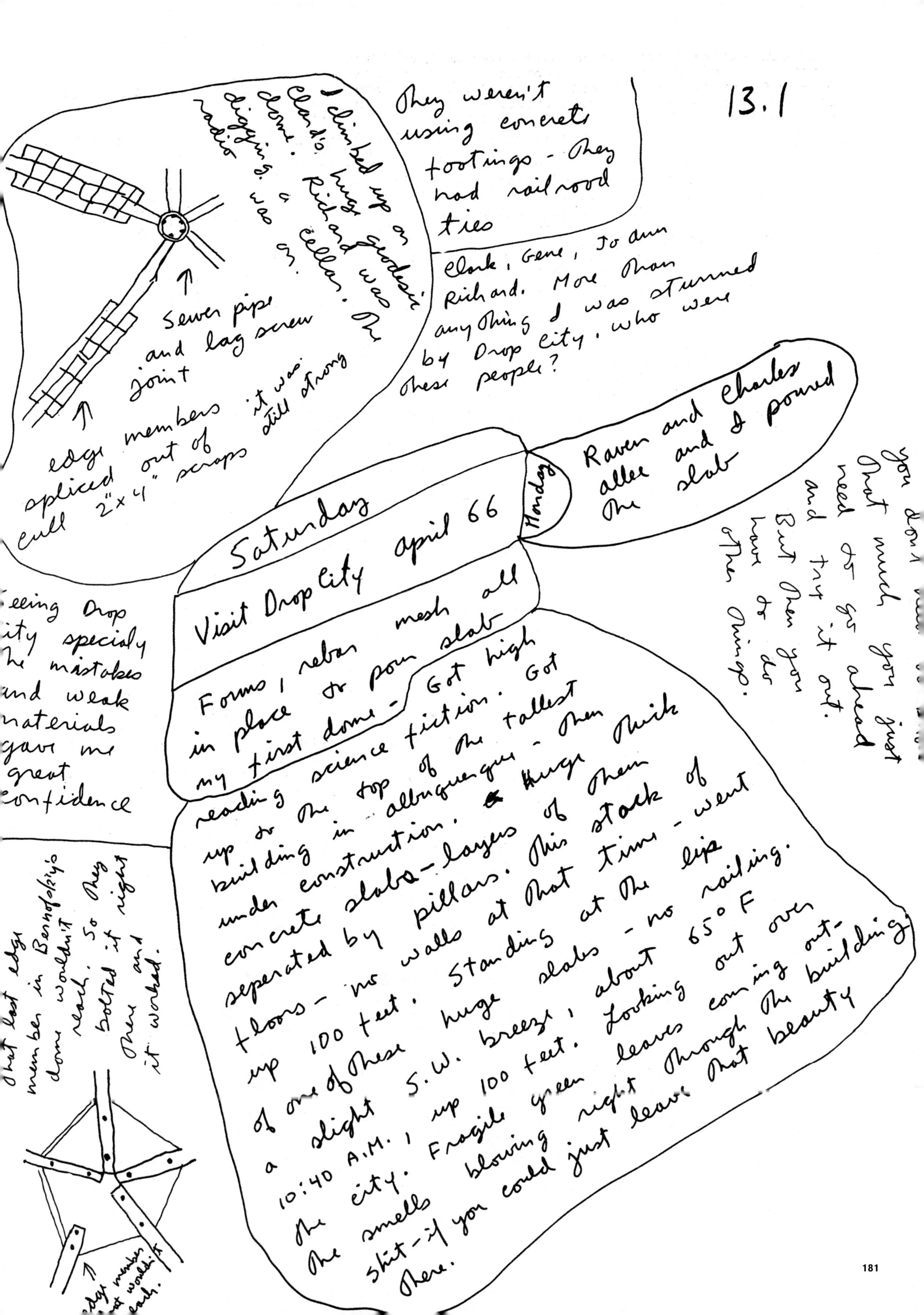
13.1
They weren't using concrete footings - they had railroad ties
I climbed up on Clard's huge geodesic dome. Richard was digging a cellar. The radio was
Sewer pipe and lag screw joint
edge members spliced out of cull 2"x4" scraps
it was still strong
Clark, Gene, Jo Ann Richard. More than anything I was stunned by Drop City. Who were these people?
Raven and Charles allee and I poured the slab
Monday
Saturday
Visit Drop City April 66
Forms, rebar mesh all in place to pour slab
Got high my first dome -
Got high reading science fiction. Got up to the top of the tallest building in Albuquerque - then think under construction. Huge concrete slabs - layers of them seperated by pillars. This stack of floors - no walls at that time - went up 100 feet. Standing at the lip of one of these huge slabs - no railing. a slight S.W. breeze, about 65° F 10:40 A.M., up 100 feet. Looking out over the city. Fragile green leaves coming out - the smells blowing right through the building - shit - if you could just leave that beauty there.
You don't need much you just need to go ahead and try it out. But then you have to do the things.
Seeing Drop City specially the mistakes and weak materials gave me great confidence
That last edge member in Bernofsky's dome wouldn't reach. So they bolted it right there and it worked.
edge member that wouldn't reach.

as a constant stream of visitors. They were running out of room. The twenty-foot-diameter Icosadod was no longer adequate as a communal kitchen/eating space, so a meeting was held and it was agreed that Baer—now known by his Drop name, "Luke Cool"—would be invited to design a large communal building. Baer accepted the challenge and made a model of a multipurpose structure with three intersecting zomes, each measuring thirty-five feet in diameter, what he described as a "triple-fused cluster of truncated icosarhombic dodecahedra." The building would contain a community kitchen, dining area, communal bath, open living area, and workroom. The Droppers approved the plan and started work in October 1966.

At first they tried to sew the metal panels together with lengths of ten-gauge wire looped through holes drilled in the corners of each panel. This proved to be too loose an arrangement, so they used gusset plates made from pieces of car-top metal. But building zomes at Drop City wasn't just about known geometries. At one point there were problems fitting a pentagonal panel into place. The Droppers were stumped so they decided to stop working and take the rest of the day off. That afternoon a warm Chinook wind began to blow and the next morning the pentagon dropped right into place. "This strong wind must have cooked the whole structure," recalled Baer.[21]

The new kitchen complex was a patchwork of random shapes cut from the roofs of old Chevys and Plymouths. Windows and doors were salvaged from old buildings and set into the sloping walls at odd Dr. Seuss angles. Some of the cladding panels were triangular, some were square, some were irregular zonagons. One facet had white squares and red triangles that combined to make a star-shaped pattern. The crowning touch, however, was a gold-painted pentagon that had been chopped from the roof of a 1952 Cadillac.

Drop City continued to grow with a zome-shaped outhouse and two icosohedrons to house the chickens and goats. The octagonal foundation of a dwelling called "The Hole" was blasted out of a shale knoll. Its walls were made with railroad ties and stones and then topped with a dome. Compared to the psychedelic patchwork of the newer zomes, the first few domes seemed almost bourgeois by this point, so Dean Fleming, a visiting artist, painted them in bright geometric patterns, one in sunburst orange and red, another in sky blue with outlines of black and white. Steve Baer invented a solar heating system for Mike and Shirley's do-decahedron. A long trench was filled with stones and covered with black corrugated plastic. Warm air funneled up the trench and into a storage chamber filled with large insulating rocks. The air was then circulated into the dome through a vent. (This was one of the first solar heating systems in the country.)

When all ten domes were finished, they made a striking impression. (Bucky Fuller approved and awarded Drop City the first-ever "Dymaxion Award.") Each dome was beautiful in its own funky way, made from the waste of American society. "Ten domes under the sky-dome," wrote one visitor. "Silverdomes, domes that are paintings, multicolored cartop-domes and one black dome."[22] To some they seemed like the embodiment of the Outlaw Area, as if Kesey's "new planet" had come to life in a windswept corner of Colorado. There were no signs out front. Nothing had to be explained. The strange, unearthly domes said it all. The Aquarian age had found its form.

OPPOSITE
Solar-heated dome, Drop City, 1967.

FOLLOWING PAGES
P. 184: *Drop City domes painted by Dean Fleming.*

PP. 186–187: *Baer's Zomeworks bus at Manera Neuva commune, New Mexico (photo: Jack Fulton).*

P. 188: *Zomes;* P. 189: *Baer's own, solar-heated zome home in Corrales, New Mexico.*

OPS • 18 $1.50

DROP CITY

By
PETER
RABBIT

"... the oldest and most famous of the modern communes..." ESQUIRE

First Hippie Commune Wins
The Buckminster Fuller Cymaxion Award!

Following the lessons of Fuller, Baer and the Droppers, there was a dome boom, a passionate romance with all things geodesic. "Living in a dome opens your fucking mind," said John Curl, one of Drop's founding members. "No corners to hide in. Round like the sky."[23] The dome would become one of the most recognizable symbols of rebellion. New-age settlers saw it as a means of acting out the allegorical life, for living one's life as art. "Macrocosm and microcosm are recreated, both the celestial sphere and molecular and crystalline forms," said Bill Voyd.[24] Inexpensive and unorthodox, it was a structure that enclosed the greatest amount of space with the least amount of material. It supported a kaleidoscope of struts through tension rather than compression, suggesting a holistic spirit of fellowship. "All those triangle sections coming together to make a single dome, a self-supporting thing," said a dome dweller named Peggy. "It's like what a community can be."[25] Another compared her communal family to a geodesic sphere of many facets, "each new facet making the sphere more perfect until we reach the One World Commune—a unity of all mankind, grooving together in friendship."[26] Baer saw the dome as a prime shaper, a model for rethinking the entire social paradigm, "one that will someday reveal the load-bearing pillars of today's arrangements as totally unnecessary."[27]

A few rudimentary domes were built at Morning Star and Wheeler's Ranch. The Hog Farm had a movable dome made from rubber hose and yellow parachute fabric under which group members would gather and search for their common center.[28] Garnet crystal domes,

FINE WINE

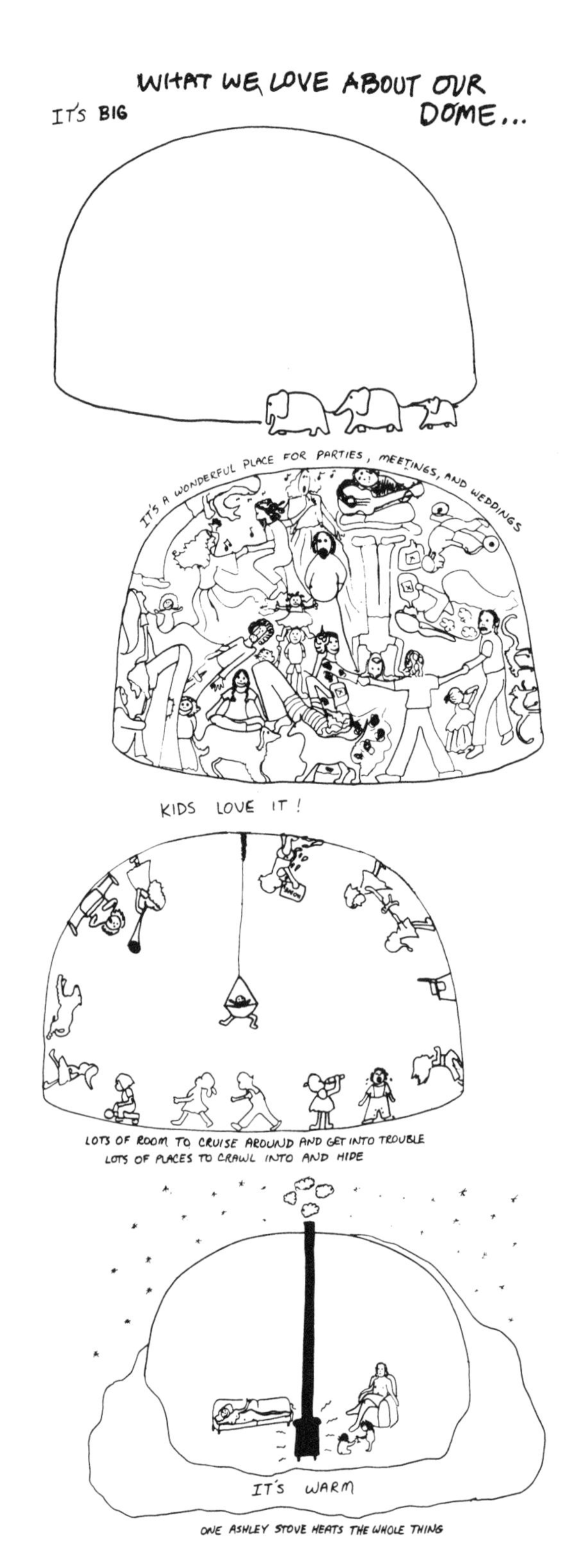

WHAT WE LOVE ABOUT OUR DOME...
IT'S BIG
IT'S A WONDERFUL PLACE FOR PARTIES, MEETINGS, AND WEDDINGS
KIDS LOVE IT!
LOTS OF ROOM TO CRUISE AROUND AND GET INTO TROUBLE
LOTS OF PLACES TO CRAWL INTO AND HIDE
IT'S WARM
ONE ASHLEY STOVE HEATS THE WHOLE THING

What the Red Rockers loved about their 60-foot-diameter dome.

FOLLOWING PAGES
P. 192: *Drawing of Libré Commune by Richard Wehrman;*
P. 193: *Unique houses at Libré.*

another Baer variation, were built at the Manerva Nueva commune in Placitas, New Mexico. A forty-two-foot dome was built at the Morning Glory commune in Canada and the first few houses at Libré commune in southern Colorado were also domes. Tony Magar, a British sculptor, built an all-white dome in Libré's lower meadow. Peter and Judy Rabbit, fugitives from Drop City, built a tripartite zome based on one of Baer's models. Dean and Linda Fleming built a double geodesic.

"We wanted to create a structure that didn't remind us of anything—a new kind of space in which to create new selves," said a member of the Red Rocker collective, a group of radical-left hippies who constructed a giant dome in the Huerfano Valley, not far from Libré.[29] The sixty-foot-diameter frame rose dramatically on its site, echoing the shape of Red Rock Mountain, which loomed in the background. Peter Coyote visited in 1970 and described it as a "huge silver bug eye."[30] Instead of building several different shelters, the Rockers chose to build only one so that they would all be together in a communal heap. "We wanted our home to have a structural bias against individualism."[31] Everything was open and exposed. During the first winter, more than twenty people slept in a circle around the perimeter wall. By the second winter the Rockers had built a sleeping platform out of logs and completed a long, narrow window that curved along the southern side to follow the arc of the sun. A single wood-burning stove heated the entire space.

The dome signified a range of subversive energies combined into collective action. "Soon domed cities will spread across the world," wrote Peter Rabbit, "anywhere land is cheap—on the deserts, in the swamps, on mountains, tundras, ice caps. The tribes are moving, building completely free and open *way-stations*, each a warm and beautiful conscious environment. We are winning."[32]

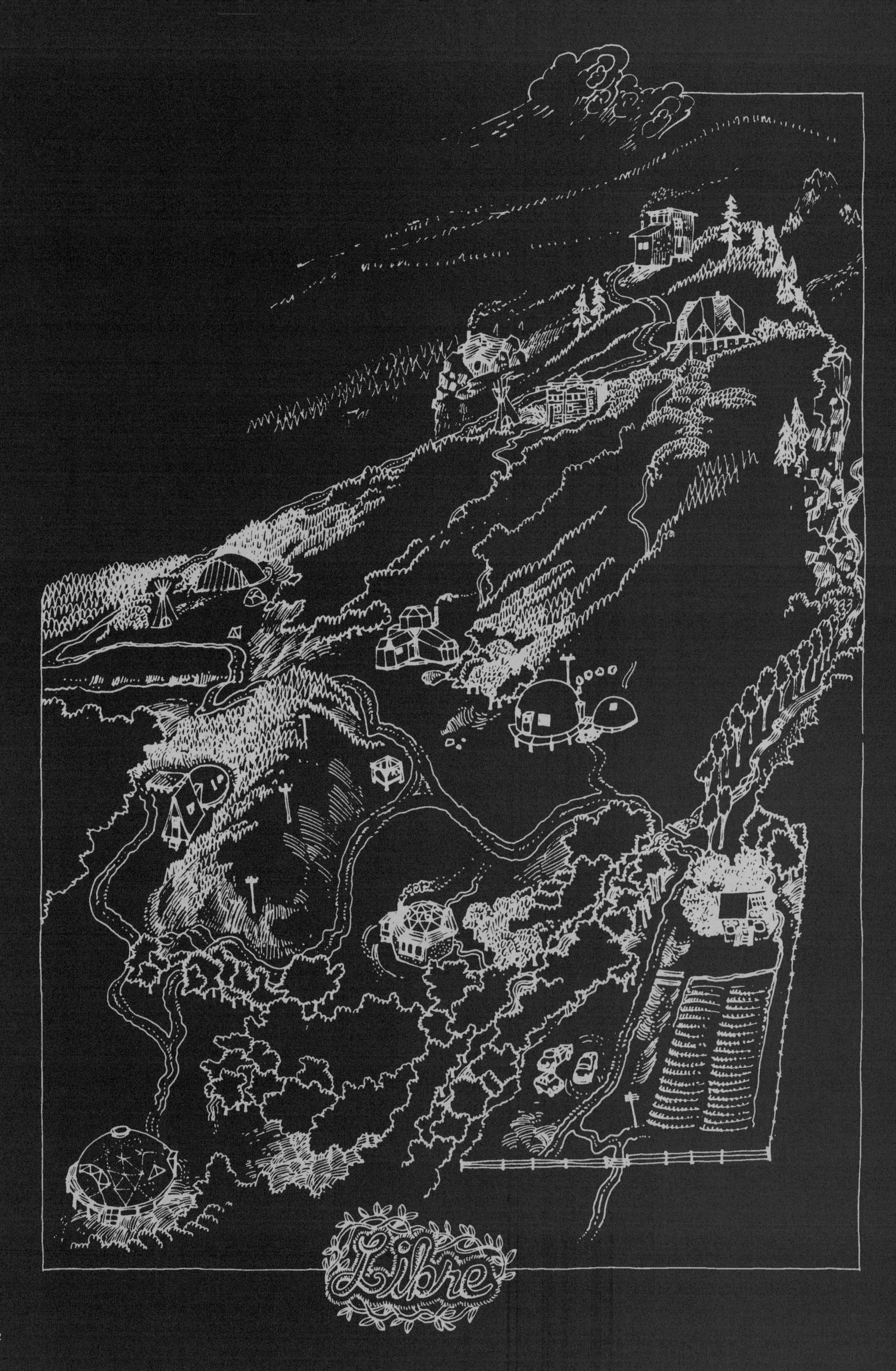
Libre

The underground press ran wide-eyed testimonials on the virtues of dome living. The coast-to-coast network of fellow dome-heads met at annual pow-wows like the Alloy Conference in New Mexico to trade secrets and compare notes. Early issues of *The Whole Earth Catalog* carried information about ready-made kits like "Dyna Dome" of Phoenix, Arizona, and the "O'Dome" kit by Tension Structures of Milan, Michigan. (If those were too expensive you could write to the U.S. Patent Office in Washington, D.C., and get a copy of Fuller's geodesic patent for only fifty cents.) Steve Baer's hands-on experience led to the publication of *Dome Cookbook,* one of the first how-to guides produced within the Outlaw Area. It was written and illustrated by Baer and published in 1968 by Steve Durkee and the Lama Foundation in New Mexico.

The forty-page pamphlet was roughly printed on newsprint and stapled together by hand.[33] "Everything must be fitted together somehow," wrote Baer, who was clearly obsessed with his subject and saw everything in terms of a zome construct.[34] Technical notations are stitched together with oddly random thoughts, spaced-out reflections, and biographical asides: "Listen to everyone's advice. Don't give up.... My mother told us stories she made up about a rabbit who lived in the river bottom named Alfred."[35] Some pages are typed on a manual typewriter. Others are covered in a childish scrawl that spirals around the page. (The reader is obliged to rotate the book to follow the line of text.) The *Cookbook* was followed by other, more practical manuals like Edward Popko's spiral-bound *Geodesics* (1968); Lloyd Kahn's *Domebook One* (1970); and John Prenis's *The Dome Builder's Handbook* (1973). While they all offered helpful information on geodesic math and engineering, none had the eccentric originality of the *Cookbook.*

BELOW: *Tony Magar's Dome, Libré, 1970 (photo: © Roberta Price, all rights reserved).*

OPPOSITE
Red Rock Dome under construction, Colorado, 1970 (photo: © Roberta Price, all rights reserved).

FOLLOWING PAGES
PP. 196–197: *Interior, Red Rock dome (photos: Jack Fulton).*

FOURTH NOBLE TRUTH IS:
THE EIGHTFOLD PATH
(FOR GETTING RID OF DESIRE)
VHICH SAYS:
ET YOUR
LIFE
STRAIGHT
BELIEF
THOUGHT
SPEECH
ACTION
LIVELIHOOD
EXERTION
REMEMBRANCE
MEDITATION
O YOUR WORK.
DO EVERYTHING
YOU'VE
GOT TO DO.
VATCH YOUR SPEECH. WATCH YOUR THOUGHT.
VATCH YOUR CALMNESS. GET YOUR CALM
CENTER GOING. LIVE YOUR LIFE IN SUCH A
VAY AS TO GET YOURSELF STRAIGHT, TO
GET FREE OF ATTACHMENT THAT JUST
KEEPS SUCKING YOU IN ALL THE TIME.
MERCURY
(DIVINE MIND)
LOGOS
MARS
(ACTION)
COURAGE
3
ANIMAL
4
HUMAN
CONSCIOUSNESS
VEGETABLE
2
MINERAL
1
SELF-CO
SCIOUSNES
JUPITER
(EXPANSION)
PROSPERITY
SATURN
(CONTRACTION)
DISCIPLINE
HILLS OF THE CONSCIOUS
NEPTUNA
(ANIMA)
INTUITION
URANS
(ANIMUS)
IMAGINATION
SUB-
PLUTO
THE COLLECTIVE,
UNDIFFERENTIATED
UNCONSCIOUS
(NON-INDIVIDUALITY)
INSTINCT
WATERS OF THE UNCONSCIOUS
ABOVE TRIANGLE
TERA FIRMA

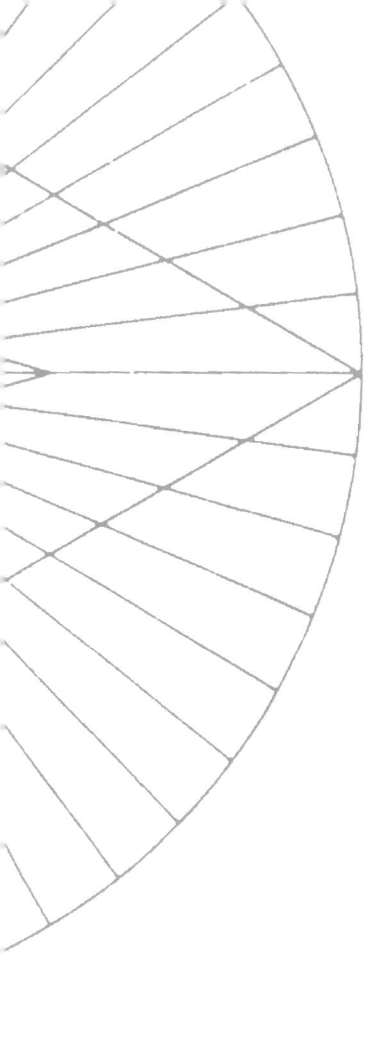

CENTERING

Since one of the goals of the movement was "getting centered," what could be better than living inside a structure that embodied the essence of *center?* "In a dome, there is an inward focus," wrote dome builder John Prenis. "You feel that you are at the center of things," but at the same time, the dome's mysterious geometry seemed to expand ever outward, toward the infinite.[36] "Like a giant retina, the dome scans the heavens... its translucent skin registers each energy transformation of the cosmic lightshow."[37] The inherent symmetry and concentric energy had particular appeal to those devoting themselves to a more spiritual path: "One's eyes can easily center on any of the mandalas formed by the struts," said Alan Schmidt, who saw the dome as an extension of his meditation, an architectural form of yoga. "All vibrations—sound, light, heat and all our awareness—begin in the center and radiate outward and rebound back and forth from the center."[38]

Swami Kriyananda (J. Donald Walters), an American-born disciple of Paramhansa Yogananda, compared the dome to the Lotus of a Thousand Petals, the seventh chakra at the top of the head. "In its roundness it represents our modern desire for continuous mental expansion, for reaching out to the universe instead of boxing ourselves in protectively against its immensity." The swami oversaw the construction of an entire dome village at the Ananda Meditation Retreat in the foothills of California's Sierra Mountains. "The dome is expressive of our new approach to the universe," said Kriyananda.[39] The main temple took the form of a forty-four-foot-diameter geodesic that stood conspicuously at the center of the complex. Its wooden frame was covered with burlap and sprayed with polyurethane foam. Rising behind the altar was a high multifaceted window that flooded the interior with natural light.

Barbara Durkee was pregnant with her second daughter, Shanti, when she and her husband met Herman Rednick, a sixty-five-year-old mystic who advised them to build a spiritual community without drugs. What started out as Solux, the Durkees' sprawling utopian vision, their "spiritual dude ranch," shrank to an earthy enclave of a few hardy souls. "As soon as we laid down the rule about no LSD, our following dropped from several hundred to about three," said Barbara.[40] Following Rednick's advice, the couple bought one hundred acres on a mountain north of Taos. An old sign on the property read "La Lama," so they called it Lama, and in 1966 they incorporated it as a nonprofit foundation dedicated to the pursuit of self-knowledge. For preliminary shelter, they built A-frame structures. Word soon spread, and a number of like-minded individuals joined them. Like the Durkees, they were tired of the self-destructive cycle of the psychedelic scene and were ready to seek a higher path through meditation and building a series of beautiful domes. "We praise God by building domes," said Barbara.[41]

Compared to most communes the daily schedule at Lama was quite rigorous with everyone rising at 5:30 a.m. for meditation, followed by a period of yoga and chanting. At 7:30 a.m. a vegetarian breakfast was served in the communitarian kitchen and then, for the rest of the day, residents were expected to perform manual labor. In the early years this took the form of working on the domes, but even this was seen as a form of yoga, an opportunity for spiritual growth: "Building at Lama is our medium for teaching and learning many things on many levels: trust, care, practicality... patience, craftsmanship, and the art of hard work," read the Lama brochure.[42]

"There are no priests here because everybody is a priest," said Steve Durkee, who wanted the architecture of the buildings to

Domes were seen by some as an architectural form of yoga.

OPPOSITE
UPPER LEFT: *"Eightfold Path," a page from* Be Here Now; RIGHT: *Swami Kriyananda, in the Temple Dome, Ananda Meditation Retreat, California, 1967.*

reflect Lama's eclectic blend of east and west.[43] "Lama is a place where people can meditate, practice Tai-Chi and yoga, Sufi dance, fast for Ramadan, welcome Shabbat, or praise the Lord in any way they want," said Barbara Durkee. Various gurus and teachers passed through, including Herman Rednick, Murshid Sam Lewis ("Sufi Sam"), Baba Hari Dass, and Richard Alpert, Leary's former partner at Harvard and Castalia who, after an enlightening visit to India, stopped doing acid and changed his name to Baba Ram Dass.

The Center was a place where the entire community would be able to gather for meetings, meditation, chanting, and communal bathing. The architecture would be a synthesis of all the cross currents Durkee had been exploring since his days as a multimedia artist with USCO. "In some way, all of these disparate things have to be woven into one seamless garment, and that's what this is an attempt to do," he said.[44] Technically speaking, the Center's domed roof was a thirty-two-foot-high *enenacontrahedron*, a shape that drew energy from the earth while also celebrating the sky and sun. A helix of diamond-shaped sections echoed the peaks of the Sangre de Cristo Mountains, while one-story wings tapered down on either side hugging the ground. One wing contained a communal bathhouse and the other housed a library and prayer room. The outer walls were made from traditional adobe bricks, packed and stacked in the style of the local Pueblo Indians. All doors in the eight-sided building pointed east, and all windows were positioned in alignment with the sun and moon. Light streamed through the star-shaped skylight and played across the walls of the great meditation space. An eight-foot-high octagonal window—something like a third eye—looked west toward the Rio Grande.

News of Lama's all-is-one lifestyle spread beyond the mountain retreat by word of mouth and a series of unconventional in-house publications that included Baer's *Dome Cookbook; The Sayings of Baba Hari Dass; Buddha Is the Center of Gravity;* and *Be Here Now* by Baba Ram Dass, which sold over a million copies. (Durkee had once apprenticed to a printer in New York and designed many of the books himself.) But the most curious of all the Lama publications was *SEED,* a book that took the form of an elaborate game, loosely based on the Glass Bead Game in Hermann Hesse's *Magister Ludi:* "a universe of possibilities and combinations." Each page carried four images printed on perforated stock, something like new-age flash cards, that could be torn out and used in the game. "Take about 40 cards and arrange them however you want on an empty wall." Sacred iconography was juxtaposed with pop imagery and current news items. Page twenty-nine, for instance, matched a Tantric wheel with a radio telescope, an astrology chart, and a circle of Busby Berkeley showgirls. There were planets and steam engines next to Bedouin tents and electric chairs, next to mushroom clouds, lighthouses, vaginas, KKK rallies, insects, Shiva, Hitler, microbes, and Hopi villages. "Allow all the associations to come and allow them to go. Just watch."

Again, as he did with Lama's architecture, Durkee was acting as a human synthesizer, pulling together hundreds of disparate influences and weaving them into a single, luminous kernel, being the *seed* of the book's title. "What you hold in your hands is a pod in the form of a book," read the introductory page. "The contents of this pod are meant to be released," but he never fully explained how the game was actually played.[45]

OPPOSITE AND FOLLOWING PAGES
Lama Foundation, New Mexico.

ACCUMULATED ERROR

"The students were suddenly stoned, sexy, and mystical," recalled a teacher who taught at Pacific High, a Summerhill-type free school that was located in the Santa Cruz Mountains, an hour and a half south of San Francisco.[46] The school was founded in 1961, but by the mid-sixties the "stroboscopic energies" of Haight-Ashbury were drifting down the peninsula and changing the institution from a progressive day school into an anarchic collective of hippie kids. In 1967 the standard curriculum was replaced by an unstructured schedule of yoga, photography, poetry, drumming, expressive dance, kayaking, and various independent study projects—one student built a working submarine out of old oil drums—but the most popular activity was building geodesic domes.

Unlike Lama, Pacific High lacked a single, guiding vision: "No grand design, no master plan," but the domes gave the school a sense of purpose that it otherwise lacked. Self-build guru Lloyd Kahn came in 1968 and taught the students everything he knew about domes. As shelter editor of *The Whole Earth Catalog*, he had already built a few, including his own twenty-six-foot-diameter house in Big Sur. By the spring of 1971 seventeen domes had been erected on the forty-acre grounds. "[It was] a community forming itself, created with no real plan other than the need to live together," said Kahn. "An exercise in expanded awareness."[47]

Students and teachers shared their visions and premonitions, learning about tools and basic geometry and, more important, how to work and live as a cooperative entity. "Most every night we would sit and get stoned together and let out all of our wild fantasies and dreams about the dome," said a student named Jon Smith. "We all worked our asses off for a few days cutting struts and assembling panels for the frame. We had never worked this hard before.... We were proud. Oh, were we proud."

There was the "Green Dome," the "White Dome," the "Om Dome," the "Pod Dome," and the "Pillowdome." Some were big and some were tiny, housing only a single resident. "Horny Mountain" was an all-male dome built high on a slope. The "Ferrostone Dome" looked like an igloo made from Portland cement troweled over a wire-mesh frame. Yoga instructors Alan and Heath Schmidt made a translucent vinyl dome into the Om Dome, "an oasis of love and calm in an otherwise chaotic place."[48] Scale models were fashioned from Popsicle sticks and drinking straws but no plans were ever drawn or consulted. The construction process followed on the vibes of the moment, aided by luck and the occasional hit of acid, which could generate random, spur-of-the-moment changes. "Everyone rushing to get their dome built," scribbled Kahn in his notebook during the Spring of 1969. "Things moving along of their own accord, no one directing."[49]

All kinds of funky contraptions—triangular doors and porthole windows with homemade hinges—were devised by the students, who ranged in age from fourteen to eighteen and had no prior building experience. To be expected, there were mistakes made along the way. Some of the domes had no doors at all and were entered through a trapdoor cut in the floor. The first few domes followed a basic formula. Platforms measured twenty-four feet in diameter. Struts were two-inch-by-three-inch Douglas fir attached with metal hubs and clad in weatherproofed plywood ("Duraply"). Interiors were of Dorvan polyurethane foam and painted on the outside with house paint. (The average cost was about $1,200.) As students and faculty gained confidence, the designs grew more inventive.

"I am delighted to have such a shell to protect the seed of my developing consciousness," said Martin Bartlett, a music teacher who built himself a fifteen-foot-diameter "Pod

Pacific High, an anarchic collective of hippie kids who built their own domes.

OPPOSITE
Students and faculty enjoy a communal dip in the Bathtub Dome, 1969.

AT 9:00 - ZOMEWORKS
PUTTING UP Jungle Jim
+ STRUCTURES SEMINAR
ANT FARM HERE TOO.

Pacific
School

THE STUDENT
RUN
SCHOOL

FOLLOWING PAGES
PP. 208–209: *Students and faculty built seventeen different domes on the school's forty-acre grounds.*

Dome" using sheets of plywood that he shaped like the petals of a flower.[50] He added a Plexiglas bubble for a window and covered the exterior with rough-split shakes that gave it the look of a scaly prehistoric bug. (Others saw a prickly pear, a pinecone, or the feathers of an owl.) Bartlett himself called it the "Temple of Accumulated Error" in honor of the miscalculations that had led to its final form.[51]

The students were delighted to be part of such a radical experiment in living. "With the dome around me, I feel like the pit inside an apricot, butterfly inside cocoon," wrote one.[52] Even when they leaked, the hemispherical roofs seemed imbued with magic geometry. "I feel infinitely large and small at the same time," wrote another.[53] "We would rather live in imperfect domes that we designed and built ourselves and be wet, than live in dry, old-style housing."[54]

Peter Calthorpe, a nineteen-year-old intern from Antioch College, came to Pacific High in 1969 bursting with ideas and energy: "I think I'll build a pod, no I'll do a triacon . . ."[55] He had started tripping in his early teens and was a founding member of the Black Shit Puppy Farm, a psychedelic lightshow group in San Francisco. Working with students, Calthorpe adapted the basic geodesic formula and created two different kinds of elliptical domes. One was stretched vertically and called the "Egg Dome." The other was stretched horizontally and called "Zapoche." As with Baer's zomes, these nonspherical variations gave more internal flexibility. Frames were made from wood, covered in burlap, and sprayed with polyurethane foam. "For plastic buildings they feel very mellow," said Calthorpe, who followed his work at Pacific High with a seventy-foot "Zafu" elliptoid for the 1969 International Design Conference in Aspen, Colorado.

The "Pillowdome" was an invention of Jay Baldwin, a young associate of Fuller who had also come to teach at Pacific High. The frame was made from EMT electrical conduit and covered with transparent vinyl pillows inflated with nitrogen. (The triangular pillows were made in a local shop that specialized in inflatable toys.) The two-ply vinyl allowed for transparency while also providing a buffer of insulation. Another one-of-kind creation was the aluminum triacon, conceived by Lloyd Kahn and built in a day with the help of twenty students. "I kept thinking how spacy a shiny dome would look in a field, reflecting the surrounding trees and grasses," said Kahn, who purchased a roll of .025-inch-thick aluminum from a local supplier and used it to clad the twenty-four-foot structure.[56] Some held the floppy panels in place while others riveted them together to make a frameless, self-supporting pod. ("We finished it in the moonlight," recalled Kahn.)

While there was no official opening, it felt like an unveiling of sorts when Bucky Fuller showed up in late January of 1970. He borrowed a pair of rubber galoshes and tramped through the muddy grounds, inspecting all the different domes. He visited the Pillowdome and took a catnap on the waterbed, but before leaving, he gave the students a crash course in spherical trigonometry.

Some of the more unusual domes were published in the underground press and Kahn started to get dozens of letters asking for more information. Instead of replying, he decided to write a book. "As we started building at the school I kept notes, on paper bags, anything lying around, throwing them all in folders," said Kahn. By the spring of 1970 he had gathered enough material to publish a fifty-six-page pamphlet called *Domebook One* ($3). It was filled with how-to diagrams, templates for cutting panels, as well as firsthand accounts of the trial-and-error process ("much error!"). While some of the prose is fairly technical and dry, there are also

Pacific High.

ABOVE: *The Om Dome.*

OPPOSITE
Jay Baldwin's Pillowdome.

FOLLOWING PAGES
PP. 212–215: *Variations on the standard 24-foot-diameter dome (photos: Jack Fulton).*

personal anecdotes and haikus about the glories of dome living:

Last night,
the wind howling around us...
Strange sensation...
[Our dome] feels delicate;
we've spun a thin light membrane over our heads.[57]

All seventeen domes were completed by 1971 and Kahn published a second volume containing almost twice as much information as the first book. ***Domebook Two*** ($4.25) became one of the hottest guidebooks of the hippie hegira and sold more than 175,000 copies. Dog-eared copies were passed from hand to hand at communes, crash pads, and college campuses. Besides technical information, there's a theme of common purpose conveyed by the text, as if to say: you are not alone. Dome freaks from around the world wrote in eagerly, sharing their experiences. Jon Sobel, who staked out a wilderness outpost in Wasilla, Alaska, described how he built a twenty-six-foot dome covered with industrial felt coated with tar. "Our dome is similar to a melon on a pedestal within a salad bowl," wrote Wendell Spencer, oddly, from Hamilton, Ohio.[58]

But all was not so copacetic on the communal front. After the initial euphoria had passed, there were grumblings about leaky seams and loose fittings. Most furniture was made for ninety-degree walls and didn't fit properly. Nor was everyone happy about living in the round without partitions or privacy. The actual building process was also tricky. Hundreds of tripped-out hippies wandered into the wilderness with vague notions of creating domed utopias but were frustrated when they learned how much discipline (and patience) it really called for. The geodesic formula was exacting and didn't allow for much flexibility. "You are

locked into abstract math," said one disenchanted dome builder who discovered that he wasn't able to improvise the way he might have with a four-square structure.[59] Many first-time builders found the process too demanding and simply gave up.

"The whole process is clumsy, slow, awkward, bitchy, often a drag to be doing," wrote Chico Drake, resident builder at a Vermont commune, who was challenged by the assembly of a thirty-two-foot-diameter dome and warned others to reconsider before going geodesic.[60] One of the early structures built at Twin Oaks commune ("Walden II") was a dome made from lengths of oak covered with polyethylene plastic. While the communards followed plans in *Popular Science* magazine, the basic principles eluded them. Their dome sagged at the center and had to be propped up with poles. It continued to collapse and was eventually abandoned.

Even Lloyd Kahn was growing tired of the movement he had helped to inspire. "After four years living in domes, the excitement of moonlight through overhead windows has worn off," he wrote.[61] In place of struts and hubs, he yearned for low ceilings, snug rooms, and old stone fireplaces. Sometimes it was healthy to have partition, but domes were difficult to divide into separate rooms, so every-

UPPER: *Steve Baer, garnet dome cluster, Manera Nueva, New Mexico;* LOWER LEFT: *Jim Anderson's cedar shake dome;* RIGHT: *Shingled dome house, Woodstock, NY.*

Wholeo Dome, a fourteen-foot-diameter geodesic dome clad with curved, stained glass panels. It was designed by Caroling, who completed the structure in 1974.

LEFT: *Caroling in front of "Bump", Harmony Ranch, California;* UPPER RIGHT: *Bump seen from Wholeo Dome;* LOWER RIGHT: *Wholeo Dome.*

FOLLOWING PAGES
PP. 218–219: *Interior view of Wholeo Dome (photo: © Chuck Henrikson, courtesy wholeo.net).*

one was obliged to share the same sounds, smells, and vibes. Life in the Red Rockers' sixty-foot dome in Colorado grew almost intolerable. There was no place to hide or escape the group. Noises and echoes were amplified by the great arcing space, especially at night, with babies crying and couples making love, as others tried to sleep. "After three years of living in a heap, most of us have decided that in order to keep growing and changing we need more privacy," said one sleepless Rocker.[62] Most decided to move out and build smaller shelters, while the big dome would be kept as a central meeting space. "Times have changed and so have we."

By the early seventies the geodesic dome was already beginning to seem dated, as predictably clichéd for hippie housing as the split-level ranch had been for postwar suburbia. Some anarchist homesteaders found it too formulaic, too predictable for their living needs. They wanted to break free from all preconceived notions of sheltering space. For them, the dome was just another urban construct, another by-product of white-man technology. Dropped into the wilderness, it referred shamefully back to itself, exerting its own kind of tyranny.

7 FRONTIER MYSTICS

"SIMPLE IS LIFE AMONG THE FRONTIER MYSTICS."

—ALLEN COHEN[1]

While self-build hippies continued to try domes and zomes, many others were starting to build with a looser, more spontaneous approach, making things up as they went along and adopting their own kind of intuitive process. "I was tired of domes," said Edmunsen, a backwoods settler who set out to build a twenty-four-foot-diameter geodesic but only got as far as finishing the foundation. He had a change of heart and built a nautiluslike dwelling instead, erecting a center pole and then working his way outward with no particular notion of where it would lead—"I knew I wanted it to spiral"—relying on mystical insights, acid visions, and the occasional clue from one of his dreams. Beams radiated out from the king post and were capped with what he described as a seven-sided-off-center-spiraling-pinwheel-inspired roof.

Something similar happened to Ela who, with daughter Mountain Pony, moved into the woods of Sonoma County to live in harmony with the elements. Like Edmunsen, she started on a dome but grew impatient with its complex geometry and decided to build something less formulaic, a house that would be more reflective of her own psychic growth.[2] "A centered life-space encompasses and encourages the use of structure while embracing the ever-changing moment," said Ela, who gathered redwood and cedar logs, split them with a hatchet, peeled back the bark, and smoothed the wood with an adze. Her home gradually evolved into a ten-sided self-portrait called the Mandala House. Every element was treated with love and concentration. The outer walls were made from triangular sections. Supporting beams and buttressing arches were framed with gnarly bits of driftwood. Windows were made from weathered strips of apple wood.

Little enclaves of homesteaders like Ela and Edmunsen sprang up across the country, in the Berkeley Hills, and up along the rocky coast of Big Sur, interspersed through the redwood forests of northern California, into Oregon and Canada, farther southeast into Colorado, New Mexico, and Arizona. Similar clusters arose in the northeast, in the wooded hills around Woodstock, New York and the Berkshires, and scattered across Vermont, New Hampshire, and Maine. They weren't really intentional communes so much as loosely knit entities, more like old-fashioned rural settlements, where independently minded individuals could stake a claim, build a house, and mind their own business. Many were tired of the communal scene, and while willing to share tools and knowledge, they weren't interested in charismatic gurus telling them how to think or behave. "Anarchy is our basic rule," said a settler named Douglas Patrick, who preferred to rough it on his own.[3]

Middle-class kids imagined they could move into the wilderness and make new lives with total abandon. They settled in rural areas, squatting illegally, sometimes scraping together enough money to buy a cheap piece of land, an inaccessible ridge, or an abandoned goat farm. The sense of interconnectedness they had first experienced on LSD was now rekindled in the rigors of self-sufficiency. They rediscovered forgotten folk wisdom and learned how to survive without running water, refrigeration, or central heating. They learned how to douse for drinking water, make compost heaps, and preserve vegetables for winter. They built humble huts, lean-tos, yurts, free-form pods, and Hobbitt hovels.

Along with copies of the *I-Ching*, they brought Bradford Angier's *How to Stay Alive in the Woods* and Scott Nearing's *Living the Good Life. The Whole Earth Catalog* offered many kinds of back-to-the-land accessories and basic building manuals like D. C. Beard's classic *Shelters, Shacks, and Shanties*, and Calvin Rustrum's *The Wilderness Cabin*, which

STAINED GLASS
HIP RAFTER
LOFT
OLD WINDOWS
CUTAWAY VIEW A
TOP VIEW BEFORE FRAMING, SHOWING POLES, GIRDERS AROUND THE FLOOR, PIERS AND
GIRDERS
PIERS
POLES
OUTSIDE STORAGE UNDER EAVES

The Indian Tipi
Its History, Construction, and Use
Reginald & Gladys Laubin
With a History of the Tipi by STANLEY VESTAL

BED
ALTAR
FIRE
TWO DOZEN
WILLOW ROD
BACK REST
R11
F8
F7
F6
F5
FIRE VENT

"All you have to do is start . . ."

Shelter becomes an act of personal transformation and revelation.

THIS PAGE AND OPPOSITE
Mongolian-style yurts in Texas and Maine, 1966–1972.

PREVIOUS PAGES
P. 222 UPPER LEFT: *Ela's Mandala House, California, c. 1969;* LOWER LEFT: *Chris Roberts, The Owl houseboat, Sausalito, California;* P. 223 UPPER RIGHT: *Chris Roberts, The Madonna houseboat, Sausalito.*

P. 224 UPPER: *Tipis under rainbow, New Buffalo Commune, Aroyo Hondo, New Mexico, 1967 (photo: Lisa Law).*

PP. 226–227: *Morning shampoo, Gila National Forest, Arizona (photo: Paul Dembski).*

showed how to cut and notch logs to make rustic walls and roofs. But many relied on their faith in the almighty moment and proceeded to build without any specific plans in mind, each house evolving as a poetic kind of place making: tree houses with rope-ladder stairs, gull-wing roofs, walls woven from saplings, skylights in the shape of Yin-Yang symbols.

The new settlers would live out their lives as heroic allegories among the ferns and toadstools, simplifying their days to such an extent that time itself would slow to a barely perceptible crawl, almost a standstill. Then came an ecstatic moment, so it was hoped, when a magic door would open and they would be able to reach the other side.[4]

"A wise man never says what he's gonna' do. He just does it," said Coyote, a free-land visionary who advised his friends to stop worrying about mundane technicalities like septic systems and building codes.[5] "All you have to do is start," said a homesteader named Feather, who moved into the forest of northern California determined to live on the land as lightly as her adopted name suggested.[6] She had never built anything before, not even a bookcase, but managed to construct a templelike house with a little help from an itinerant carpenter. "Throw away all your plans," he had said, encouraging her to persevere. "Go ahead! You can do it."

Feather made innumerable mistakes along the way but accepted them as part of the learning process. She started with a simple twelve-foot-by-twelve-foot box, tight enough to keep out rain and wild animals. "The house grows and you serve its growth," said Feather, who added a kitchen and a deck as her confidence level grew. "Once I learned that it's not so difficult to hammer two-by-fours together, there was no stopping me." She lined the interior with saplings, built a fireplace, and fashioned a Japanese-style gate out of pine boughs. She worked on her house for six months and spent a total of $950, which, at the time, was considered a lot of money. (Her nearest neighbor, in comparison, built a house from scavenged lumber for less than $50.) "I didn't design this house," explained Feather. "It designed itself. I was just a servant."[7]

In the funky, self-build revolution, making shelter was seen as an act of personal transformation and revelation. The mantra was always the same: "Simplify. Open your heart to the flow. Listen to the land. Observe the movement of sun and moon. Study the contours of the land. Dream about your space and it will reveal itself."

After sharing their acid epiphany on a boulder in Colorado, Roberta Price and her husband, David Perkins, decided to build their house right on that very spot. "Gently running our fingers over the glowing, fuzzy lichen... we realized that we should build our house *around* it," wrote Price, referring to the rock that told them where and what to build.[8] It would be an octagonal structure made from stacked railroad ties, and the boulder would stand at the center of their lives, providing both a psychic and structural armature while rough-hewn vigas would support the earthen roof.

After several days of wandering through the redwoods of Northern California, a hippie named Kent came upon a glen filled with giant ferns and carpets of moss. The forest spirits spoke to him and told him to stop and rest. This was the right place, the place of stone and shadows. "Direction for the building was provided by the wind, moon, and the changing patterns of energy," he said, lopping the tops off several Douglas firs and using their stumps as a foundation. His roof was made from old boards, and his windows were scavenged from an abandoned building. He improvised as he went, shaping logs with an adze but never using any kind of level or measuring device.

OPPOSITE
Working on the Rock House, Libré Commune, Colorado, 1970 (photos: Roberta Price).

Earth-cast forms of Paolo Soleri.

RIGHT: *Studies for cactus-like towers;*
BELOW: *Soleri drawing in his studio at Cosanti Foundation, Scottsdale, Arizona, c. 1964.*

OPPOSITE
North Studio, Cosanti Foundation, 1961.

"It gets me high not to be able to tell what it's going to look like when I'm done," he said.[9] "To live in Tao is to live invisibly—melt into the holy nature web of the land," said another frontier mystic, who taught himself to build without plans or permits.[10]

The self-build credo was spread by word of mouth, by contact high, and by a kind of telepathic interconnection that was also known as *grokking.*[11] It was just there, somehow, in the air, the back-to-nature vibe, the need to make shelter, the need to uncomplicate one's life. "Building is like yoga," said a long-haired builder named Douglas. "You can't do it any other way than one nail at a time. It's a constant surrender. 'Look at that hammer hit that nail!' As within, so without."[12]

Revolutionary forms for housing and community could be found everywhere in nature: in birds' nests, spiderwebs, and beehives. "We want our homes to spring from the soil like trees," said one outlaw builder.[13] While working on his Endless House in the early sixties, Frederick Keisler studied the architecture of termite mounds and beaver dams. In his fervently utopian proposals for Mesa City, Paolo Soleri looked to seedpods and stamens for inspiration. His prolific notebooks were filled with sketches for buildings that looked like fungi and cactus plants.

Hundreds of self-taught architects pursued the dream of a free-form, asymmetrical kind of shelter that featured curving

FOLLOWING PAGES

PP. 236–237: *Aleksandra Kasuba, interior view of Cocoon Dwelling at night.*

PP. 238–239: *Kasuba, Cocoon Dwelling.*

P. 240: *Foam House, fabricated by students from the Yale School of Art & Architecture, 1968;*
P. 241: *Pod houses, Woodstock, New York.*

PP. 242–243: *James Hubbell, "Ilan-Lael" Compound, Santa Ysabel, California, 1958–1970.*

P. 244: *Hubbell, Waldorf School, Fairoaks, California, 1973;*
P. 245: *Hubbell, Davidson House, Alpine, California, 1972.*

walls, undulating roofs, and womblike interiors—some called it "biotecture"—to better harmonize with the natural rhythms. An itinerant hippie named Teddy envisioned a cocoon-shaped dwelling hanging fifty feet up a redwood tree. It would be made from rubberized macramé woven like the nest of a weaverbird. When this proved impossible to achieve, Teddy settled for a house in the shape of a giant mushroom, a fitting abode for someone whose spiritual awakening came on magic mushrooms.[14]

"When we think of reality as flowing, as dynamic, as growing, then we begin to build houses that are more like flowers, more like buds," wrote Thad Ashby, an underground journalist who envisioned new forms of communal housing based on botanical models. "Imagine, for example, the absolute ecstasy of living inside a big orange flower about a block wide," wrote Ashby. "We'd ride around on large, trained butterflies."[15]

Aleksandra Kasuba fabricated a cocoon-like dwelling on the edge of a pond in Woodstock, New York. As with all of her soft environments, the process was nonlinear and intuitive. She followed signals from the light, the wind—the natural elements of the site. "The approach was spontaneous throughout," said Kasuba. "We let the shape happen and did not fuss with it later."[16] A system of ropes, hoops, and wooden strips served as a basic armature, but it was the trunks and branches of the trees that provided the structural integrity. Loose edges of fabric were sewn together by hand. Piles of stones were used to anchor the fabric to the ground. "The Woodstock project made me realize that tension is not an adversary but a silent partner," said Kasuba. "It cannot possibly err." (Fourteen people lived inside the ghostly membrane of Kasuba's cocoon at *Whiz Bang City East*, an alternative building conference held in the summer of 1972.)

ABOVE: *Teddy and his Mushroom House.*

OPPOSITE
Aleksandra Kasuba, Cocoon Dwelling, Whiz Bang City East, Woodstock, New York, 1972.

Biologist D'Arcy Thompson's book, *On Growth and Form* was a popular reference for new-age utopians, as it recognized a divine geometry in all forms of natural growth and offered examples of non-Euclydian engineering in shells, sponge formations, honeycombs, and fish vertebrae. "There are no exceptions to the rule that God always geometrizes," noted Thompson. Stewart Brand had studied biology at Stanford and was an avid reader of Thompson's work. He speculated about the possibility of houses made from living vegetable tissue, a truly green kind of architecture. "Start with the nearest seed-pod," wrote Brand. "The walls take up your

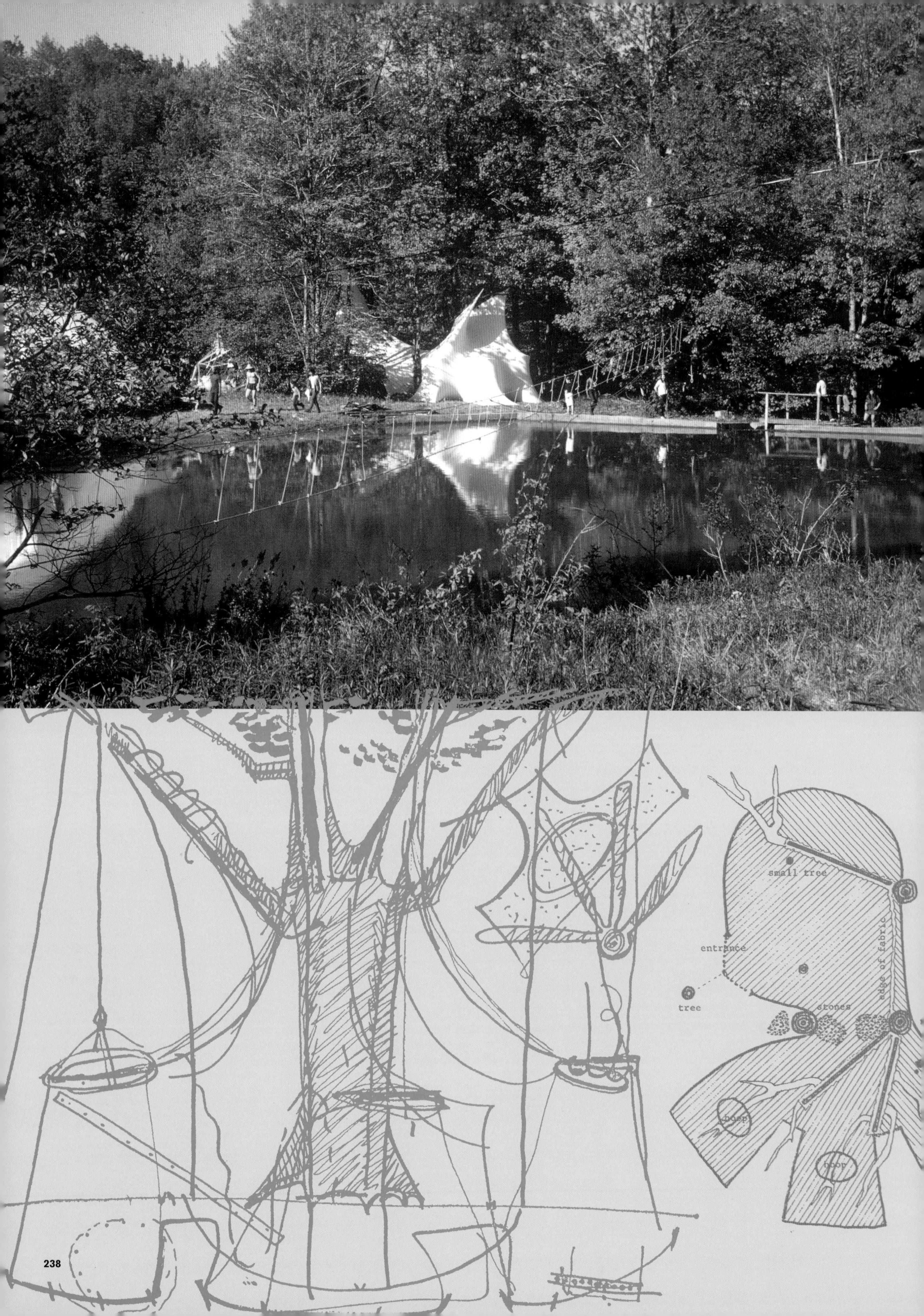
small tree
entrance
edge of fabric
tree
stones
hoop
hoop

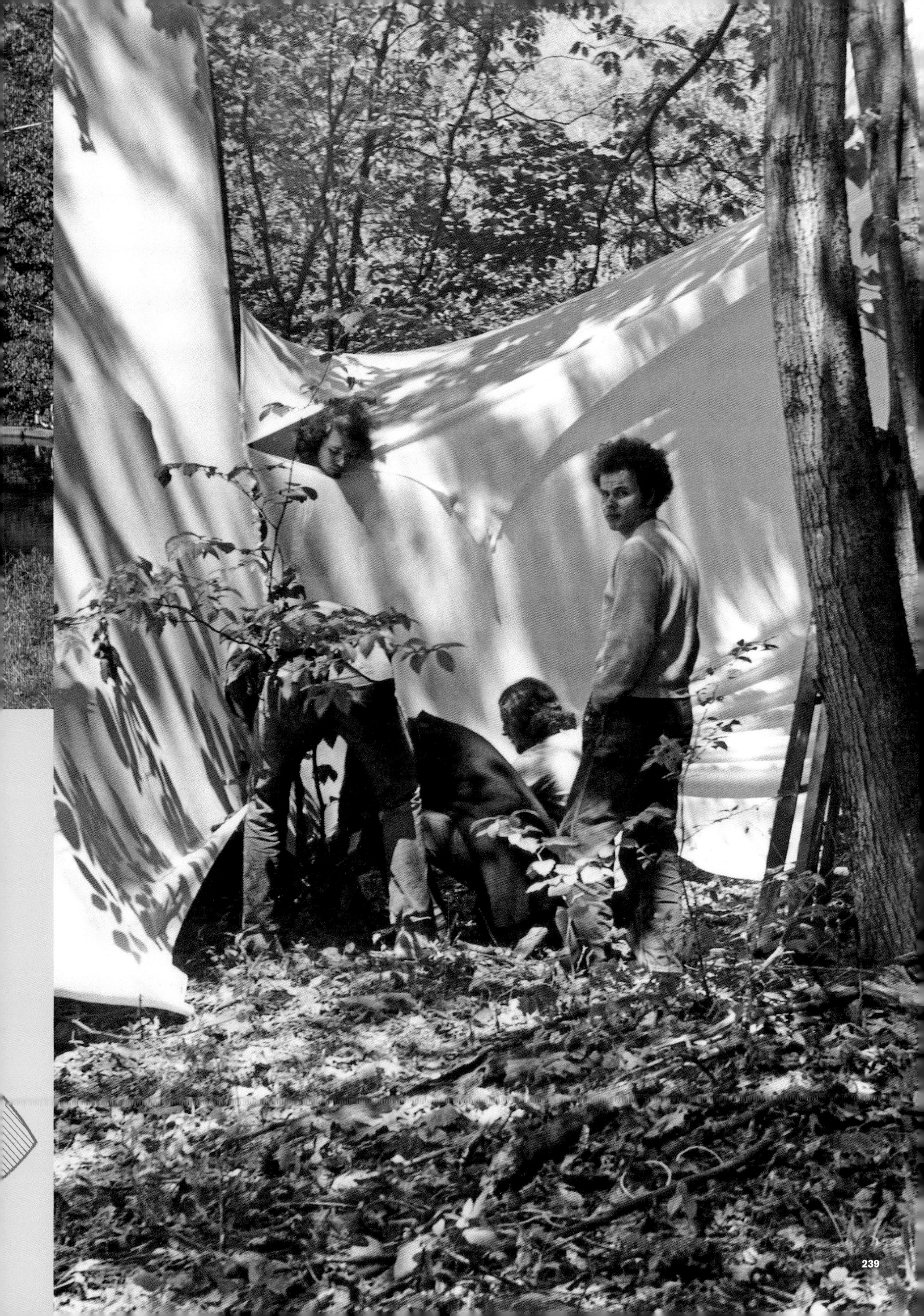

CO_2 and return oxygen. . . . Dweller and dwelling domesticate each other."[17]

But the true father of the organic moment was Keisler. His "Endless House" was a biomorphic shell of reinforced concrete in which all corners dissolved. Cavelike rooms, or "space-nuclei," flowed from one to the next, unrestricted by conventional walls or columns. "The 'Endless House' is called 'Endless' because all ends meet, and meet continuously," wrote Keisler, who compared conventional houses to voluntary prisons.[18] Liberated builders of the late sixties looked to Keisler for inspiration and made up their own variations, with molded macaroni roofs and eyelike openings. A wooden frame could be covered with chicken wire and coated with plaster or concrete. Almost any shape was possible with new, lightweight synthetics like sprayed-on polyurethane. Space could be stretched and twisted. Rooms and passageways could take the form of softly folded coves.

Some, borrowing Soleri's silt-casting techniques, built mounds of earth, covered them with concrete, and simply scooped out the dirt when the concrete had set. "I like geodesic domes, but they're not architecture," said free-form sculptor/architect James

KINDERGARTEN
WALDORF SCHOOL

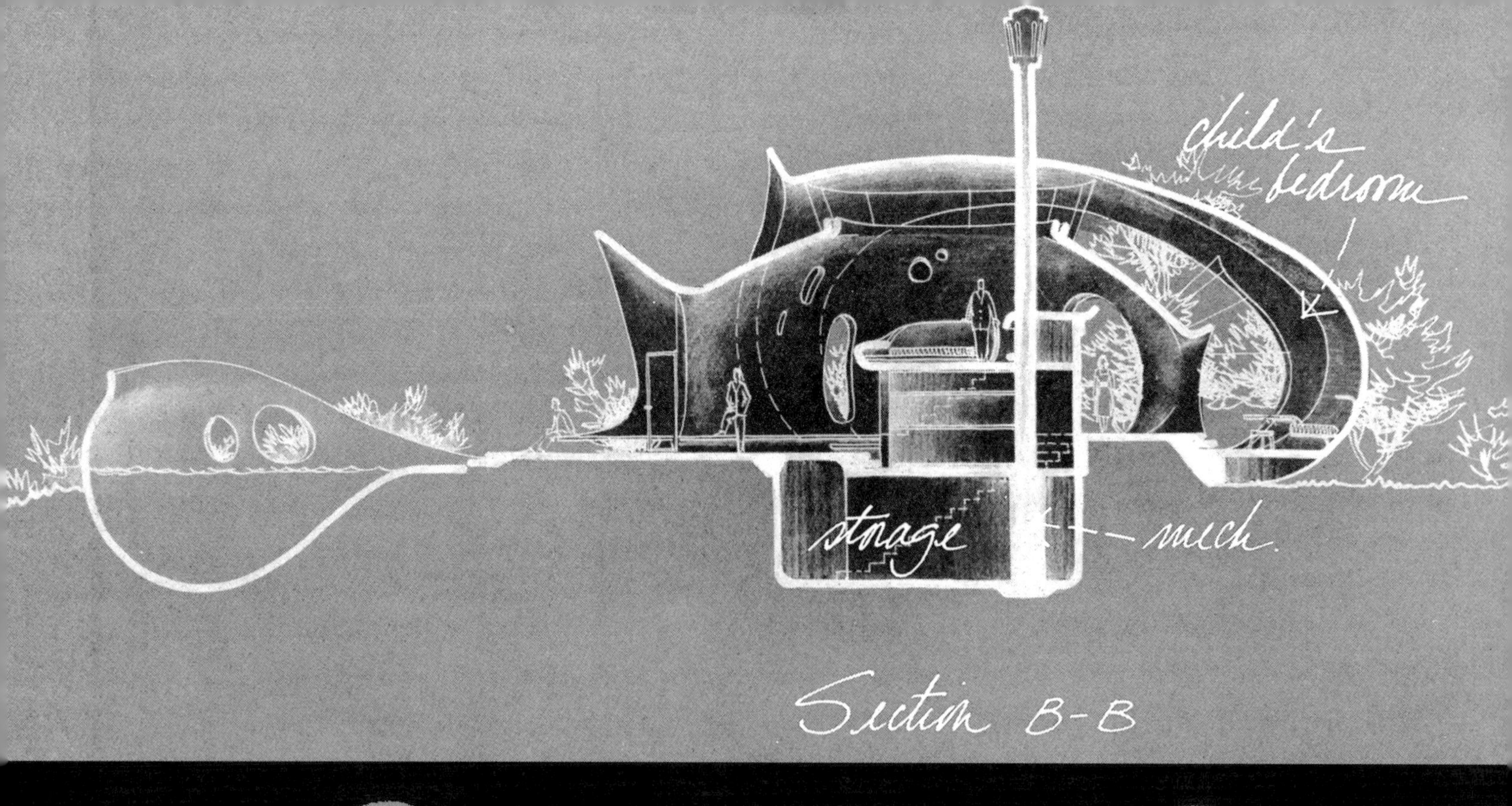
child's bedroom
storage
mech.
Section B-B

BELOW AND OPPOSITE
Bob De Buck, desert house, Truchas, New Mexico, 1969 (photos: Jack Fulton).

PREVIOUS PAGES
P. 246 UPPER: *John M. Johansen, Spray-Form House, 1959;* LINE ART: *Frederick Keisler, Endless House;* LOWER: *Daniel Grataloup, Villa d'Anieres, Geneva, Switzerland, 1970.* P. 247 UPPER: *Roger Dean, Organic City, 1970;* LOWER: *Mark Mills, "Limp Penis House,"Carmel, California, 1969.*

Hubbell, who created "Ilan-Lael," an entire compound of anthropomorphic buildings that appeared to grow out of the rocky soil of Santa Ysabel, California. Hubbell shaped the buildings by hand with trowel and concrete, giving each a unique form and integrating it into the natural landscape with pools and terraces. Interiors were decorated with swirling patterns of mosaic tiles and multicolored stained-glass skylights. During the same period, architects John Johansen and Mark Mills were experimenting with Gunite sprayed over skeletal steel armatures, while André Bloc was creating wild architectural improvisations using plaster over lathe.

Some saw the desert home of Bob De Buck as a giant spiderweb. Others were reminded of a human anthill. Steve Baer drove by one afternoon and mistook it for a heap of garbage until he got closer and began to see the beauty of its weird, fractured anatomy. The deliriously free-form house was built near Truchas, New Mexico, by De Buck and his friend Jerry Thorman. It defied all architectural conventions. A series of old bridge timbers radiated out from a hub of cast-concrete columns and supported a tentlike roof made from chicken wire and concrete. De Buck was a hippie jeweler and saw the project as a gigantic piece of jewelry, mutating into unforeseen patterns. He started by *untraining* himself, trying to forget all preconceived notions about what a house was supposed to be. "Tools not to have: straightedge, square, level, plumb," advised De Buck.[19] As a result, there wasn't a level line or a right angle in the whole place.

Scrap plywood and old timbers were scavenged from building sites around Albuquerque. As soon as the pile got big enough, De Buck would add another room. Short-end two-by-fours were nailed together in a crudely hexagonal kind of honeycomb that twisted and rose in rippling, concave waves toward a mesalike mound near the center of the roof. De Buck compared the building process to something in a dream: "An illusion of completeness, of fulfilling, exasperation."

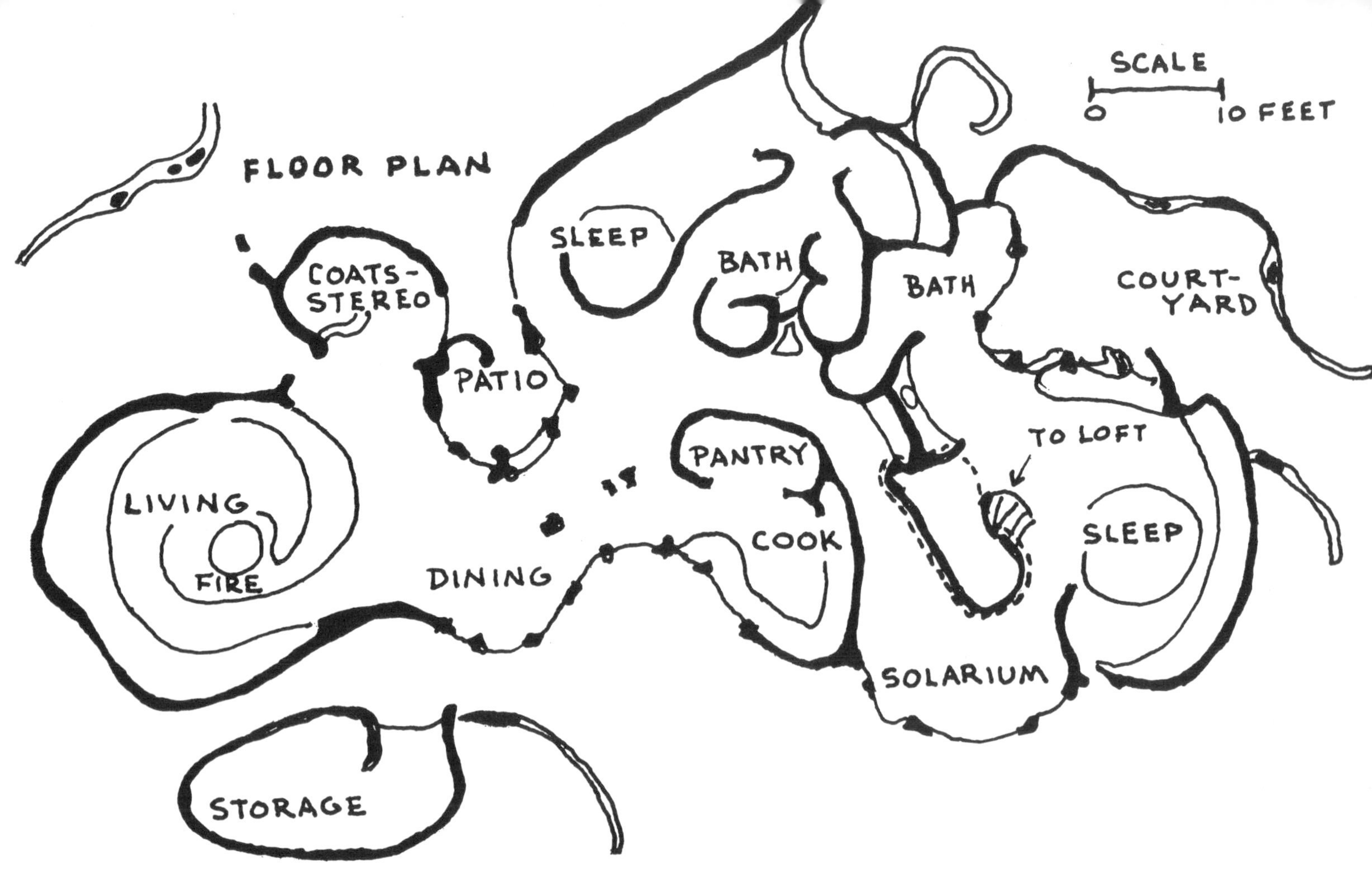

The house's self-supporting canopy allowed for internal flexibility, so partitions could be placed anywhere. Some of the rooms burrowed into the desert floor. Others appeared to hover in spectral light. Doorways, shelves, and cubbyholes were sculpted in the same biomorphic rhythm as the rest of the house.

"The place is a maze of wandering space," said one visitor, who was reminded of the spatial mutations of LSD. "You never know exactly where you are."[20] Tinted Plexiglas skylights cast spacey colors on the walls and floors. According to De Buck, inspiration for these lighting effects was the "star gate" sequence in Stanley Kubrick's *2001: A Space Odyssey*, "where the dude had finally split out of the satellite and was heading toward Jupiter."

Charles Harker, founder of the Tao Design collaborative, took the free-form aesthetic to another extreme in 1970, when he and his friends built Earth House on six acres of hill country west of Austin, Texas. The house appeared to sprout directly from the earth, hence the name, as if volcanic magma had bubbled up and been frozen in place, rising skyward in bulging masses or dipping downward with undulating fins that served to buttress the main forms of the structure.

It was an experiment in living, a "full-scale model" that was not so much built as it was sculpted in a process that Harker called "supramorphics." Long strands of flexible PVC piping were bent and woven into a structural skeleton that was then sprayed with polyurethane foam. Once set, the foam could be carved and smoothed for the desired effects. Like De Buck, the Tao builders worked without plans or conventional design documents. They set out with a basic idea and improvised, adding new walls and imaginative shapes, weaving strands of PVC into nestlike configurations. "All design is spontaneous," said Harker, who compared the process to the metamorphosis of a butterfly. "The visualization is in a constant state of flux." The foam was forgiving, and mistakes could be corrected in minutes. "We were riding high on a frail bubble of mutual assent and understanding," he said.

Earth House was published in several alternative journals of the day and seemed like the ultimate expression in free-flow living. Hundreds came to visit, including Frank Zappa of the Mothers of Invention, who showed up one day wearing a white tuxedo and red sneakers. "Zappa picked up so quickly on what was going on," recalled Harker. "He wasn't even stoned."[21]

ABOVE: *Charles Harker/Tao Design, Earth House, floor plan, Westlake Hills, Texas, 1970.*

OPPOSITE
Undulating walls and sinews were made with polyurethane foam sprayed over PVC piping.

FOLLOWING PAGES
P. 252: *Spraying polyurethane, Earth House.*

PP. 254–255: *Harker/Tao Design, Bloomhouse, Westlake Hills, Texas, 1973.*

P. 256: *Strider, New Buffalo commune, Arroyo Hondo, New Mexico, 1970 (photo: Roberta Price)*; P. 257: *Page from* Shelter, *1973.*

P. 258: (UPPER): *Dragon House, New Mexico, 1970;* (LOWER): *Summer solstice, New Buffalo, 1974;* P. 259: *Adobe fireplace, New Mexico (photo: Wayne McCall).*

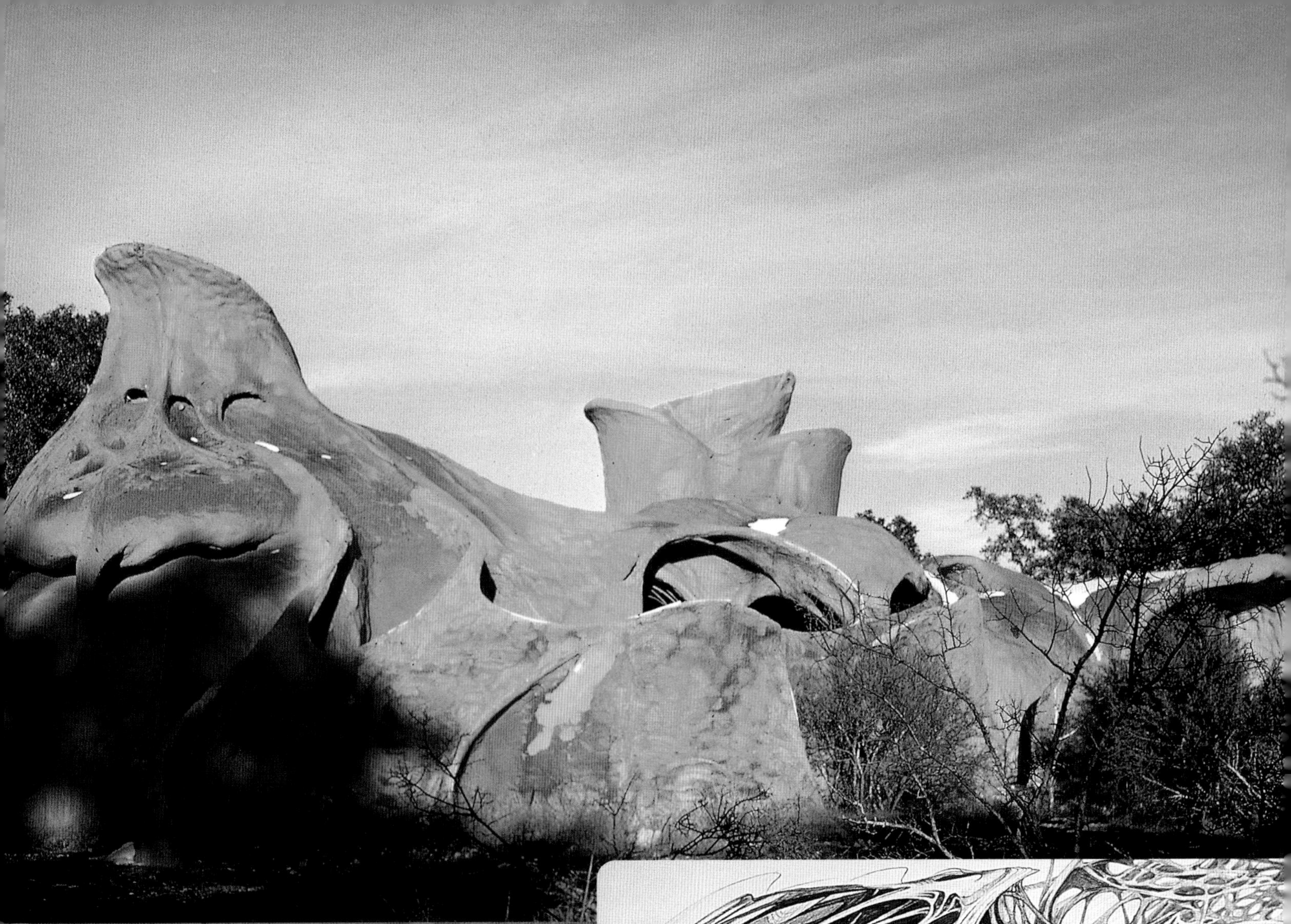
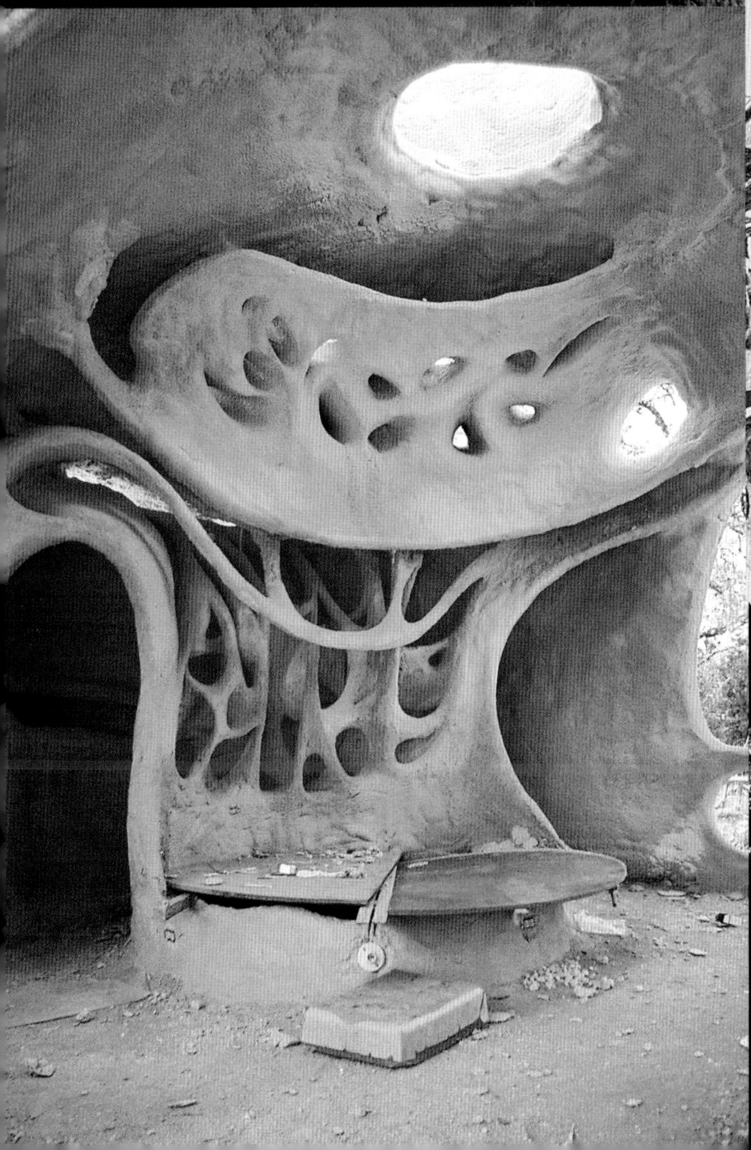
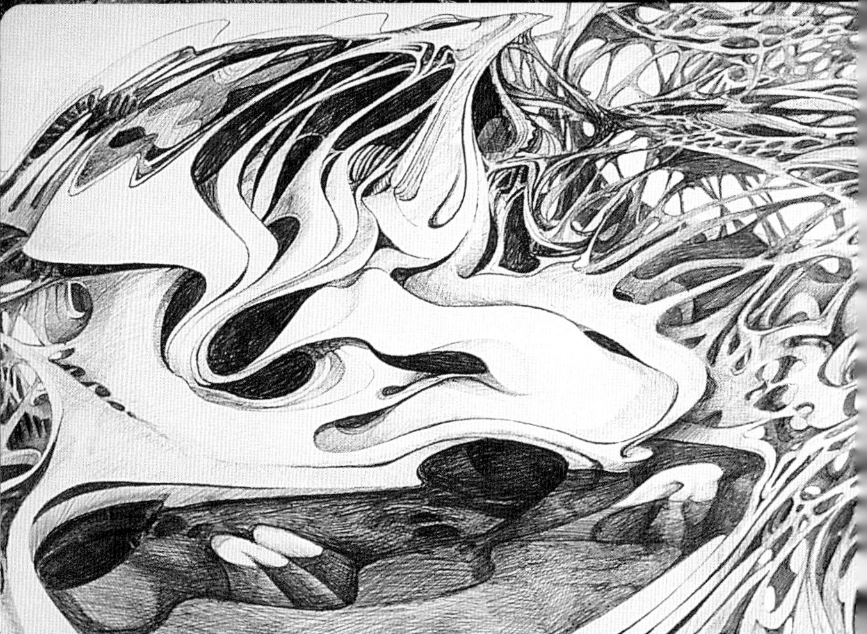
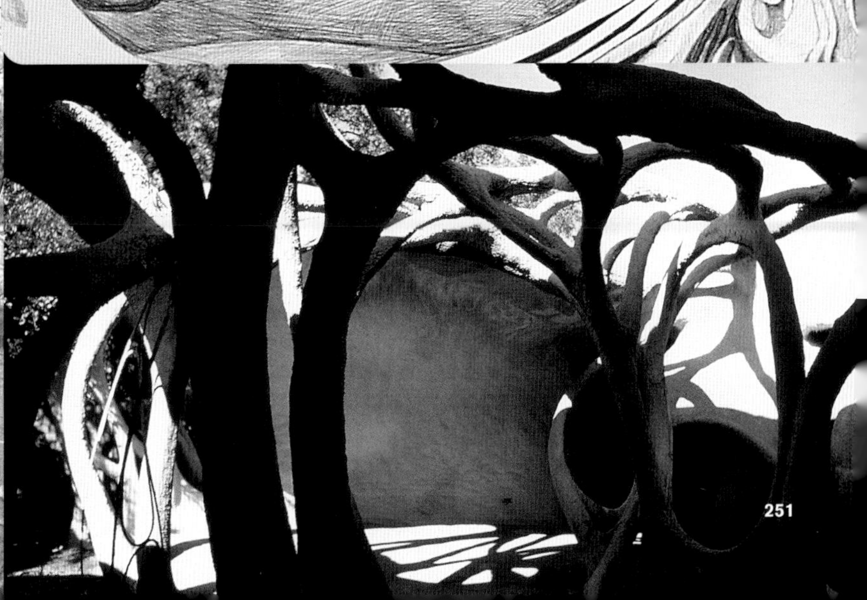

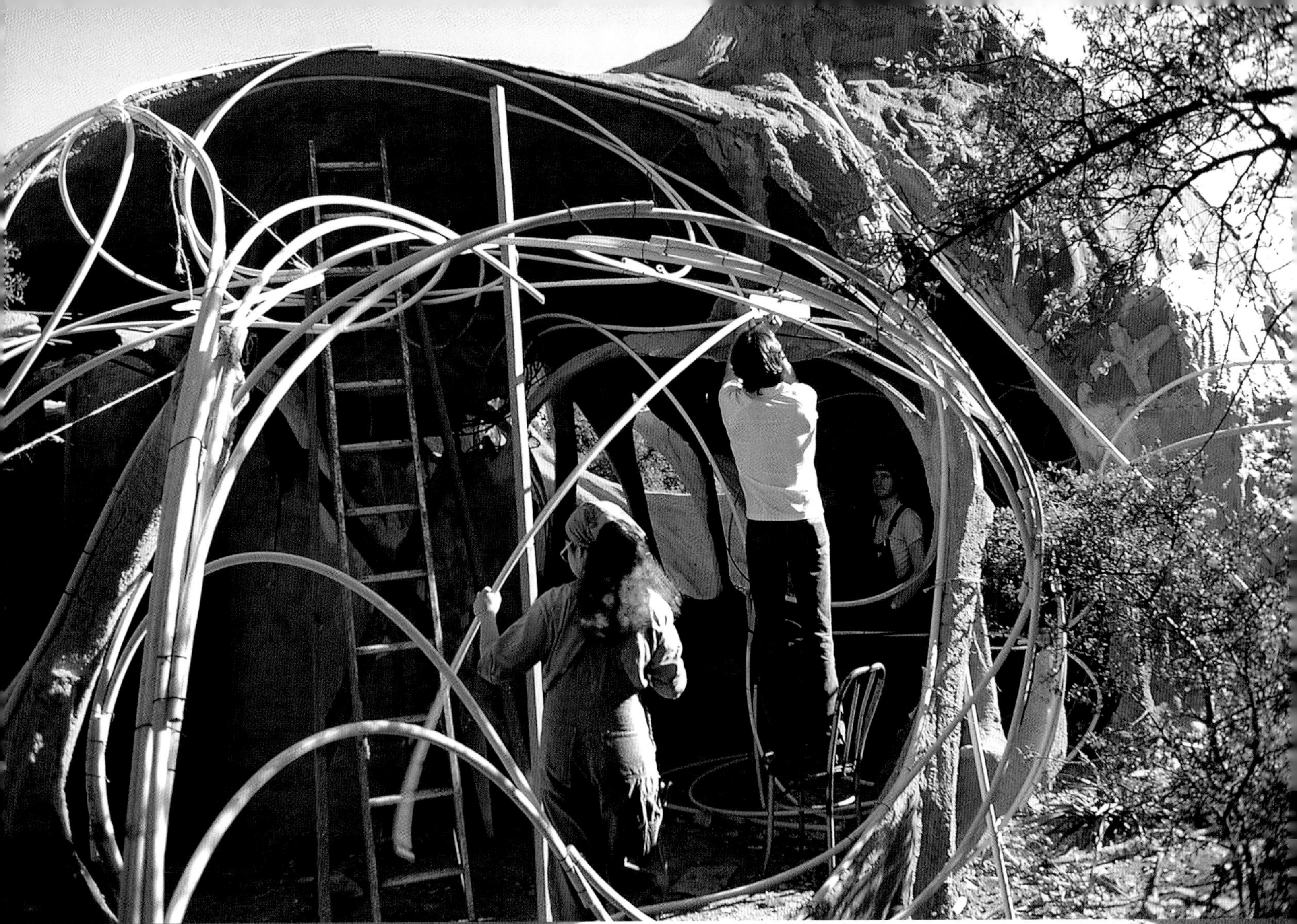

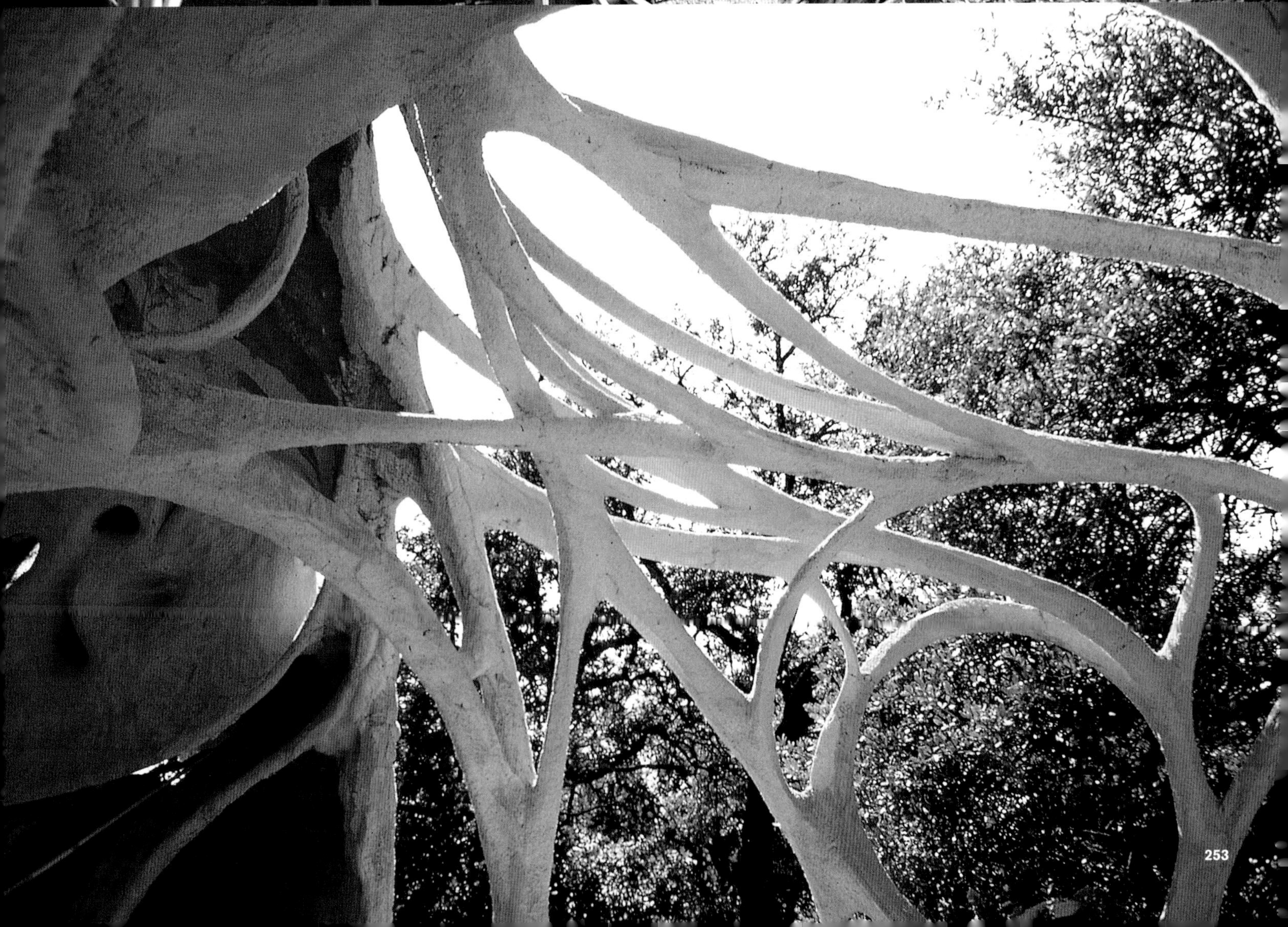

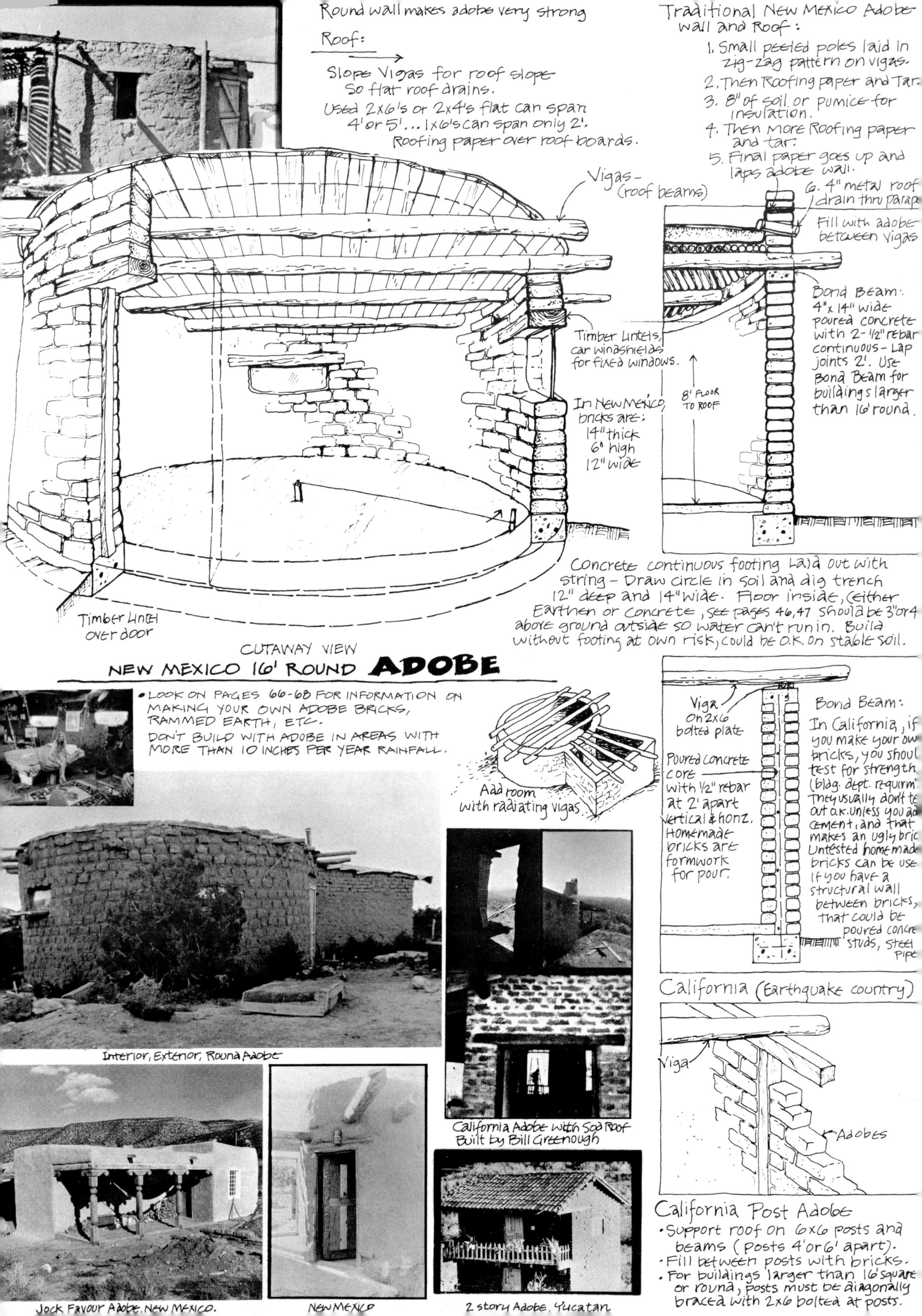

Round wall makes adobe very strong
Roof:
Slope Vigas for roof slope so flat roof drains.
Used 2x6's or 2x4's flat can span 4' or 5'... 1x6's can span only 2'.
Roofing paper over roof boards.
Traditional New Mexico Adobe wall and Roof:
1. Small peeled poles laid in zig-zag pattern on vigas.
2. Then Roofing paper and Tar.
3. 8" of soil or pumice for insulation.
4. Then more Roofing paper and tar.
5. Final paper goes up and laps adobe wall.
6. 4" metal roof drain thru parape
Fill with adobe between vigas
Vigas - (roof beams)
Bond Beam: 4"x 14" wide poured concrete with 2 - 1/2" rebar continuous - Lap joints 2'. Use Bond Beam for buildings larger than 16' round.
Timber Lintels, car windshields for fixed windows.
8' FLOOR TO ROOF
In New Mexico, bricks are: 14" thick 6" high 12" wide
Concrete continuous footing laid out with string - Draw circle in soil and dig trench 12" deep and 14" wide. Floor inside, (either Earthen or concrete, see pages 46, 47 should be 3" or 4 above ground outside so water can't run in. Build without footing at own risk, could be O.K. on stable soil.
Timber Lintel over door
CUTAWAY VIEW
NEW MEXICO 16' ROUND ADOBE
• LOOK ON PAGES 66-68 FOR INFORMATION ON MAKING YOUR OWN ADOBE BRICKS, RAMMED EARTH, ETC.
DON'T BUILD WITH ADOBE IN AREAS WITH MORE THAN 10 INCHES PER YEAR RAINFALL.
Add room with radiating vigas
Viga on 2x6 bolted plate
Poured concrete core with 1/2" rebar at 2' apart vertical & horiz. Homemade bricks are formwork for pour.
Bond Beam: In California, if you make your ow bricks, you shoul test for strength (bldg. dept. requirm They usually don't te out o.k. unless you ad cement, and that makes an ugly bric Untested homemade bricks can be use if you have a structural wall between bricks, that could be poured concre studs, steel pipe
California (Earthquake country)
Viga
Adobes
California Post Adobe
• Support roof on 6x6 posts and beams (posts 4' or 6' apart).
• Fill between posts with bricks.
• For buildings larger than 16' square or round, posts must be diagonally braced with 2x6 bolted at posts.

Interior, Exterior, Round Adobe

California Adobe with Sod Roof Built by Bill Greenough

Jock Favour Adobe, New Mexico.

New Mexico

2 story Adobe, Yucatan

FROM ED ALLEN:
...TO BUILD A DOME OF MUD WITHOUT FORMWORK, WORK UPWARD IN TIGHTENING SPIRAL. IT'S NOT DIFFICULT, EASIER AS YOU CLOSE TOWARDS TOP. TO BUILD VAULTS WITHOUT FORMS, START FROM END WALL, AND BUILD OUT A SLOPE. AT RIGHT, SKETCH OF MUD HOUSE BUILT BY ED AS COLLEGE THESIS PROJECT. WOULD BE PRACTICAL IDEA IF ARCHITECTURE STUDENTS COULD LEAVE BEHIND A HOUSE UPON GRADUATION.
TUBE TO NORTH STAR
TUBE TO EAST
THE MUD HAS CRACKED BADLY-NEEDS CONSTANT REPLASTERING.
CUTAWAY VIEW OF MUD HOUSE

SELF-BUILD ENCLAVES

There was a concentration of frontier-anarchists gathering in the wooded hamlet of Canyon, in the foothills east of Berkeley. One or two of them managed to complete geodesic domes, but the majority invented their own kinds of eclectic shelters, fabricating them without deeds or building permits. "You come out of the womb equipped to live in nature," said a settler named Doug. "It's possible to do anything that you want to do."[22] One squatter incorporated the rusting hulks of abandoned cars into his house. Another converted an old chicken coop into a humble shelter and, in the process, learned to let go of his materialist past. "It took me six years to get my standard of living low enough so I wouldn't have to do what I didn't want to do for money," he said.[23] Farther up the same trail, a hippie named Astro built a one-room cabin using old salvaged windows. His all-window house was built around the stump of an oak tree. "I knew that there was a center of myself somewhere that was truly me, and that I had got off center," he said, explaining how his tree house had helped him to reclaim that missing center.

The quintessential hippie shelter of the Canyon area was the wall-less home of Barry Smith, who began by camping out on the site, getting in tune with the geni loci, and waiting for those spirits to tell him how to proceed.[24] "I didn't know what I was going to do here when I started," confessed Smith, but he had seen the picture of a hyperbolic paraboloid roof in an architecture magazine. Its curving, self-supporting surface would allow him to build his house without walls or partitions. There had been an old cabin on the site, and Barry recycled some of its logs, setting them into the hillside in a sequence of steps that spiraled up to a single, symbolic post. Long eucalyptus logs were attached to this central column and splayed out, crisscrossing like the spokes of a bicycle wheel. (Unlike most of his neighbors, Smith had some basic construction knowledge. He had spent a summer working at Cosanti, Soleri's desert community in Arizona.) The twisting plane of the roof took the shape of an owl's head peering over the crest of the hill with crescent-shaped openings for eyes.

Smith's dream was to dwell in total solidarity with the elements. "I got to thinking a lot about what walls were for," he said. "The Indians used to live around here without much shelter at all—just something to keep the rain off—and they lived outside most of the time."[25] There were no partitions, nothing to constrict his movements or those of birds that flew through the rafters. As one visitor noted: "The deeper you go inside his house, the more you seem to move outdoors."[26] There was, however, one interior wall made from thick planks to help break the chill of the north wind. Smith built a rudimentary kitchen with redwood counters, an old ceramic sink, and a Rube Goldberg tangle of scavenged pipes and faucets. It was here that he prepared his simple fare of brown rice, homegrown vegetables, and tea made from local sassafras root.

For a heady moment it seemed like Canyon, with its live-and-let-live tolerance, might become the ideal hippie community, but that didn't last long. State and county authorities swept in and started harassing settlers in a way that was reminiscent of Morning Star's demise. In February 1969 more than forty outlaw builders were cited for violations by county inspectors and given forty-eight hours to vacate their nonconforming homes or face the consequences. Some stayed to do battle; others moved on to more remote destinations.

One such refugee, Tim Biggins, moved north to an isolated island in Canada. Another found his way to New Mexico and lived alone in a cave on the Hondo River. "Cave Dave," as he came to be known, took a vow of silence and only communicated by

OPPOSITE
UPPER: *Funky plumbing, Barry's house, Canyon, California, 1968.*

PREVIOUS PAGES
PP. 260–261: *Making adobe bricks, Reality Construction Company commune, Arroyo Seco, New Mexico, 1969 (photo: Roberta Price).*

FOLLOWING PAGES
PP. 264–265: *"Anarchy is our basic rule . . ." Self-build shelters in the woods of California;*

PP. 266–269: *Open-air bathing.*

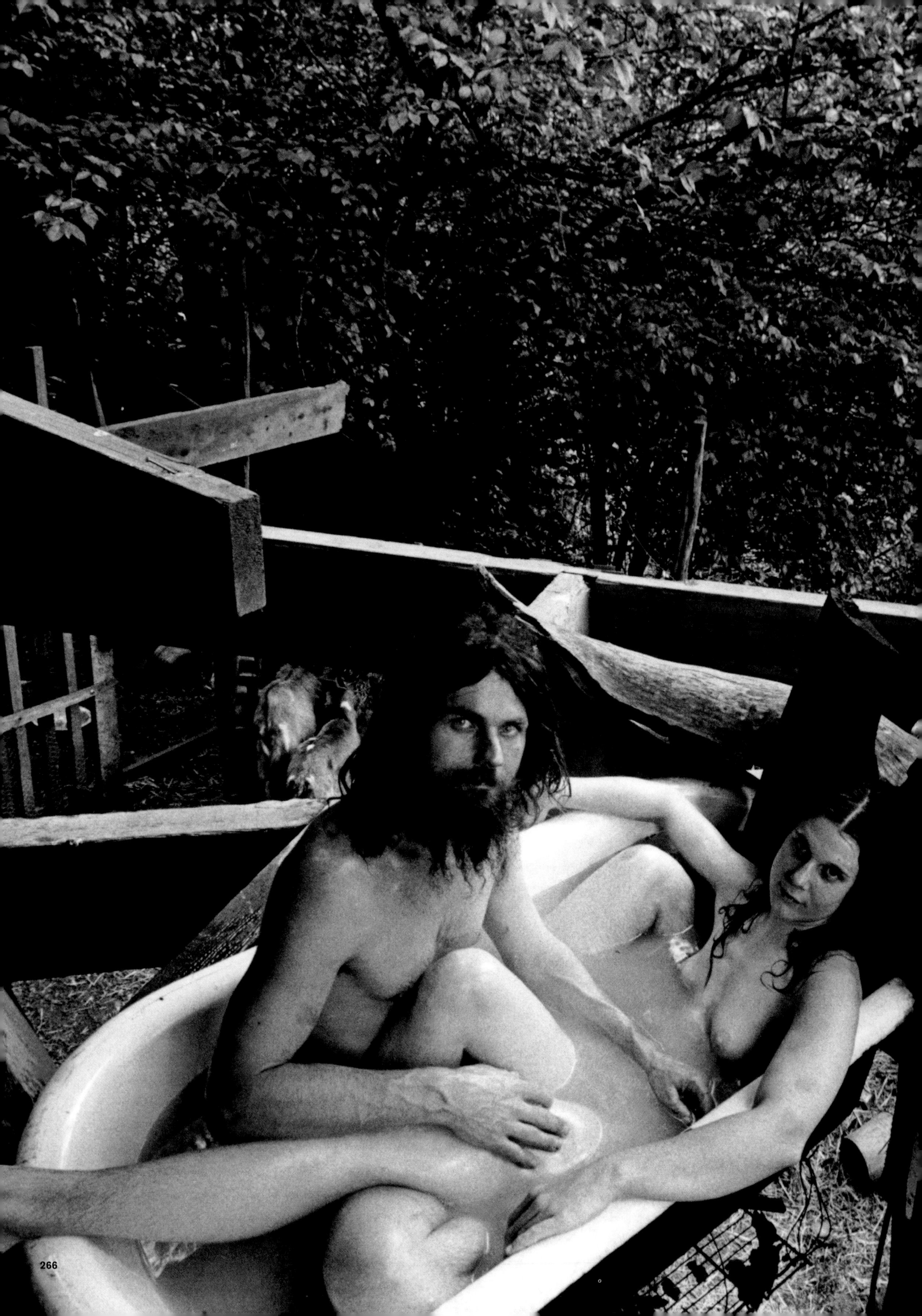

POSTED
NO
FISHING

writing on a chalkboard. A gnomelike hippie named Teddy wandered up the California coast and settled in among the seals and kelp beds. For a time, he tried to live on one of the offshore rock masses at Big Sur, surrounded by fog and crashing surf. He rigged up a rope bridge to get back and forth and made a temporary shelter out of flotsam and jetsam, but he almost drowned one day and decided to move inland.

Farther up the same coast, an entire community of driftwood houses arose. Dick Keigwin propped his house in a V-shaped ravine, between two sloping rocks. Karen and Roger Knoebber built theirs with a framework of sea-washed logs covered in a rippling skin of shingles fashioned from small pieces of driftwood. The house had a fairy-tale look, something like a Victorian boot. The Knoebbers and their three little girls lived on mussels, fish, and New Zealand spinach that grew wild along the shore. After a few idyllic months, the U.S. Coast Guard invaded the driftwood enclave and bulldozed all the houses back into the sea.

Much farther north, another kind of driftwood community was forming itself on a fog-enshrouded island in British Columbia. Hornby Island became the mecca for many self-build hippies, offering freedom from prying officials and a safe haven for draft dodgers. New arrivals were free to build whatever they liked, since there were no building codes or zoning restrictions. Most chose to work with the abundant supply of felled pines that washed up on the island's rugged shoreline. "The beach [here] is like a mill-yard and a supermarket . . . a temptress," said one Hornby settler.[27] What came to be known as the "Hornby Style" was characterized by artfully arranged beach logs, post-and-beam frameworks, sod roofs, hand-split shakes, and a preference for improvising on the spot. "I never did have a design, just a napkin with a dream on it," said Arthur Corner, who framed his own house using forty-five-foot-long poles hauled up from the beach.[28]

Tim Biggins, the American fugitive from the clamp-downs in Canyon, built a circular structure propped on stilts. The centerpiece of his "Log-Rythmic" house, was a gravity-defying umbrella of driftwood that spiraled around a central post. Each gnarly log retained its own personality, with lumps, knots, and twisted stumps intact, while Biggins patiently balanced, notched, bolted, or strapped them into place with various fasteners and bits of metal. A rope was hung from one of the rafters so Biggins, like Tarzan, could swing from room to room. "A man needs space to swing," he said.[29]

A driftwood community grows on Hornby Island, British Columbia.

OPPOSITE
Tim Biggins, Log-Rythmic House, 1969.

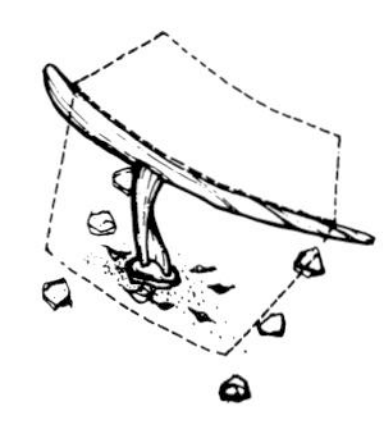
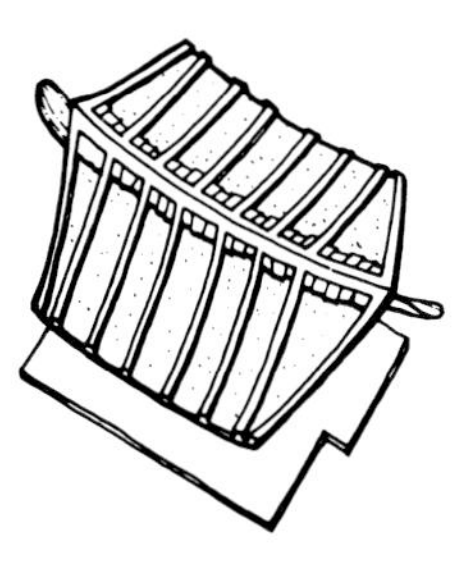
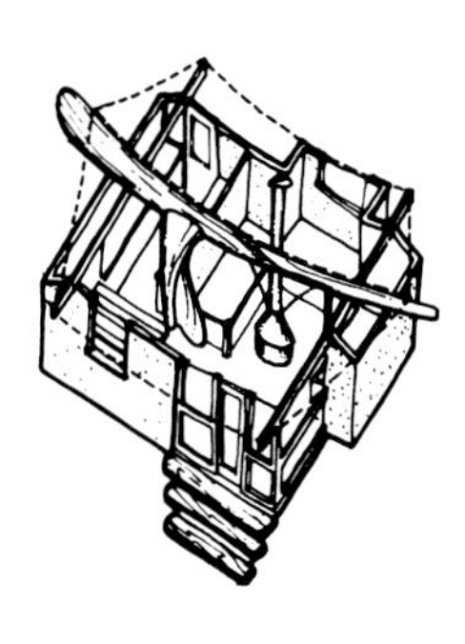
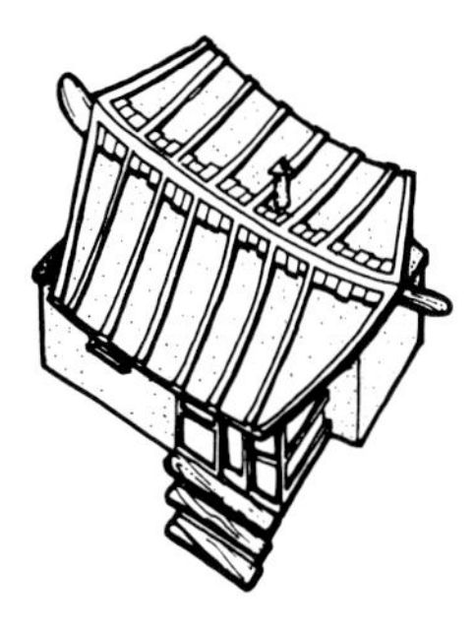
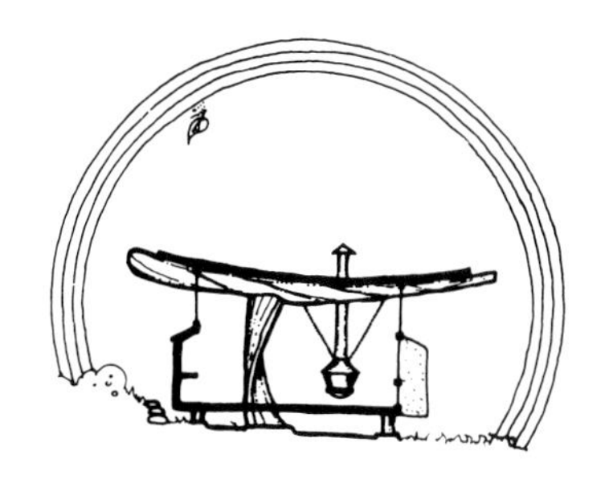

ABOVE: *Leaf Retreat evolves around a single piece of driftwood;* BELOW LEFT: *Wayne Ngan, studio door, 1969;* BELOW RIGHT: *Tim Burrows, Cliff-Top Mound, view from beach.*

OPPOSITE
ABOVE: *The "Shire," 1968;*
BELOW: *Lloyd House, Leaf Retreat, 1970;*

FOLLOWING PAGES
P.274: *Tim Burrows, notes and sketch for Cliff-Top Mound;*
P. 275: *Driftwood portal, Community Center, 1974 (all photos: Blue Sky Archive, Bo Helliwell and Michael McNamara).*

The "Leaf Retreat" started with a particularly sculptural piece of driftwood that builder Lloyd House noticed one day. "As I walked along the beach it said 'Take me.'" He knew right away that this was meant to be the roof's primary support. A few days later, House found a long, gently curving log that made a perfect complementary beam. "The ridge log turned up on the beach the morning it was needed," said House. "This building is essentially a falling leaf and the log is the leaf's stem."[30] He covered the roof with rough-hewn cedar boards, leaving the eaves frayed to further evoke the image of the leaf.

Tim Burrows, another Hornby resident, wanted an "invisible house" that would merge with the landscape of a sixty-foot cliff overlooking Tribune Bay. With its sod roof, driftwood frame, and hyperbolic roof, the house hardly registered as a man-made structure. A deck was cantilevered over the cliff and equipped with an ingenious pulley-and-winch system for raising more logs from the beach.

From May to September '73 I lived in the completed section and worked on the foundations for the remaining 2/3 of the structure, and the winching platform/deck and then again returned to Vancouver.

In May 74 I moved permanently into the structure and completed the second 1/3 of the living space and the basement under it by the following winter.

The remaining 1/3, including the main heating system built from a 1/4" steel marker buoy found on the beach, was completed by the winter of 1975.[1]

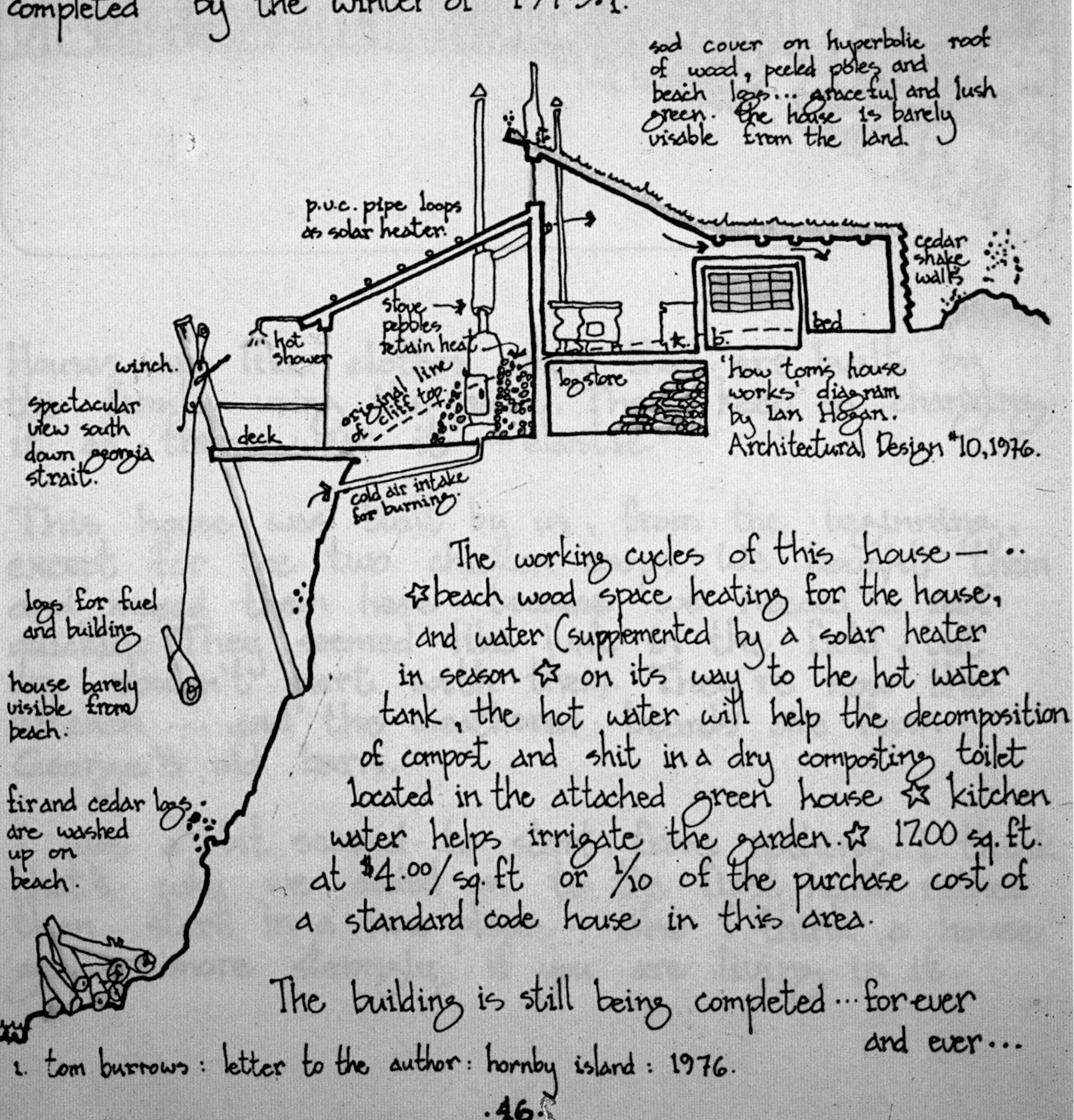

The working cycles of this house— ☆ beach wood space heating for the house, and water (supplemented by a solar heater in season ☆ on its way to the hot water tank, the hot water will help the decomposition of compost and shit in a dry composting toilet located in the attached green house ☆ kitchen water helps irrigate the garden. ☆ 1200 sq. ft. at $4.00/sq. ft or 1/10 of the purchase cost of a standard code house in this area.

The building is still being completed ... forever and ever ...

1. tom burrows : letter to the author : hornby island : 1976.

Prickly Mountain, Warren, Vermont.

ABOVE: *Dave Sellers, Bill Reienecke, Tack House/Sellers Residence, 1966–1970.*

OPPOSITE *Wadsworth House, 1966 (photo: Alastair Gordon).*

Prickly Mountain, an alternative community outside of Warren, Vermont, was founded by a group of Yale architecture students who felt alienated by the dehumanizing qualities of modern architecture and the corporate detachment of the profession.[31] They bought six hundred acres on the spruce-covered mountain and built their own designs, working together, and sharing ideas and expenses. It was a liberating experience after the stultifying atmosphere of architecture school. "They were dressed in plaid lumberjack shirts over surfers' pullovers, pants hung on wide elastic clip-on suspenders, and construction boots," recalled critic C. Ray Smith, who visited Prickly Mountain in 1966.[32] "It was a free-for-all," said Louis Mackall, one of Prickly's pioneers. "A place where people felt empowered to express themselves."[33] Hardly any plans were drawn, but the houses reflected a passion for natural materials, hand-hewn craftsmanship, and spontaneous thinking.

The first to be built was the "Tack House," a multilevel crash pad built atop the post-and-beam frame of an old sugarhouse. Dave Sellers and Bill Reienecke lived there with others who drifted in and out. The interior space rose in a succession of open, loftlike levels connected by handmade ladders and rickety steps, ascending all the way to a crow's-nest sleeping perch. The roof sloped to a steep peak for shedding snow and echoing the vertical thrust of the surrounding pines. The south and east sides were faceted with kaleidoscopic panes of multicolored glass, something like a psychedelic solar collector. The interior was left raw. Plumbing and electrical conduit were exposed, and furniture was made from barn timbers crudely bolted into place. An old rake became a clothes rack. A sink was carved from a block of wood. The Tack House served as a template for other buildings at Prickly, such as the Wadsworth House (1967), a steeply pitched pyramid covered in slate shingles and topped with a barrel-vaulted skylight.

Most structures were single-family dwellings, but there was a compound near the

base of Prickly Mountain called "Dimetredon," where twenty-five people lived communally. The name referred to a type of dinosaur that had a large, spiky sail on its back that was thought to act as a solar collector. "We were a little tribe," said Jim Sanford, who had come north from the architecture program at the University of Pennsylvania. "We'd learn how to make something," he said. "It would fail and then we'd try something else."[34] The idea was to have one giant solar collector connected to a series of small living pods that would feed off the central source. During dark winter months there was recourse to a huge wood-burning furnace, and every man in the compound was assigned a certain week when he had the responsibility of keeping the cast-iron monster stoked.

Another group of disaffected architecture students—Steve Badanes, John Ringel, Jim Adamson, and Greg Torchio—emerged from Princeton's architecture program and established a roving design-build collaborative called Jersey Devil, named after the legendary creature of the New Jersey Pine Barrens. The Devils worked with a sense of humor, humility, even self-deprecation. They liked to get their hands dirty and usually camped out on the construction sites. "A building has a life of its own," said Badanes, who was inspired to become an architect builder after a visit to Prickly Mountain in 1968.[35] "Our emphasis is always on craft, sustainability, and social justice," he said.[36]

Like Ant Farm, they started by making inflatable environments but soon moved on to more permanent structures like "Arthurpod" and "Sphincter House," and the "Snail House" that was built in the Pine Barrens in 1972. Essentially, it was a dome that spiraled outward like the volutes of a shell. The unusual shape was achieved by attaching curving rafters to a concrete core, then cladding the frame with cedar boards, spraying polyurethane foam over the siding, and sealing it with a layer of concrete plaster.

Another elaboration on the dome, even more radical in concept, was the Helmet

ABOVE: *Tack House/Sellers Residence, Prickly Mountain,* LOWER: *Swimming in Mad River, Warren, Vermont.*

OPPOSITE
UPPER LEFT: *Dimetredon, Prickly Mountain;* UPPER RIGHT: *Tack House;* LOWER LEFT & RIGHT: *Jersey Devil, Helmet House, Goffstown, New Hampshire, 1974;* MIDDLE RIGHT: *Bill Wadsworth, Dave Sellers (fiddle), Carl Bates playing music at Prickly Mountain, c. 1975.*

ABOVE: *Jersey Devil, Snail House, Forked River, New Jersey, 1972 (photo: Alastair Gordon).*

OPPOSITE
John Ringel of Jersey Devil sitting on Snail House foundation.

House that the Devils built in the woods of New Hampshire. Initial inspiration came from an outcropping of granite that sat overlooking a lake. The idea was to let the rock itself be the interior of the house, leaving the natural contours of the stone, complete with ferns and moss and no partitions, as open space. Again, Badanes and his partners began with prefabricated barn rafters. They covered the elliptical frame with Homasote boards, chicken wire, and ferrocement. Long, curving skylights, resembling the visors of a helmet, filled the interior with natural light. A rustic boulder staircase led to a dining/kitchen area, and the living room was perched on a rock ledge. A shower was ingeniously contrived within a vertical crevice of rock, while a sleeping loft was suspended among the rafters.

Like so many of the outlaw architects that preceded them, the Devils rejected high design concepts and the arrogant persona of the professional architect. Their houses were a good deal more sophisticated than the average hippie shelter, however, and while still unconventional in their methods, the Devils had actual clients who paid them for their work. (Some of the houses even had running water and flush toilets.)

Ideas that had first started to circulate in the communes and frontier outposts of the mid- to late sixties were, by the 1970s, starting to reach the outer fringes of mainstream society. Some backwoods pioneers simply assimilated into local communities and took on adult responsibilities without necessarily selling out, bringing with them a commitment to sustainable design, alternative medicine, environmental activism, whole-grain foods, natural child birthing, and other new-age contributions that would filter into the general culture and transform it quietly from within.

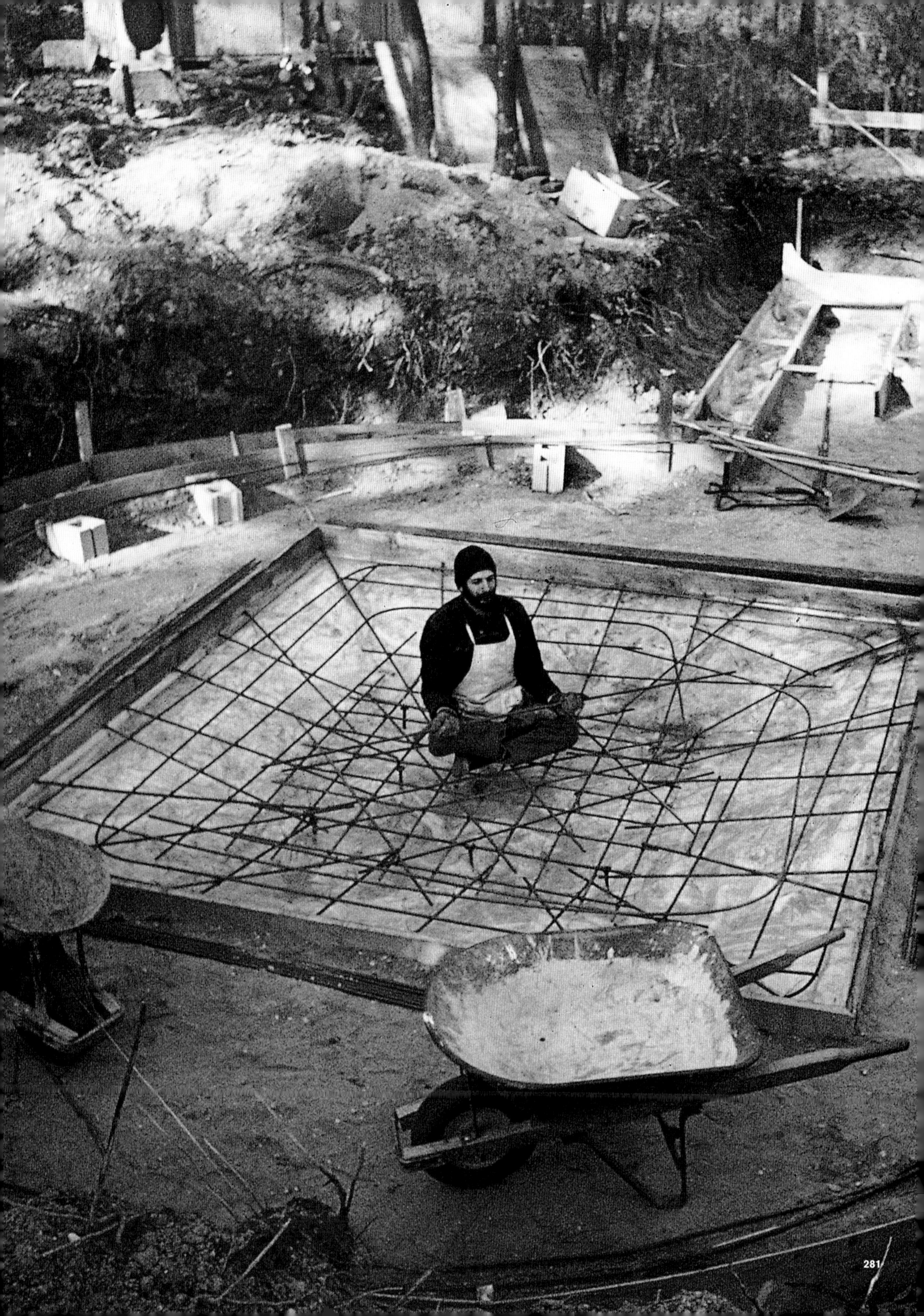

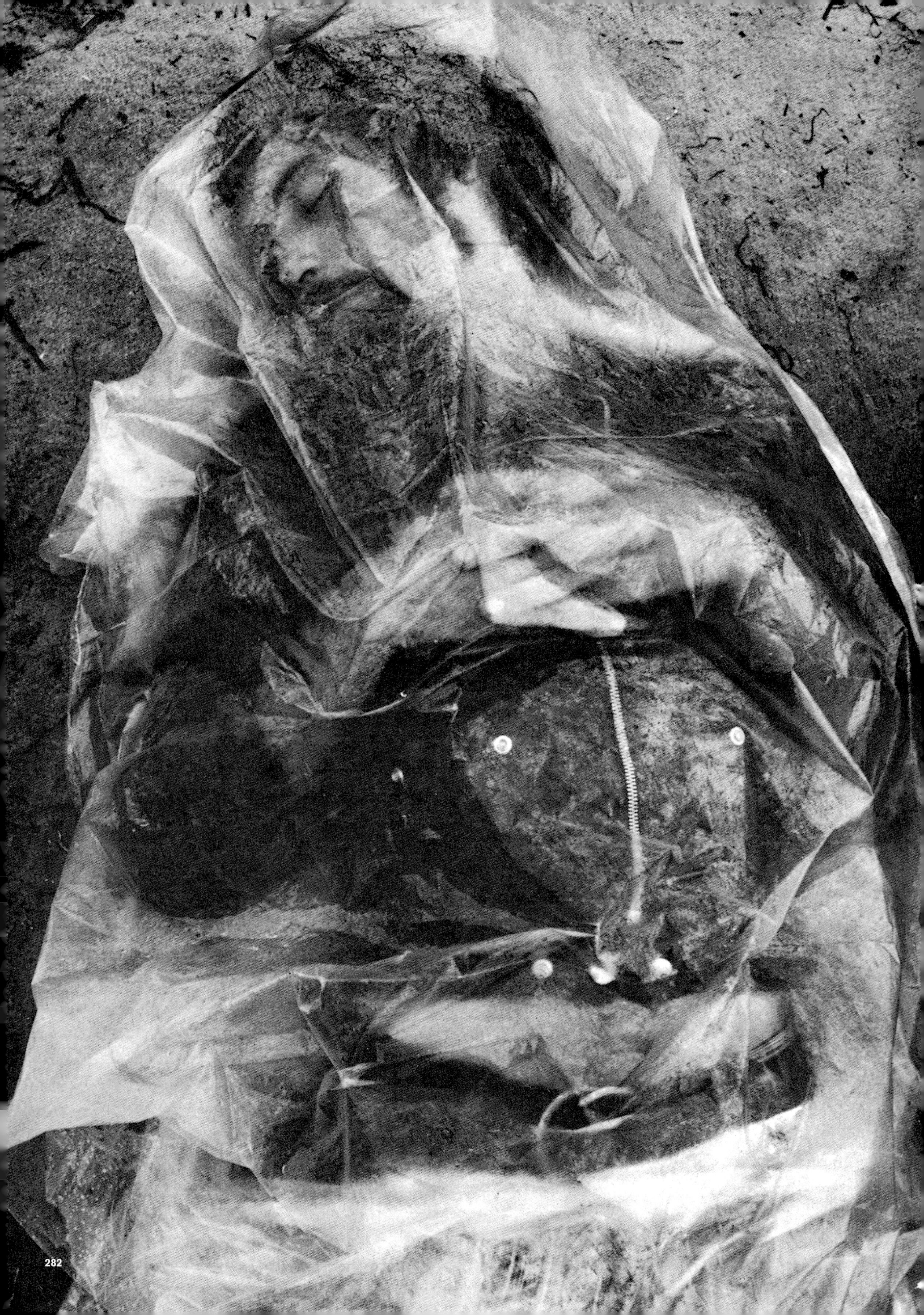

EPILOGUE THE FALL OF DROP

"LET THERE BE NO MORE MORNING STARS."
—RONALD REAGAN, 1967

For some, the tipping point came with the bloody insurrection in Chicago. For others it was the pool-cue assault at Altamont, the Tate-LaBianca murders, the breakup of the Beatles, or Watergate. The freaky, freeform era faded into the self-conscious seventies. The momentum was lost, as if everyone had taken an amnesia pill and resumed a former level of mediocrity. What had seemed epic was now mocked and marginalized, reduced to a cliché. Yippies became Yuppies. LSD and pot gave way to cocaine and meth. Disco ascended the charts, as did big hair and heavy metal, and many were left with a feeling of premature withdrawal, emotional *coitus interruptus.* Jimi Hendrix, Janis Joplin, Jim Morrison, and other icons were dead from overdose. The sunny optimism of the Summer of Love was suddenly overshadowed by death and destruction. The press, who had done so much to mythologize the counterculture in the first place, washed their hands of the movement, and the flower-power stories of the sixties were replaced with lurid tales of addiction, squalor, sexual depravity, and violence. Charismatic gurus competed for ascendancy while open-door communes gave way to mind-controlling cults. Charles Manson, with satanic eyes glaring, became the new poster child for hippie culture.

What started as an exploration of inner space through utopiate drugs like LSD shifted to a reckless longing for other levels of being, instant karma, nirvana, distant worlds. (The idea of Stewart Brand's Outlaw Area would lose much of its appeal when outlaws like Manson were in the mix.) Some were driven to despair and gave up on planet earth altogether. "I keep getting the vision of the planet as a plant which has flowered and wants to go to seed," wrote psychedelic trailblazer Ramon Sender.[1] Dean Fleming, co-founder of Libré, called for a "totally integrated colony in Free Space." Brand himself announced that outer space was now the preeminent frontier, the ultimate Outlaw Area, "too big and dilute for national control."[2] Paolo Soleri proposed giant man-made asteroids with names like "Astermo" that would provide sustenance for seventy thousand ex-earthlings. Pop physicist Gerard O'Neill drew controversial plans for a cylindrical space colony, an "inside-out planet," of one million inhabitants, complete with artificial mountains and rivers. But not everyone was convinced. "I anticipate a continuous vague low-key 'airplane fear,'" warned zome inventor Steve Baer.[3]

Things started to unravel in 1968 when Tim Leary, Richard Alpert, and their band of Castalian mystics were evicted from Millbrook and forced to abandon the dream of an LSD-based utopia. Art Kleps, former resident, returned a few months later and found the place in ruin. The furniture had been stolen and the electricity shut off. "The fifty-room mansion was full of dog shit, cat shit, goat shit, and phantasmagorical images of cherished people and grand scenes, now long gone."[4] (In 1970, Leary escaped from a minimum-security prison in San Luis Obispo and became a fugitive from justice.)

Ken Kesey's cabin at La Honda was abandoned and the Merry Pranksters went on a perpetual road trip. Disillusioned with what he called the "communal lie," Kesey moved back to Oregon with his family while the famous painted bus was left to rust in a nearby field.[5] By 1970, Drop City was also passing into oblivion as all the original droppers moved on to other scenes. Drop's flamboyant zomes became hideouts for runaways and motorcycle gangs. Peter Rabbit, one of the founding members, went by in 1971 and found the place deserted. "Sad hippy ghost town

Fre
ACID +

MAN LETS
GET TOGETHER
BUILD DOMES
& LIVE IN
PEACE
LEAVE THE WORLD
START A NEW
WORLD BEYOND
TO LIVE IN PEAC
AND HARMONY
LIVING AND
LOVING, SH
AND CARING.
LETS BUILD A
COMMUNE. O

OH!!
HERE ARE THE PEOPLE TOO!!

BUT BETTER STILL
HERE IS A COMMUNE
HERE ARES DOMES

LETS GET
THIS
IS DEAR TOGETHER

OPPOSITE
Graffiti, Drop City, Colorado, 1972 (photo: Jack Fulton).

PREVIOUS PAGES
P. 282: *Hippie under plastic (photo: Anders Holmquist).*

with a huge pile of human shit deposited on the drain board next to the sink," he wrote. "There were ghosts behind every broken window and half-off-the-hinges door."[6]

Other Aquarian experiments were quite literally going up in smoke. A fire at Johnson's Pastures commune in Vermont killed four residents and set a pall over the whole back-to-the-land movement. The main building at Oz, a commune in Pennsylvania, was destroyed by arson while fifty hand-built shelters at Wheeler's Ranch were burned to prevent squatters from returning. "At dawn we torched the last house on the Knoll," said Bill Wheeler.[7]

The graffiti on a building in Taos, New Mexico, made it clear how local residents felt about the new settlers there: "The only good hippie is a dead hippie."[8] There were drive-by shootings, random beatings, and widespread intimidation of the longhair population. A VW van was dynamited, a macrobiotic restaurant was destroyed, and Steve Durkee, former USCO partner and founder of Lama, was beaten while sitting in his truck. A group of vigilantes attacked the Kingdom of God commune near Guadalupita, killing one communard, and raping and wounding others while survivors fled to the mountains.[9] There were also murders at the Lower Farm, a commune in Placitas, not far from the zomes of Manera Nueva. "HIPPIE HAVEN DOUBLE SLAYING" read the headlines in the Albuquerque *Tribune*.[10]

The all-inclusive, open-door spirit of the communes may have spelled their demise from the start, but sensationalized press coverage didn't help. As Richard Fairfield, editor of *The Modern Utopian,* noted: "Publicity is the death of a community."[11] Hundreds of magazine and newspaper reports brought unwanted visitors and unforeseen tensions. "The powers of the media won out," said Gene Bernofsky of Drop City. "Too much, too early, and it was the end."[12]

Most communes were collapsing from internal problems anyway. Ego battles, ennui, leaky roofs, and poverty took their toll. "After a brief summer of orgies and fun in the sun, the long winter sets in and darkness brings dissatisfaction and disillusionment," wrote Fairfield after making an extensive tour of the communal front in 1970.[13] People grew tired of living on top of one another, sharing possessions, and eating from the same pot.

There was a romantic return to the virtues of pitched roofs, vertical walls, right-angled corners, and private rooms in place of single, open spaces. *Shelter*, Lloyd Kahn's 1973 guide to alternative living, marked a significant change in attitude. It featured examples of hand-crafted dwellings made from natural materials. Only a few geodesic domes were included. "There is far more to learn from wisdom of the past... than from any further extension of whiteman techno-plastic prowess," wrote Kahn.[14]

Domes and zomes leaked and were difficult to expand. (By 1973, all seventeen domes at Pacific High had been abandoned and fallen into disrepair.) Inflatables deflated. Tree houses, hand-woven bowers, yurts, tents, and tepees were only temporary solutions at best. Free-form structures sprayed with polyurethane were, it turned out, potentially lethal. (Polyurethane emitted toxic gasses and could burst into flame.) The Tao design collaborative abandoned work on Earth House in 1973 and left its undulating roof of plastic foam to bake in the Texas sun.[15]

But not all was dispersal and decay. There were success stories too. Anarchist homesteaders in Canyon, California, chose to stay and fight and eventually won a victory over zoning authorities there. Libré in Colorado, Lama in New Mexico, and the Farm in Tennessee managed to grow with the times and prosper as viable alternatives. (All three communities continue to exist today, as does,

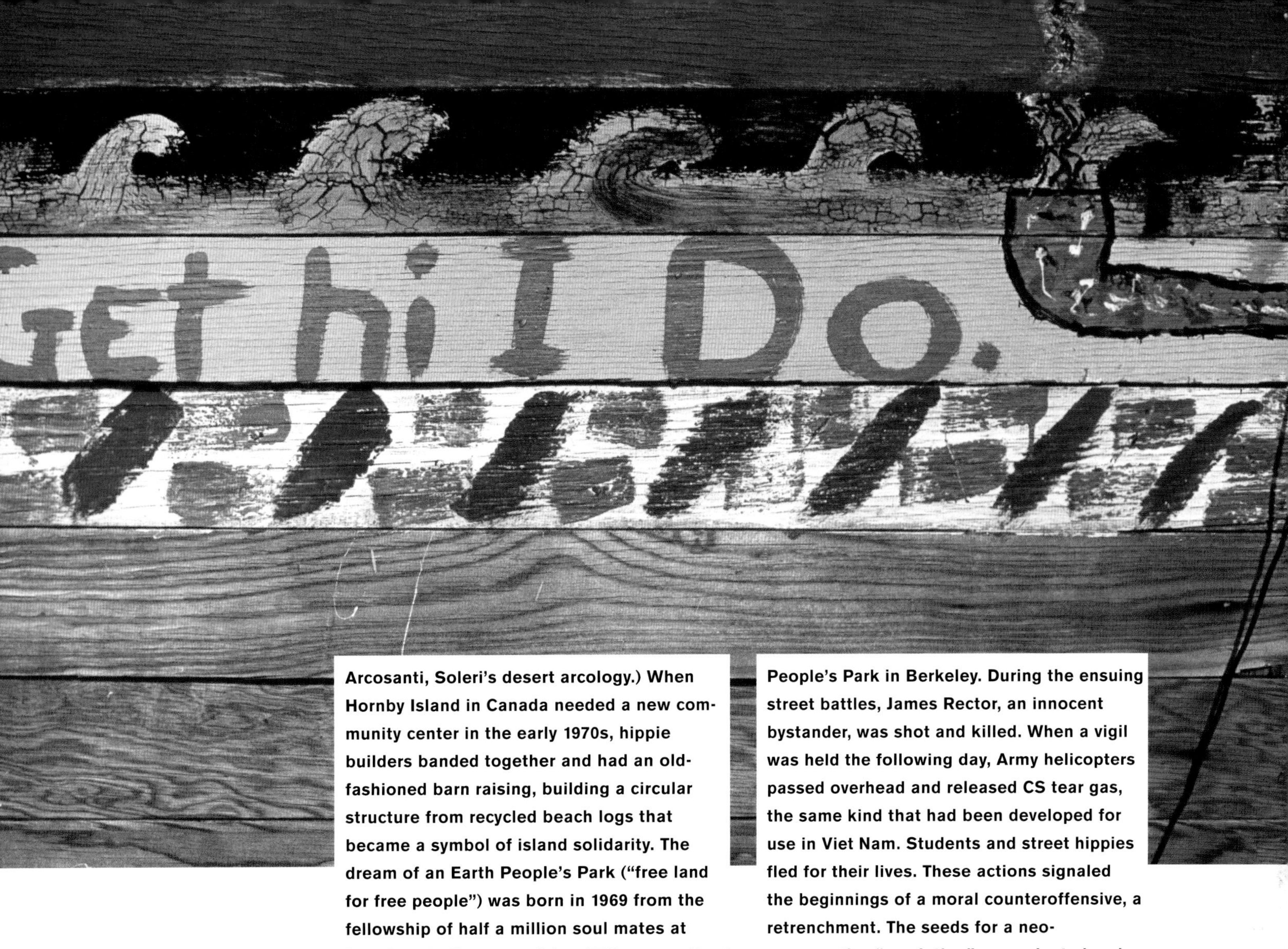

ABOVE AND OPPOSITE
Drop City in ruin, 1972 (photos: Jack Fulton).

FOLLOWING PAGES
P. 288: *Yab-Yum (photo: Paul Kagan)*; P. 304: *Drop City (photo: Jack Fulton).*

Arcosanti, Soleri's desert arcology.) When Hornby Island in Canada needed a new community center in the early 1970s, hippie builders banded together and had an old-fashioned barn raising, building a circular structure from recycled beach logs that became a symbol of island solidarity. The dream of an Earth People's Park ("free land for free people") was born in 1969 from the fellowship of half a million soul mates at Woodstock. Two years later, EPP was realized as a self-contained hippie republic in Vermont with no laws or taxes. The 600-acre settlement continued to grow for several more years until the federal government seized the land, threw out the homesteaders, and turned it into a public park.[16]

During his campaign for governor of California in 1967, Ronald Reagan appealed to the insecurities of his white, suburban constituency by promising to "clean up the mess at Berkeley" and contain the hippie contagion. "Let there be no more Morning Stars," he pronounced, referring to the Sonoma County commune founded by Lou Gottlieb who, along with other free-land advocates, had dared to challenge the very essence of American-style ownership. Something raw and seemingly uncontrollable had been let loose. Reagan and his fellow right-wing ideologues saw it as their duty to put the genie back in the bottle. In May 1969, Reagan called in the National Guard and 49th Infantry Brigade to quell dissent and forcibly clear People's Park in Berkeley. During the ensuing street battles, James Rector, an innocent bystander, was shot and killed. When a vigil was held the following day, Army helicopters passed overhead and released CS tear gas, the same kind that had been developed for use in Viet Nam. Students and street hippies fled for their lives. These actions signaled the beginnings of a moral counteroffensive, a retrenchment. The seeds for a neo-conservative "revolution" were planted and Reagan rode the sentiment all the way to the White House. Many are still wondering what happened and how so much was lost in the ensuing years.

I started to write this book in response to the culture of control that arose after September 11, 2001. It seemed like the right time to invoke a period of free-spirited, all-out independence. As one Haight-Ashbury hippie put it: "Hold on by letting go."[17] The sixties legacy lingers on, influencing everything from the Internet and sustainable design to Freak Folk music, anti-globalism, organic cuisine, alternative healing, and rave clubs. Behind the liberated parks, communes, crash pads, and painted busses was the struggle for a certain mental space, a place without boundaries or divisions that would foster wild creativity, nurture new experiences, and even change human consciousness. That dream never died but the story needs retelling.

ACKNOWLEDGMENTS

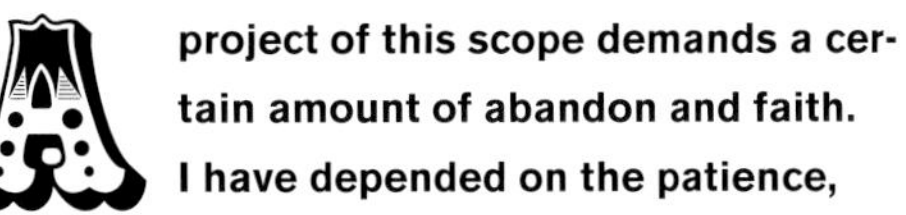

A project of this scope demands a certain amount of abandon and faith. I have depended on the patience, trust and blessings of many people who supported its underlying spirit. (Several became friends in the process.) I start by thanking the trailblazers who were generous with their insights and memories. Everyone has his or her own version of the sixties and it's not always easy going back through the looking glass. I am indebted to Ramon Sender, Gerd Stern, Tony Martin, Aleksandra Kasuba, Bill Wheeler, Steve Baer, Clark Richert, Nooridin (Steve Durkee), Asha Greer (Barbara Durkee), Steve Badanes, Dean Fleming, Linda Fleming, Peter Calthorpe, Jay Baldwin, Robert Forte and Roberta Price. (An interview with Paolo Soleri and a visit to Arcosanti provided the initial spark seven years ago.) Heartfelt admiration goes to the late William Chaitkin for his pioneering work on the counter culture, to Lloyd Kahn for his thoughtful books on alternative habitation, to Timothy Miller for his research on communes, and to Stewart Brand for the freewheeling vision that produced *The Whole Earth Catalog.* Their work provided inspiration and guidance throughout the shaping of this book.

Numerous individuals and institutions provided archival assistance including Connie Lywellen and Stephanie Cannizzo at the Berkeley Art Museum; Paul Smith and the American Crafts Council; Mark Weimar of Regent Press for access to *The Oracle of the City of San Francisco* archives; Liz Ryan of Wolfgang's Vault (www.wolfgangsvault.com); Adrienne and Michael Callahan of Museum Technology Source, Inc. for opening the USCO Archives; and everyone at the Cosanti Foundation, keepers of the Soleri collection. Additional thanks go to all the multi-media artists, designers, filmmakers and architects who kindly shared their thoughts and/or lent their works for reproduction including Isaac Abrams, Ant Farm, Alicia Bay Laurel, Tim Biggins, Tim Burrows, Jackie Cassen, Wendell Castle, Ivan Chermayeff, William S. Coperthwaite, Gamal El-Zoghby, Harry Fischman, Charles Forberg, Caroling Geary, Tom Geismar, Charles L. Harker, Haus-Rucker Co., James Hubbell, Ken Isaacs, Jersey Devil, Swami Kriyananda, Chip Lord, Tom Luckey, Mark Mills, Ugo La Pietra, Bill Rienecke, Jim Sanford, Dave Sellers, Rudi Stern, John Storyk, Sim Van der Ryn, Richard Wehrman, Joshua White, and Jud Yalkut.

I thank the photographers whose imagery has been specially featured: Gene Anthony who captured the cultural vortex of Haight Ashbury; Paul Dembski who documented the communal spirit of New Mexico; John Elliott for his images of hand-built dwellings in and around Woodstock; Dean Fleming who recorded the people and buildings of Libré commune; Jack Fulton for his inspired documentation of alternative building throughout the southwest; Bo Helliwell and Michael McNamara (Blue Sky Archive) for their documentation of Hornby Island; Barry Shapiro for his classic shots of handmade houses on the west coast; Bill Wheeler for his photos of Wheeler's Ranch; Jane Pincus Lidz and her shots of mobile dwellings; Ben Martin who, as a *Time* photographer, recorded the crash pads of the East Village; Clark Richert who recorded the evolution of Drop City; and Roberta Price for her remarkable photographs of Libré and other radical outposts of the period. (Roberta's work is featured in: *Huerfano, A Memoir of Life in the Counterculture,* University of Massachusetts Press, 2004.) I thank all the other photographers and archivists who also lent work: Gordon Adelman, Sally Bailey, Adam Bartos, Bruce Davidson, Richard Crone, Richard Fairfield, Charles Harker, Chuck Henrikson, Anders Holmquist, Paul Kagan, Lisa Law, Wayne McCall, Terrence Moore, Jerry Oshinga, David Perkins, Otto Rigan, Amalie R. Rothschild, Curtis Schreier, Michael Schulman of Magnum Photos, Barry Shapiro, Anne Simpkin, Don Snyder, Dennis Stock, John Veltri, and Bill Wadsworth. My sincere apologies to anyone who has been accidentally overlooked or misrepresented.

I was fortunate to receive heroic support from the staff at Rizzoli International who remained gracious under pressure. I give my gratitude to publisher Charles Miers for his enthusiasm and my editor, Dung Ngo, who managed to sustain a consistent vision throughout editing and design. I also thank Richard Olsen for his early counsel. It was a particular delight to work with designer Sara Stemen on this our third book. Sara managed to weave together hundreds of disparate images and make them flow as one. I also wish to acknowledge the tireless editorial and production efforts of Maria Pia Gramaglia, Meera Deean, Alexandra Tart, Henry Casey, Tricia Levy, Lee Cerré, and Kaija Markoe at Rizzoli.

I wouldn't have accomplished anything without the collaborative forces of my wife and partner Barbara de Vries who worked on every aspect of *Spaced Out.* My four children provided insight and motivation and graciously tolerated my own spaced-out work habits so I give extra special thanks to Iain, Kiki, Leila and my free-spirited daughter Iona, to whom this book is lovingly dedicated.

—ALASTAIR GORDON

NOTES

INTRODUCTION

1. Raoul Vaneigem, *The Revolution of Everyday Life,* (London: Rebel Press/Left Bank Books, 1994), 266.
2. Rasa Gustaitis, *Turning On* (New York: The Macmillan Company, 1969), 94.

CHAPTER 1

1. Timothy, Leary, *High Priest* (New York: The World Publishing Company, 1968), 194.
2. Ralph Metzner, *The Ecstatic Adventure* (New York: The Macmillan Company, 1968), 4.
3. Rolf Von Eckartsberg, "A Kind of Harmonious and Convincing Equilibrium," in Metzner, *The Ecstatic Adventure*, 39.
4. Alan W. Watts, *The Joyous Cosmology: Adventures in the Chemistry of Consciousness* (New York: Pantheon Books, 1962), 27.
5. Kleps was a long-term resident at Millbrook and founder of the Neo-American Church. See Art Kleps, *Millbrook: The True Story of the Early Years of the Psychedelic Revolution* (Oakland, CA: Bench Press, 1965), 27.
6. Aldous Huxley, *The Doors of Perception* (New York: Harper & Brothers, 1954).
7. "The legs, for example, of that chair—how miraculous their tubularity, how supernatural their polished smoothness! I spent several minutes—or was it centuries?—not merely gazing at those bamboo legs, but actually *being* them." Huxley, *The Doors of Perception,* 22.
8. Ibid., 36.
9. Stanley Krippner, "An Adventure in Psilocybin," in *Psychedelics: The Uses and Implications of Hallucinogenic Drugs,* ed. Aaronson, Bernard & Humphry Osmond (Garden City, NY: Doubleday & Company, Inc., 1970), 35.
10. Leary, *High Priest*, 88.
11. Humphry Osmond, "On Being Mad," in *Psychedelics*, 25–26.
12. Huxley, *The Doors of Perception.*
13. Metzner, *The Ecstatic Adventure*, 5.
14. William James, "Subjective Effects of Nitrous Oxide," *Mind*, 7: 1882. Also see William James, *The Varieties of Religious Experience,* 1910.
15. Krippner, "An Adventure in Psilocybin," 36. "There is something about synchronicity that resists [any] kind of retrospective examination," wrote Art Kleps.
16. Osmond, "On Being Mad," 25.
17. Michaux published six volumes on the subject. *Miserable Miracle: Mescaline* (New York: New York Review Books, 2002), the first of his accounts, was published in 1956. For his remarkable mescaline drawings see Henri Michaux, *Emergences/Resurgences* (Milan, Italy: The Drawing Center/SKIRA, 2000).
18. Michaux, *Miserable Miracle*, 67.
19. Ibid., 11.
20. Leary, *High Priest*, 158.
21. "tender garden of divine bliss," Leary, *High Priest*, 155. "artificial paradise," Hevelock Ellis, "Mezcal: A New Artificial Paradise," *Contemporary Review* (January 1898).
22. Osmond, "On Being Mad," 25.
23. Aldous Huxley, *Heaven and Hell* (London: Chatto & Windus, 1956), 9.
24. "shimmering filigree," Osmond, "On Being Mad." "lattice... honeycomb," Heinrich Klüver, as cited in Robert E.L. Masters & Jean Houston, *Psychedelic Art* (New York: Grove Press, 1968), 92.
25. Michaux, *Miserable Miracle*, 67.
26. Watts made every effort to scribe the ineffable and published a rambling account of his psychedelic encounters in *The Joyous Cosmology: Adventures in the Chemistry of Consciousness.* "I am trying to delineate the basic principles of psychedelic awareness," he wrote, chronicling every rush and flash of insight. Unhindered by the clinical mindset, Watts hoped to capture the elusive nature of his experience, at one point describing it as a "round dance," at another point, as a "circle of reciprocity." Watts, *The Joyous Cosmology,* 32–33.
27. Leary, *High Priest,* 159.
28. Ibid., 2.
29. Most of the photographs were taken by Wolf Strache or Barbara Gould.
30. Leary, *High Priest*, 159.
31. Watts, *The Joyous Cosmology*, 17.
32. In 1957 Hubbard began to work with Canadian psychiatrist Abram Hoffer and Dr. Humphry Osmond to develop a psychedelic therapy for chronic alcoholics. Hollywood Hospital, in New Westminster, British Columbia, was the first private Canadian clinic to use LSD therapy.
33. Hubbard, known as the "Johnny Appleseed of LSD," first worked under Dr. Ross MacLean, the medical superintendent of the Hollywood Hospital, and later at the International Federation for Advanced Study in Menlo Park, California.
34. Leary, *High Priest*, 171.
35. They were influenced by the traditions of Brook Farm, the nineteenth-century utopian community in West Roxbury, Mass., founded by George Ripley, a Unitarian minister.
36. Leary, *High Priest*, 192.
37. Leary's daughter, Susan, as quoted in Leary, *High Priest,* 85.
38. Leary, *Flashbacks,* 157.
39. Leary, *High Priest,* 169.
40. Leary, *Flashbacks,* 157.
41. Ibid.
42. Leary, *High Priest,* 320.
43. "Statement of Purpose," *The Psychedelic Review* I, No. 1 (June 1963): 6.
44. Leary, *High Priest,* 322.
45. As quoted in John Kobler, "The Dangerous Magic of LSD," *The Saturday Evening Post* (Nov. 2, 1963): 39.
46. Joseph J. Downing, "Zihuatanejo: An Experiment in Transpersonative Living," in *Utopiates: The Use & Users of LSD-25,* ed. Richard Blum & Associates (New York: Atherton Press, 1964), 142.
47. Leary, *Flashbacks*, 180.
48. Leary, *Flashbacks,* 183.
49. The house was originally built for the gas lighting magnate Charles F. Dietrich.
50. Leary, *Flashbacks*, 188.
51. Leary, *Flashbacks*, 189.
52. Ibid., 35.
53. Kleps, *Millbrook,* 50.
54. Leary, *Flashbacks*, 190.
55. Atwell published drawings in the *Psychedelic Review* and illustrated *High Priest*, the book that chronicled sixteen of Leary's trips in numbing detail. As visual counterpoint to the fractured narrative, Atwell drew tangled sinews and clumps of raw tissue drifting in liquid suspension—his attempt to capture the flux of LSD.
56. Masters & Houston, 171.
57. As cited in Kleps, *Millbrook.*
58. The Psychedelic Temple was painted in a New York City apartment. See Masters & Houston.
59. Michael Hollingshead, *The Man Who Turned on the World* (The Psychedelic Library), chapter 5, page 6.
60. Leary called it "Neurological Art." Leary, *Flashbacks,* 227.
61. Unnamed "psychedelic artist" quoted in "Psychedelic Art," *Life* (Sept. 9, 1966): 60–69.
62. Gerd Stern, as quoted in Richard Kostelanetz, *The Theater of Mixed Means* (New York: The Dial Press, 1968), 251.
63. Paul Perry, *On the Bus* (New York: Thunder's Mouth Press, 1990), 63.
64. Tom Wolfe, *The Electric Kool-Aid Acid Test* (New York: Farrar, Straus & Giroux, 1968), 58.
65. Ken Kesey, as quoted in Perry, *On the Bus,* 37.
66. Ibid., 59.
67. Ibid., 144.
68. Ibid., 105.
69. Ibid., 85.
70. Ibid., 97.
71. Ibid., 93. "I felt like we were a pastoral Indian village invaded by a whooping cowboy band of Wild West saloon carousers," recalled Richard Alpert, as quoted in Leary, *Flashbacks,* 206.
72. Perry, *On the Bus,* 55.
73. Wolfe, *The Electric Kool-Aid Acid Test*, 72.
74. Perry, *On the Bus*, 59.
75. Ibid., 91.
76. Ibid., 43.

CHAPTER TWO

1. Frank Popper, *Kunst Licht Kunst* (Eindhoven: Stedelijk van Abbe-Museum, 1966).
2. *Life* (Sept. 9, 1966). According to LIFE, 1966 was the Year of Turning On without Drugs.
3. Buckminster Fuller, as quoted in Gene Youngblood, *Expanded Cinema* (New York: E. P. Dutton & Co., 1970) 20.
4. The first photographs showing planet Earth in its immaculate blueness were sent back from Apollo 4 on November 9, 1967.
5. Alan Harrington, "A Visit to Inner Space," in *LSD: The Consciousness-Expanding Drug,* ed. David Solomon (New York: G. P. Putnam's Sons, 1966) 72.
6. Jay Stevens, *Storming Heaven* (New York: Grove Press, 1987), 143.
7. "Neuronauts," in Timothy Leary, *Flashbacks, An*

Autobiography (Los Angeles: J. P. Tarcher, Inc., 1983), 160; Timothy Leary, *High Priest* (New York: The World Publishing Company, 1968), 67.
8. Alan W. Watts, *The Joyous Cosmology* (New York: Pantheon Books, 1962), 67.
9. From the march against the Pentagon on October 21, 1967, quoted in Norman Mailer, *The Armies of the Night* (New York: The New American Library, 1968), 121.
10. Robert E.L. Masters & Jean Houston, *Psychedelic Art* (New York: Grove Press, 1968), 84.
11. Joshua White, interview by the author, November 26, 2006.
12. Thoman Tadlock, interview by Jud Yalkut, July 2, 1969, *The East Village Other*, vol. 4, no. 31.
13. "The electric light is pure information. It is a medium without a message, as it were, unless it is used to spell out some verbal ad or name." Marshall McLuhan, *Understanding Media* (Cambridge, Mass: MIT Press, 1996), 8.
14. Leary, *Flashbacks*, 230.
15. Jonas Mekas, as quoted in Masters & Houston, 126.
16. Gene Youngblood, *Expanded Cinema* (New York: E. P. Dutton & Co., 1970) 135–36.
17. Youngblood, *Expanded Cinema*, 136.
18. Mailer, *The Armies of the Night*, 86.
19. Öyvind Fahlström, as quoted in Douglas Davis, *Art and the Future* (New York: Praeger, 1972), 72.
20. Isaacs was influenced by McLuhan and the *nouvelle vague* of French filmmakers, in particular Jean Luc Godard and his belief that narrative was the enemy. Kenneth Isaac, interview by the author, March 21, 2006
21. Paul Welch, "The Way You Feel Inside the Box," *Life*(Sept. 14, 1962): 112.
22. VanDerBeek, as quoted in Davis, *Art and the Future,* 49.
23. Kranz, *Science & Technology in the Arts,* 240.
24. Gerd Stern, telephone interview by the author, May 2004.
25. Gerd Stern interview in Richard Kostelanetz, *The Theatre of Mixed Means: An Introduction to Happenings, Kinetic Environments, and other Mixed-Media Performances* (New York: The Dial Press, Inc., 1968), 244.
26. Kostelanetz, *The Theatre of Mixed Means,* 246.
27. Popper, *Kunst Licht Kunst,* 1966.
28. Kostelanetz, *The Theatre of Mixed Means*, 259.
29. The exhibition was called *Down by the Riverside* and ran from May 8 to June 19, 1966, at the Riverside Museum, 310 Riverside Drive at 103rd Street.
30. Kostelanetz, *The Theatre of Mixed Means*, 263.
31. Gerd Stern, telephone interview by the author, June 14, 2005.
32. *The Village Voice,* June 13, 1968, republished in Jill Johnston, *Marmalade Me* (New York: E. P. Dutton & Co., 1971), 161.
33. GRAV mounted their first New York installation in 1965 at the Contemporaries Gallery, 992 Madison Avenue, from February 16 through March 6, 1965. See Davis, *Art and the Future,* 131–34.
34. The *Vibrations* installation ran from December 14, 1967, to January 11, 1968. See Youngblood, *Expanded Cinema,* 398, and Kranz, *Science & Technology in the Arts,* 198–99.
35. "Transistorized Tunnel of Light," *Time* (June 7, 1968).
36. Ralph, T. Coe, *The Magic Theater* (Kansas City: The Circle Press, 1970), 228.
37. Ibid., 193.
38. R. C. Kenedy, "The Kansas City Magic Theater," *Art International* (Sept. 20, 1968), 28. See also Coe, *The Magic Theater,* 209.
39. "Wild New Flashy Bedlam of the Discotheque," *Life* (May 27, 1966), 72.
40. Robert Christgau, "Filmotheques," *Popular Photography* (January 1967).
41. "New Madness at the Discotheque," *Life* (May 27, 1966).
42. USCO combined eighteen slide projectors, closed-circuit TV, as well as several 16-mm movie projectors. "Wild New Flashy Bedlam," 72. The World was originally supposed to be called "Murray the K's World" after the famous New York disc jockey who was going to be the master of ceremonies.
43. Harold Edgerton invented the first electronic strobe light in 1931 as a way to study machine parts in motion.
44. Theologian James N. Lapsley visited New York's Electric Circus in 1968 and wrote about it in "A Psycho-Theological Appraisal of the New Left," *Theology Today* (January 1969).
45. Joseph Mathewson, *The Love Tribe.* (New York: The New Americn Library, 1968), 59.
46. Alvin Toffler, *Future Shock.* (New York: Random House, 1970), 310.
47. "Light shows, split-screen movies, high decibel screams, shouts and moans, grotesque costumes and writhing, painted bodies create a sensory environment characterized by high input and extreme unpredictability and novelty," wrote Toffler. Toffler, *Future Shock*, 310.
48. EPI combined a simultaneous onslaught of imagery and sound with films by Warhol, slides, and stroboscopic lighting effects by Danny Williams and Paul Morrissey, music by the Velvet Underground, and dancing by Gerard Malanga and other Warhol regulars. Andy Warhol and Pat Hackett, *Popism, The Warhol Sixties* (New York: Harcourt, 1990), 118.
49. Michael Erlewine, "Interview with Light Show Artist Bill Ham," February 19, 2003, ClassicPosters.com.
50. Martin's "painting in time," as he called it, emerged from the work he did at the San Francisco Tape Music Center in the early 1960s with Ramon Sender, Morton Subotnick, and Terry Riley.
51. "Visual Music Light Show: The Electric Collage," http://electriccollage.com.
52. Gene Youngblood describing the lightshow work of Single Wing Turquoise Bird in *Expanded Cinema,* 94.
53. John Leo, "Swinging in the East Village Has Its Ups and Downs," *The New York Times* (July 15, 1967). Also see Robert A. M. Stern, et al, *New York 1960: Architecture and Urbanism Between the Second World War and the Bicentennial* (New York: The Monacelli Press, 1995), 258.
54. Lapsley, "A Psycho-Theological Appraisal."
55. Dan Sullivan, "Cerebrum: Club Seeking to Soothe the Mind," *The New York Times* (Nov. 23, 1968).
56. Youngblood, *Expanded Cinema,* 363.
57. "Sex, Shock and Sensuality," *Life* (April 4, 1969): 29; "Mattress for the Mind," *Time* (Dec. 13, 1968): 87.
58. Sullivan, "Cerebrum."
59. Toffler, *Future Shock,* 203.
60. The bomb was reportedly planted by a member of the Black Panther party. The Electric Circus closed its doors in August 1971 just a few months after the closing of the Fillmore East.

CHAPTER THREE

1. William Hedgepeth, "Inside the Hippie Revolution," *Look* (August 22, 1967): 59.
2. Richard Honigan, "Flower from the Street," *San Francisco Oracle* (August 1967).
3. *The Hippies* (New York: Time, Inc., 1967), 4.
4. The story was about the Blue Unicorn coffee shop. "A New Haven for Beatniks," *San Francisco Examiner* (Sept. 6, 1965).
5. *I-Ching or Book of Changes* (Princeton: Princeton University Press, 1977), 190.
6. Yayoi Kusama, interview by Jud Yalkut, *The New York Free Press & West Side News* (Feb. 15, 1968). Reprinted in *Yayoi Kusama* (London: Phaidon Press, 2003), 112.
7. Don McNeill, "Be-In, Be-In, Being: Central Park Rite is Medieval Pageant," *The Village Voice* (March 30, 1967).
8. Ibid.
9. It was at 164 Avenue A. As quoted in *The Hippies.*
10. "A Flower from the Street," *San Francisco Oracle* 1, no. 9 (August 1967). Timothy Leary, as quoted in Lewis Yablonsky, *The Hippie Trip*, (New York: Pegasus Books, 1968), 199.
11. Jay Thelin, as quoted in H. Burton Wolfe, *The Hippies* (New York: Signet Books, 1968), 45–46.
12. Jerry Mander/Zev Putterman and Associates.
13. Free City Collective flier, 1967: "The Underground Press Syndicate is a Self-Indulgent Bore & Rigged-Up Bullshit Fraud," FC_B11a, summer 1967. See www.diggers.org.
14. *Digger Free News* (April 25, 1968).
15. Leonard Wolf, ed., *Voices from the Love Generation* (Boston: Little, Brown and Company, 1968), 249–63.
16. From a statement of purpose by Allen Cohen. Charles Perry, *The Haight-Ashbury,* (New York: Wenner Books, 2005), 122.
17. Press release for the Human Be-In, Barney Hoskyns, *Beneath the Diamond Sky* (New York: Simon & Schuster, 1997), 129.
18. Stephen Gaskin, *Haight Ashbury Flashbacks* (Berkeley, CA: Ronin Publishing, 1990), 46.
19. Helen Swick Perry, *The Human Be-In,* (New York: Basic Books, 1970), 88.
20. Tom Wolfe, "Putting Daddy On," in *The Kandy-Kolored Tangerine-Flake Streamline Baby* (New York: Farrar, Straus & Giroux, 1965), 287–89.
21. Yablonsky, *The Hippie Trip*, 100.
22. Jess Stearn, *The Seekers: Drugs and the New Generation* (Garden City, New York: Doubleday & Co., 1969), 109.
23. Yablonsky, *The Hippie Trip,* 100.
24. Wolfe, *The Hippies*, 108.
25. Yablonsky, *The Hippie Trip,* 115.
26. Allen Ginsberg, "Unshaven Rooms" in *Howl* (San Francisco: City Lights Books, 1956).
27. *Time*, July 7, 1967.
28. Yablonsky, *The Hippie Trip,* 102.
29. Hedgepeth, "Inside the Hippie Revolution," 60.
30. "The Spread and Perils of LSD," *Life* (March 25, 1966).
31. "Inside S.F. Pad: The New Beatnik Life," *The San Francisco Chronicle* (March 15, 1966), 1.
32. Joan Didion, "Hippies: Slouching Towards Bethlehem," *Saturday Evening Post* (Sept. 23, 1967), 26–31.
33. Kate Kelly, "The East Village Others" in *The Hippies: Who They Are, Where They Are,* ed. Joe David Brown (New York: Time, Inc., 1967), 82.
34. Katie Kelly and James Kent Willwerth, "The East Village Others," in Brown, *The Hippies* 88–89.
35. Thad and Rita Ashby, "Ecstatic Living," *The Oracle of Southern California* (October 1967), reprinted in Jerry Hopkins, ed., *The Hippie Papers* (New York: Signet Books, 1968), 206.
36. Ibid.

CHAPTER FOUR

1. *Design for Life: The Architecture of Sim Van Der Ryn* (Salt Lake City: Gibbs Smith, 2005), 37.
2. Reyner Banham called it "Hallucinogenic design." Reyner Banham, *Megastructure: Urban Futures of the Recent Past* (London: Thames and Hudson, 1976), 208. "LSDesign" was used in

C. Ray Smith, *Supermannerism: New Attitudes in Post-Modern Architecture* (New York: E. P. Dutton, 1977), 146.
3. Smith, *Supermannerism,* 140.
4. "L.S.D.: A Design Tool?" *Progressive Architecture* (August 1966), 147–53. Also see Eric Clough, "Toward the City of the Future" in *The Ecstatic Adventure,* ed. Ralph Metzner (New York: The Macmillan Company, 1968), 202–11.
5. Henrik Bull, "The Designs were More Free" in Metzner, *The Ecstatic Adventure,* 185–90.
6. Clough, "Toward the City of the Future," 210.
7. Norma Skurka and Oberto Gili, *Underground Interiors: Decorating for Alternate Life Styles* (New York: Galahad Books, 1972), 25–26.
8. "Environment for Casting the *I Ching*" (1969) in *Contemplation Environments*, ed. Paul Smith (New York: The Museum of Contemporary Craft, 1970). A knob could be turned, which controlled a series of blinking lights. Various combinations of lights-on or off-represented the hexagrams of the *I-Ching.*
9. Skurka and Gili, *Underground Interiors,* 37.
10. *Design for Life,* 37. Stewart Brand, *The Whole Earth Catalogue* (Spring 1970), 98.
11. Hall applied for a patent in 1969 and established the Innerspace Corp. to market his waterbed product. Allen Salkin, "Waterbeds: The Next Big Wave?" *The New York Times* (August 14, 2003).
12. *Contemplation Environments.*
13. *Home Furnishings Daily* (May 15, 1968), 10.
14. Sixteen experiments in womb-style living were shown in *Contemplation Environments,* an exhibition curated by Paul Smith at the Museum of Contemporary Craft, New York City, in January 1970. Castle's "Enclosed Reclining Environment for One" was originally produced for this exhibition.
15. "Time for Spaces," *Time* (February 2, 1970), 43.
16. Heino R. Möller, as quoted in Alexander von Vegesack and Mathias Remmele, *Verner Panton: The Collected Works* (Weil am Rhein: Vitra Design Museum, 2000), 176.
17. Smith, *Supermannerism,* 147.
18. Ibid.
19. "Supergraphics," *Progressive Architecture* (November 1967): 132–37.
20. See Smith, *Supermannerism*, 151.
21. Marshall McLuhan, *Understanding Media: The Extensions of Man* (Cambridge, Mass: MIT Press, 1996), 130.
22. Smith, *Supermannerism*, 297.
23. "The Synthetic Environment," *Progressive Architecture* (October 1968).
24. Skurka and Gili, *Underground Interiors*, 34.
25. Kasuba, telephone interview by the author, March 12, 2007.
26. See "Imagining the Future" on www.kasubaworks.com.
27. The color odors were designed by Danutė Anonis. The complementary sounds were composed by Emanuel Ghent.
28. Skurka and Gili, *Underground Interiors*, 30.
29. Barbara Plumb, *Young Designs in Living* (New York: The Viking Press, 1969), 24–25.
30. Gamal El Zoghby, interview by the author, April 2006.
31. Peter S. Stevens devoted an entire chapter to the subject in his *Patterns in Nature*. Peter S. Stevens, *Patterns in Nature* (Boston: Little, Brown and Company, 1974), 167–98.
32. Edward T. Hall, *The Hidden Dimension,* (Garden City, NY: Anchor Books, 1966), 149.
33. Buckminster Fuller, as quoted in Joachim Krausse and Claude Lichenstein, eds., *Your Private Sky: R. Buckminster Fuller, The Art of Design Science* (Baden, Switzerland: Lars Müller Publishers, 1999), 457.
34. Peter S. Stevens, *Patterns in Nature* (Boston: Little, Brown and Company, 1974), 153.
35. Stewart Brand, ed., *The Last Whole Earth Catalogue* (June 1971), 107.
36. Reyner Banham, "Monumental Windbags," *New Society* (April 1968). Reprinted in Marc Dessauce, ed., *The Inflatable Moment: Pneumatics and Protest in '68* (New York: Princeton Architectural Press, 1999), 31.
37. The full title was *The Environment-Bubble: Transparent plastic bubble dome inflated by air-conditioning output. Renyer Banham,* "A House is Not a Home," *Art in America* (April 1965).
38. A version of Webb's Cushicle was demonstrated by David Greene at the Milan Triennale in 1968. Peter Cook, *Archigram* (New York: Princeton Architectural Press, 1999), 64
39. Banham, "Monumental Windbags."
40. Jim Burns, *Arthropods: New Design Futures* (New York: Praeger Publishers, 1972), 65.
41. The event was sponsored by the Museum of Contemporary Crafts in June 1970. See "N.Y.A.S.A.R.S.R.W.," *Time* (June 15, 1970), 62.
42. "Such extraordinary event-structure interferences can force a dissolution (disillusion) of the present compulsively noninformational engineering of the world surface," read one ERG manifesto. See Jim Burns, *Arthropods: New Design Futures* (New York: Praeger Publishers, 1972), 112.
43. Banham, "Monumental Windbags."
44. Brand, *The Last Whole Earth Catalogue,* 107.
45. Ant Farm, *Inflatocookbook* (Sausalito, CA: Rip Off Press, 1970), unpaginated.
46. Ibid.
47. Ibid.
48. Ibid.
49. Smith *Supermannerism*, 305–06.
50. Rolf Von Eckartsberg, "A Kind of Harmonious and Convincing Equilibrium," in Metzner, *The Ecstatic Adventure*, 39.
51. Negroponte was founder of MIT's Media Lab and author of *Soft Architecture Machines* (Cambridge, Mass., MIT Press, 1975), 147.
52. Brand, *The Last Whole Earth Catalogue*, 107.
53. Percival Goodman and Paul Goodman, *Communitas: Ways of Livelihood and Means of Life* (New York: Vintage Books, 1960), 134.
54. Peter Cook, *Experimental Architecture* (New York: Universe Books, 1970), 110.
55. Constant Nieuwenhuys, "Lecture at the ICA, London (November 7, 1963)" in *Another City for Another Life: Constant's New Babylon,* Drawing Papers 3 (New York: The Drawing Center, 1999), a12–a13.
56. Sean Wellesley-Miller, "Intelligent Environments," in Negroponte, *Soft Architecture Machines*, 125.
57. W. M. Brodey, "Soft Architecture—The Design of Intelligent Environments," *Landscape* 17, No. 1, 8–12 (1967). Cited in Negroponte, *Soft Architecture Machines,* 143.
58. Jim Burns, *Arthropods: New Design Futures* (New York: Praeger Publishers, 1972), 65.
59. "In the morning, suburbs might come together to create cities, and at night move like music to other moorings for cultural needs or to produce the socio-political patterns that the new life demands." William Katavolos, as quoted in Justus Dahinden, *Urban Structures for the Future* (New York: Praeger Publishers, Inc., 1972), 205.
60. Rudolf Doernach, as quoted in Dahinden, *Urban Structures for the Future*, 194–196.
61. Peter Cook, Warren Chalk, Ron Herron, Mike Webb, Dennis Crompton, David Greene.
62. Cook, *Archigram*, 68.
63. Ibid., 86.
64. McLuhan first used the expression "global village" in *The Gutenberg Galaxy*, 1962, page 31: "The new electronic interdependence recreates the world in the image of a global village..."
65. McLuhan, *Understanding Media,* 4–5.

CHAPTER FIVE

1. Bill Voyd, "Funk Architecture" in *Shelter and Society,* ed. Paul Oliver (New York: Frederick A. Praeger, 1969), 159.
2. Griffin, as quoted in Rasa Gustaitis, *Turning On* (New York: The Macmillan Company, 1969), 94.
3. Robert Houriet, *Getting Back Together* (1971), 403.
4. *The Digger Papers* (August 1968), www.diggers.org.
5. Joan Didion, "Hippies: Slouching Towards Bethlehem," *Saturday Evening Post* (September 23, 1967): 93.
6. William Hedgepeth, "Inside the Hippie Revolution," *Look* (August 22, 1967): 63.
7. As quoted in Joan Didion, *Slouching Towards Bethlehem* (New York: The Noonday Press, 1990), 101.
8. As quoted in Lewis Yablonsky, *The Hippie Trip* (New York: Pegasus Books, 1968), 163.
9. *Time* (October 20, 1967).
10. Yablonsky, 105.
11. Fred Richardson, as quoted in Stewart Brand, *The Last Whole Earth Catalog* (Menlo Park, California: 1971), 111.
12. Walter Bowart, "The Return to the Land," *East Village Other* (December 1, 1967), republished in Jesse Kornbluth, ed., *Notes from the New Underground* (New York: Ace Publishing, 1968), 206.
13. Houriet, *Getting Back Together,* 7.
14. *The Digger Papers* (August 1968), www.diggers.org.
15. Van Arsdale met Steve and Barbara Durkee in Taos and helped to build some of the first buildings at the Lama Foundation. See Iris Keltz, *Scrapbook of a Taos Hippie: Tribal Tales from the Heart of a Cultural Revolution* (El Paso, Texas: Cinco Punto Press, 2000), 121.
16. Ann Halprin was founder of the San Francisco Dancers' Workshop Company.
17. Lawrence Halprin, *The RSVP Cycles* (New York: George Braziller, Inc., 1969), 31.
18. Emmet Grogan, *Ringo Levi, A Life Played for Keeps* (Boston: Little, Brown and Company, 1972), 367.
19. Stephen Gaskin, *Haight Ashbury Flashbacks* (Berkeley, CA: Ronin Publishing, 1990), 228–29.
20. Ibid, 229.
21. Stephen Diamond, *What the Trees Said: Life on a New Age Farm* (New York: Dell Publishing Co., Inc., 1971), 87.
22. Roberta Price, *Huerfano: A Memoir of Life in the Counterculture* (Amherst and Boston: University of Massachusetts Press, 2004), 46–47.
23. Raymond Mungo, *Total Loss Farm* (New York: E.P. Dutton & Co., Inc., 1970), 4.
24. Ibid., 90.
25. Estimates vary greatly on this matter. See Timothy Miller, *The 60s Communes: Hippies and Beyond* (Ithaca, NY: Syracuse University Press, 1999), xviii–xx.
26. Stephen Gaskin, as quoted in Alicia Bay Laurel, *Living on the Earth* (New York: Vintage Books, 1970), 108.
27. *Paul Steiner, Chamisa Road with... Paul & Meredith* (New York: Random House, 1971).
28. People were inspired by Henry Miller's *Big Sur and the Oranges of Hieronymus Bosch* (1957), Jack Kerouac's *Big Sur* (1962) and Elizabeth Taylor cavorting with Richard Burton in *The Sandpiper* (1965), a Hollywood drama shot in Big Sur.

29. Esalen was established in 1962.
30. Lewis Yablonsky, *The Hippie Trip* (New York: Pegasus Books, 1968), 80.
31. Richard Honigman, "Flower from the Street," *The San Francisco Oracle* (August 1967): 25.
32. "Neon Nirvanas finally overload their circuits as we snake dance thru our world trailed by a smoke-screen of reefer." See Martin A. Lee and Bruce Shlain, *Acid Dreams: The CIA, LSD and the Sixties Rebellion* (New York: Grove Press, 1985), 228.
33. This notion would be crystallized in 1969 as "Woodstock Nation" after the three-day rock concert in upstate New York.
34. As quoted in Yablonsky, *The Hippie Trip*, 200.
35. Bowart, "The Return to the Land," 207.
36. Ibid., 208.
37. Frederick Jackson Turner, "The Significance of the Frontier in American History," in *The Frontier in American History* (New York: Henry Holt and Co., 1920), 38.
"The frontier is productive of individualism," wrote Turner in 1893. According to Turner, the "ever-retreating" frontier had already vanished by 1900 but it left a deep imprint on the national soul.
38. Voyd, "Funk Architecture," 159.
39. Timothy Leary as quoted in "Changes," in Kornbluth, *Notes from the New Underground,* 172.
40. Alan Watts as quoted in Kornbluth, *Notes from the New Underground*, 145.
41. Italics by author. Ken Kesey, quoted in Paul Perry, *On the Bus* (New York: Thunder's Mouth Press, 1990), 52; "locate a better reality," 37.
42. In 1630 John Winthrop preached to his puritan flock about creating a God-fearing community in the New World that would be "as a city upon a hill."
43. Kesey, quoted in Perry, *On the Bus*, 43.
44. Lyric from *We Can Be Together,* © 1970 Jefferson Airplane.
45. Gary Snyder, as quoted in "Changes," in Kornbluth, *Notes from the New Underground,* 166.
46. "All improvement has to be made in the outlaw area," said Buckminster Fuller. Calvin Tompkins, profile of Fuller, "In the Outlaw Area," *The New Yorker* (January 8, 1966).
47. Brand, *The Last Whole Earth Catalog,* 233.
48. Ant Farm, *Inflatocookbook* (Sausolito, CA: Ripp Off Press, 1970), unpaginated.
49. Kesey, quoted in Perry, *On the Bus,* 116, 37; Lyric from *We Can Be Together,* © 1970 Jefferson Airplane.
50. Brand, *The Last Whole Earth Catalog,* 233.
51. Kornbluth, *Notes from the New Underground,* 208
52. Brand called *Walden* "the prime document of America's 3rd revolution." Brand, *The Last Whole Earth Catalog,* 47.
53. Henry David Thoreau, *Walden* (Boston: Ticknor & Fields, 1854), 243.
54. Kathleen Kinkade, *A Walden Two Experiment: The First Five Years of Twin Oaks Community* (New York: William Morrow & Company, Inc., 1973), 14.
55. Tom Wolfe, *The Electric Kool-Aid Acid Test* (New York: Farrar, Straus & Giroux, 1968), 231
56. Brand, *The Last Whole Earth Catalog,* 107.
57. "Interview with Ant Farm," in *Ant Farm*, eds. Constance M. Lewallen and Steve Seid (Berkeley: University of California Press, 2004), 49.
58. Italics by author. Richard Kostelanetz, *The Theatre of Mixed Means: An Introduction to Happenings, Kinetic Environments, and other Mixed-Media Performances* (New York: The Dial Press, Inc., 1968), 270.
59. Barbara Durkee (as told to Iris Keltz), "Mama Lama," in Iris Keltz, *Scrapbook of a Taos Hippie: Tribal Tales from the Heart of a Cultural Revolution* (El Paso, Texas: Cinco Punto Press, 2000), 128.
60. The Durkees based the design of the Solux dome on the Aribindo Ashram in India.
61. Kostelanetz, *The Theatre of Mixed Means,* 271.
62. John Curl, *Adventures in the Counterculture of the 1960s,* unpublished manuscript, 2002. http://www.red-coral.net/DropCity.html
63. Clark Richert, interview by the author, February 27, 2004
64. Ibid.
65. Curl, *Adventures in the Counterculture of the 1960s.*
66. Jo Ann Bernofsky as quoted in Miller, *The 60s Communes, 33.*
67. Richert, telephone interview by the author, February 27, 2004.
68. Voyd, "Funk Architecture," 159.
69. Ibid, 158.
70. Peter Rabbit as quoted in "Communes in the Country" in *The Hippies,* ed. Joe David Brown (New York: Time Inc., 1967), 77.
71 *The Ultimate Painting* was exhibited at the Brooklyn Museum. Ibid.
72. "Candy-colored toadstools," Hedgepeth, 153.
73. The original Hog Farm group included Romney's wife, Bonnie Jean, and David Le Breun.
74. The Jacopettis were founders of the Open Theater, an early venue for multimedia events located at 2976 College Avenue in Berkeley.
75. *Home Free Home, A History of Two Open-Door California Communes*, unpublished manuscript, 59. http://www.diggers.org/home_free.htm
76. Gustaitis, *Turning On,* 158.
77. *Home Free Home, A History of Two Open-Door California Communes*, unpublished manuscript, 50. http://www.diggers.org/home_free.htm
78. *Open Land Manifesto Two*, Wheeler's Ranch, unpublished manuscript (1971), 19.
79. Ibid., 21.
80. *Home Free Home, A History of Two Open-Door California Communes*, (unpublished manuscript), 26. http://www.diggers.org/home_free.htm
81. Perry, *The Haight-Ashbury*, 149
82. Home Free Home, 33.
83. "Open Land: A Manifesto," Unohoo, Coyote, Rick and the Mighty Avengers, *The Morningstar Scrapbook* (self-published, 1972), 154.
84. Home Free Home, 27.
85. *Time* (July 7, 1967): 22.
86. Ibid.
87. *Home Free Home, A History of Two Open-Door California Communes*, (unpublished manuscript). http://www.diggers.org/home_free.htm
88. *Time* (July 7, 1967): 20.
89. Bill Wheeler, *Open Land Manifesto,* 102.
90. *Open Land Manifesto*, 92. A photograph of the interior was used to illustrate Stewart Brand's essay on the Outlaw Area. Charlotte lies naked and pregnant while a chicken scurries across the dirt floor. Brand, *The Last Whole Earth Catalog,* 233.
91. Alicia Bay Laurel, *Open Land Manifesto*, 8.
92. Alicia Bay Laurel, *Living on the Earth* (New York: Random House, 1971).

CHAPTER SIX

1. Lloyd Kahn, ed., *Shelter* (Bolinas, CA: Shelter Publications, 1973), 138.
2. Steve Baer, *Sunspots* (Albuquerque, NM: Zomeworks Corporation, 1975), 28.
3. Ibid.
4. "Communes of the Southwest USA," *Architectural Design*, No. 12, 1971.
5. Marshall Mcluhan, *Understanding Media* (Cambridge, Mass: MIT Press, 1994), 125.
6. Steve Baer, *Dome Cookbook* (Corrales, N.M.: Lama Foundation, 1968), 1.
7. Paul Oliver, *Shelter and Society* (New York: Frederick A. Praeger, 1969), 158.
8. From a letter quoted in Lloyd Kahn (ed.), *Domebook Two* (Santa Barbara, CA: Mountain Books, 1971), 50.
9. William Hedgepeth, *The Alternative: Communal Life in New America* (New York: The Macmillan Company, 1970), 156.
10. Richard Fairfield, *Communes USA: A Personal Tour* (Baltimore, MD: Penguin Books Inc., 1972), 202.
11. "Coupoles géodésiques pur l'habitat hippy," *L'Architecture d'aujourd'hui*, no. 141 (December 1968–January 1969): 82–84.
12. Richert was joined by Richard Kallweit (a.k.a. Larry Lard) and Burt Wadman.
13. Bill Voyd, "Funk Architecture" in *Shelter and Society,* ed. Paul Oliver (New York: Frederick A. Praeger, 1969), 158.
14. *Popular Science* magazine would finally publish blueprints for a geodesic dome in 1966.
15. Clark Richert, telephone interview by the author, February 27, 2004.
16. Baer, *Dome Cookbook*, 13.1.
17. Ibid.
18. Baer, *Dome Cookbook*, 21.
19. Ibid., 24.
20. Peter Rabbit, *Drop City*, (New York: Olympia Press, 1971), 33.
21. Baer, *Dome Cookbook,* 25.
22. Rabbit, *Drop City,* 26–27.
23. John Curl, *Adventures in the Counterculture of the 1960s*, unpublished manuscript.
24. Voyd, "Funk Architecture," 158.
25. Hedgepeth, *The Alternative*, 153.
26. Ibid., 118.
27. Baer, *Dome Cookbook*, 40.
28. Wavy Gravy, *The Hog Farm and Friends* (New York: Links Books, 1974), 21.
29. Kahn, *Domebook Two*, 61.
30. Peter Coyote, *Sleeping Where I Fell* (Washington, D.C.: Counterpoint Press, 1998), 246.
31. Kahn, *Domebook Two*, 61.
32. Peter Rabbit, *Drop City* (New York: The Olympia Press, 1971), 29.
33. Baer's *Dome Cookbook* cost $1 and could be bought directly from Baer's Zomeworks, the Lama Foundation, or ordered through *The Whole Earth Catalog.*
34. Baer, *Dome Cookbook*, 26.
35. Ibid., 26.
36. John Prenis, *The Dome Builder's Handbook* (1973), 1.
37. Kahn, *Domebook Two*, 50.
38. Ibid., 100.
39. The first few domes, built between 1966 and 1967, were based on the "Sundome" plans published in *Popular Science.* In 1968 four "Pease" type domes were erected as well as several smaller Icosahedra and residence domes. Kahn, *Domebook Two*, 96.
40. Barbara Durkee (Asha Greer), phone interview by the author, May 2006.
41. Robert Houriet, *Getting Back Together* (New York: Coward, McCann & Geoghegan, Inc., 1971), 368.
42. From a Lama Foundation pamphlet, as quoted in Ron E. Roberts, *The New Communes* (Englewood Cliffs, N.J.: Prentice-Hall, Inc., 1971), 64–65.

43. Fairfield, *Communes USA,* 119.
44. Steve Durkee quoted in Fairfield, *Communes USA,* 118, 121.
45. *SEED* (New York: Harmony Books, 1971), F.
46. "The students were suddenly stoned..." Peter Marin in Michael Kaye, *The Teacher Was the Sea,* (New York: Links, 1972), ix.
47. Kahn, *Domebook Two,* 33.
48. Kaye, *The Teacher Was the Sea,* 50.
49. Kahn, *Domebook Two,* 33.
50. Kaye, *The Teacher Was the Sea,* 61.
51. Ibid.
52. Lloyd Kahn, *Domebook One,* (Santa Barbara, CA: Mountain Books, 1970), 33.
53. Kahn, *Domebook Two,* 94.
54. Kahn, *Domebook One,* 33.
55. Kahn, *Domebook Two,* 34.
56. Ibid., 26.
57. Kahn, *Domebook One,* 20.
58. Kahn, *Domebook Two,* 101.
59. Kahn, *Shelter,* 136.
60. From a letter to Kahn, *Domebook One,* 104.
61. Kahn, *Shelter,* 136.
62. Kahn, *Domebook Two,* 61.

CHAPTER SEVEN

1. Allen Cohen, "Poem to Protest the Condemnation of Our Homes." See: River, *Dwelling: On Making Your Own* (Albion, CA: Freestone Publishing Co., 1974), 166.
2. Ela worked only with a chainsaw, adze, and axe.
3. Douglas Patrick, as quoted in River, *Dwelling,* 60.
4. Most outlaw builders preferred to remain anonymous, fearing discovery by park rangers, building authorities, or county health inspectors. A handful of hip writers and photographers recorded their deeds, trekking up winding pathways and steep canyons, on occasion to be rebuffed at the door. *Shelter* editor Lloyd Kahn drove across country with photographer Jack Fulton documenting dozens of funky dwellings. Arthur Boericke and Barry Shapiro explored one-of-a-kind shelters in the backwoods of northern California, while Robert Haney and David Ballantine did the same in the area around Woodstock, New York. But most of these Aquarian outposts were built in secrecy and remained undocumented for posterity.
5. Coyote, *Open Land Manifesto,* Vol. 2 (Wheeler's Ranch, CA: self-published, 1971), 29.
6. River, *Dwelling,* 67.
7. Ibid., 69.
8. Author's italics. Roberta Price, *Huerfano* (Amherst and Boston: University of Massachusetts Press, 2004), 45.
9. River, *Dwelling,* 128.
10. *Open Land Manifesto,* 31.
11. A term borrowed from science fiction writer Robert A. Heinlein, who used it in his novel *Stranger in a Strange Land.* (New York: G. P. Putnam's Sons, 1961).
12. Douglas Patrick, as quoted in River, *Dwelling,* 60.
13. Bill Voyd, "Funk Architecture," in *Shelter and Society,* ed. Paul Oliver (New York: Frederick A. Praeger, 1969), 157.
14. River, *Dwelling,* 147.
15. Thad Ashby, "Ecstatic Living," *The Oracle of Southern California* (Los Angeles: October 1967), in *The Hippie Papers,* ed. Jerry Hopkins (New York: Signet Books, 1968), 205–07.
16. Aleksandra Kasuba, interview by the author, March 2007.
17. Stewart Brand, *The Last Whole Earth Catalog* (Menlo Park, California: 1971), 84.
18. A scale model of the Endless House was exhibited at New York's Museum of Modern Art in 1959, but Kiesler never built a full-scale prototype.
19. Kahn, *Shelter,* 146.
20. Bob Easton, as quoted in Kahn, *Shelter,* 145.
21. Charles Harker, interview by the author, April 18, 2007.
22. John Van Der Zee, *Canyon: The Story of the Last Rustic Community in Metropolitan America* (New York: Harcourt Brace Jovanovich, Inc., 1971), 170.
23. Van Der Zee, *Canyon,* 157.
24. Smith's house was featured in numerous alternative publications of the day including: Boericke and Shapiro, *Handmade Houses,* 28–29; Kahn, *Shelter,* p. 58; Van der Zee, *Canyon,* pp. 90–95; and River, *Dwelling,* p. 26–31.
25. River, *Dwelling,* 26.
26. Van Der Zee, *Canyon,* 93.
27. Lloyd House, as quoted in "Hand-Built Hornby," *Architectural Design* (July 1978): 478.
28. Ibid., 451.
29. "Hand-Built Hornby," 456.
30. Ibid., 451.
31. They included Dave Sellers, Bille Reienecke, Louis Mackall, Charlie Hosford, Barry Simpson, and Tom Luckey.
32. C. Ray Smith, "Architecture Swings Like a Pendulum Do," *Progressive Architecture* (May 1966). See also Smith, *Supermannerism.*
33. Louis Mackall, interview by the author, Amagansett, New York, July 12, 2006.
34. Jim Sanford, telephone interview by the author, May 24, 2007.
35. Michael J. Crosbie, *Jersey Devil, Design/Build Book* (Layton, UT: Peregrine Smith Books, 1985), 21.
36. Steve Badanes, telephone interview by the author, August 4, 2007.

EPILOGUE

1. Brand, Stewart, ed. *Space Colonies,* New York, Penguin Books, 1977, 51.
2. Brand encouraged the idea of space colonization by publishing a compilation of information á la *Whole Earth Catalog.* Brand, Stewart (ed.) *Space Colonies.* New York: Penguin Books, 1977, 6.
3. Brand, Stewart (ed.) *Space Colonies.* New York. Penguin Books, 1977, 40.
4. Kleps, Art. *Millbrook: The True Story of the Early Years of the Psychedelic Revolution.* Oakland, CA: Bench Press, 1975, 7.
5. "We were all lying to each other, and saying that what we were doin' was righteous when we didn't really feel it." As cited in Miller, Timothy. *The 60s Communes,* 20.
6. Peter Rabbit quoted in: Kahn Lloyd (ed.), *Shelter,* 1973, 118.
7. Houriet, Robert. "Life and Death of a Commune Called Oz." *The New York Times Magazine,* February 16, 1969, pp. 30–31. "Home Free Home: The Story of Two Open-Door Sixties Communes, Morning Star and Wheeler's Ranch, as Told by Various Residents," ed. Ramón Sender Barayón, unpublished ms., University of California Library, Riverside, 133.
8. See: Jon Stewart, "Communes in Taos," *Conversations with the New Reality.* San Francisco. Canfield Press. 1971., 206.
9. Robert Houriet, *Getting Back Together.* New York: Coward, McCann & Geoghegan, 1971, 398.
10. The leader of the Lower Farm, an eccentric character named Ulysses S. Grant, was suspected of the crimes. Richard Fairlfield. *Communes USA, A Personal Tour.* Baltimore, MD. Penguin Books. 1972, 180.
11. *Communes USA,* Richard Fairfield, 3
12. Gene Bernofsky as quoted in *The 60s Communes: Hippies and Beyond,* Timothy Miller. Syracuse, NY:, Syracuse University Press, 1999, 38.
13. Richard Fairlfield. *Communes USA, A Personal Tour.* Baltimore, MD. Penguin Books. 1972, 79.
14. Lloyd Kahn, *Shelter,* (Bolinas, CA: 1973), 114.
15. The land was sold in 1990 and the house was subsequently demolished to make way for an Episcopalian Church retreat.
16. See: http://hpn.asu.edu/archives/2005–August/009385.html
17. Elizabeth Gips, *Scrapbook of a Haight Ashbury Pilgrim* (Santa Cruz, CA: Changes Press, 1991).

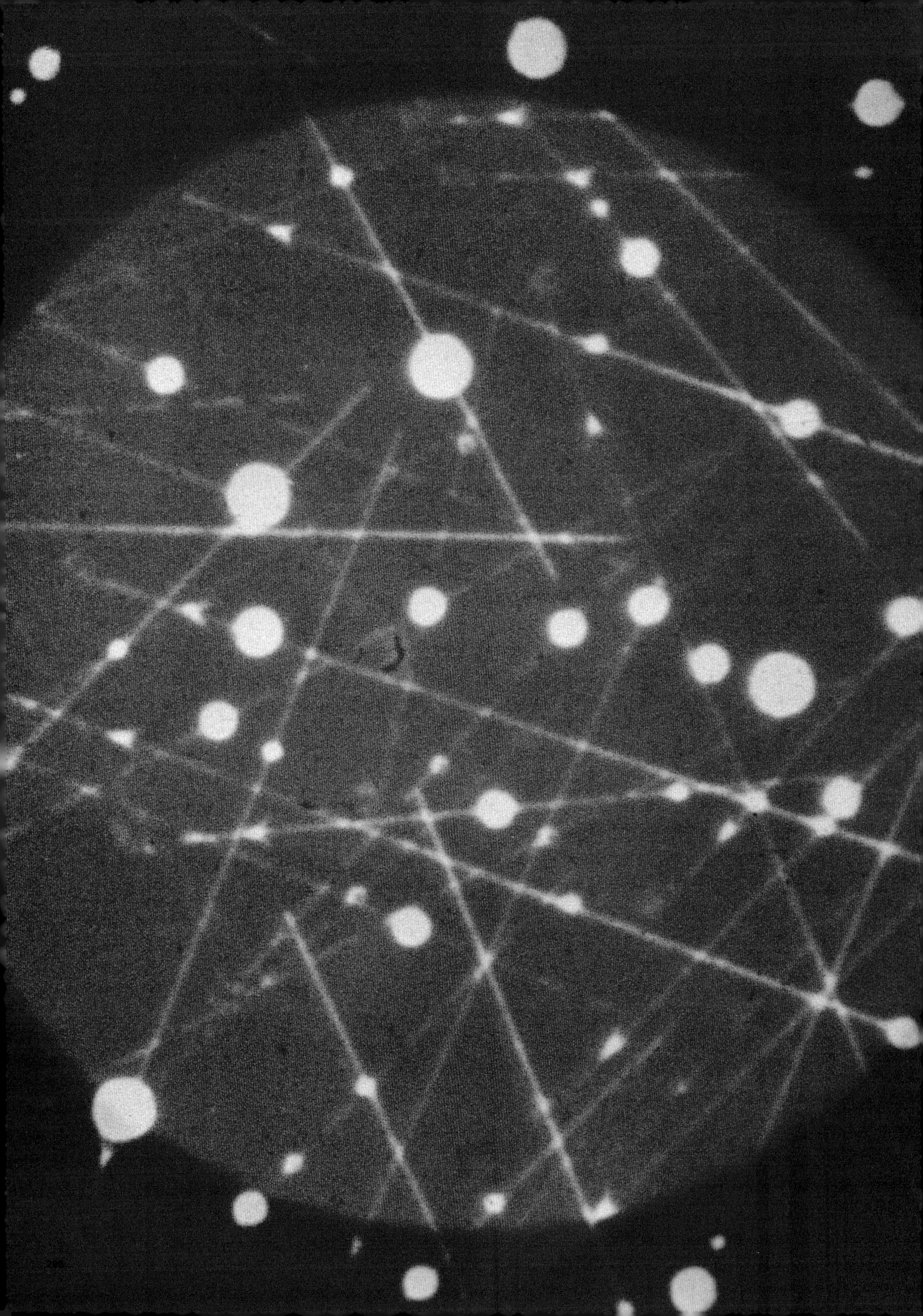

IMAGE CREDITS

Cover: Harry Fischman, 1970

INTRODUCTION

pp. 2-3: USCO light show, c. 1966, courtesy: Adrienne and Michael Callahan, USCO Archive.

p. 4: Aleksandra Kasuba, Stretched Nylon Environment, "Contemplative Environments," Americam Craft Museum, New York, NY, 1970.

p. 8: Domes, Manera Nueva, New Mexico (photo: Jack Fulton).

pp. 4–5: Rainbow Gathering, Gila National Forest, New Mexico (photo: Paul Dembski).

p. 10: Ceramics Apse, Arcosanti, Arizona (photo: Terrence Moore).

p. 12: Handmade door, Arcosanti (photo: Alastair Gordon).

CHAPTER 1

p. 16: *Solar, cellular, somatic and sensory levels of energy*, illustration from Timothy Leary, *The Politics of Ecstasy* (New York: College Notes & Texts, Inc., 1968).

p. 17: *background*: from Wolf Strache, *Forms and Patterns in Nature* (New York: Pantheon Books, 1956).

p. 18: *upper left*: woman in chair, tripping (photo: Richard Crone, *Hippie Hi* [San Francisco: self-published, 1967]); *upper right*: woman staring at lightbulb, tripping, *Life*, March 25, 1966, 30 (photo: Lawrence Schiller); *lower*: Henri Michaux, *Mescaline Drawing*, 1955.

p. 19: *Time Chamber*, International Federation for Inner Freedom, Newton Center, Mass., 1963 (photo: *Look*, November 2, 1963, 30).

p. 20: *Alan Watts, Geographer of Inner Space*, teaching at Berkeley, c. 1962 (photo: Loly Rosset).

p. 21: *Fructification of Clematis* (photo: Wolf Strache, from: Alan W. Watts, *The Joyous Cosmology: Adventures in the Chemistry of Consciousness* [New York: Pantheon Books, 1962], 53).

p. 22: *upper left*: "The Exploding Threat of the Mind Drug That Got Out of Control: LSD," *Life,* March 25, 1966, cover; *upper right*: *Bad Trip, Look*, August 8, 1967 (photos: Wayne Miller); *lower left*: "The Hidden Evils of LSD," *The Saturday Evening Post*, August 12, 1967, 19 (photo: Don Ornitz); *lower right*: "The Newly Discovered Dangers of LSD," *The Saturday Evening Post*, August 12, 1967, cover.

p. 24: *upper left*: Timothy Leary, shirtless, the League for Spiritual Discovery, Greenwich Village on the corner of Perry and Hudson streets, New York, NY (photo: Ben Martin); *upper right*: Leary sitting beneath the sacred birch at Millbrook, NY, c. 1966 (photo: Don Snyder, *Aquarian Odyssey, A Photographic Trip into the Sixties* [New York: Liveright, 1979]); *lower*: Leary speaking at the League for Spiritual Discovery (photo: Ben Martin); *line art*: Seal, the League for Spiritual Discovery.

p. 25: Timothy Leary, *High Priest*, cover (photo: Fred W. McDarrah, jacket design: Paul Bacon [New York: The World Publishing Co., 1968]).

p. 27: *upper*: Big House, Castalia, Millbrook, NY, 1967 (photo: Gene Anthony); *lower left*: man meditating, Millbrook, 1967; *lower right*: detail of Tantric painting on façade of Big House, Millbrook, NY, 1967 (photo: Gene Anthony).

p. 28: Allen Atwell, *Psychedelic Temple*, New York, NY, 1965 (photo: Robert E.L. Masters and Jean Houston, *Psychedelic Art* [New York: Grove Press, 1968]).

p. 29: *upper*: Jackie Cassen and Rudi Stern, *Liquid Light Show*, Millbrook, NY, 1966 (photo: Yale Joel, *Life*, September 9, 1966, 62); *lower*: Paul Ortloff, *Exhalation*, 1965 (Robert E.L. Masters and Jean Houston, *Psychedelic Art* [New York: Grove Press, 1968]).

pp. 30–31: Isaac Abrams, *All Things Are Part of One Thing*, 1966.

CHAPTER 2

p. 32: *left*: Francis Lee, "Experimental Motion Picture," 1967 (Robert E.L. Masters and Jean Houston, *Psychedelic Art* [New York: Grove Press, 1968]), 54; *right*: Woman under strobe lights, San Francisco, c. 1968 (photo: Anders Holmquist).

p. 33: *background*: from Wolf Strache, *Forms and Patterns in Nature* (New York: Pantheon Books, 1956).

p. 34: *upper left*: Richard Aldcroft gazing through hemispheric goggles into light patterns made by his Infinity Machine (photo: *Life,* September 9, 1966, cover); *upper right*: Jacques Kaszmacher, lattice of crystal light projections on woman's face, 1967 (photo: *Horizon,* vol. X, no. 2, Spring 1968, 22); *middle left*: *Man in Gas Mask*, from triple-projection film *As the World Turns* by Ronald Nameth, 1968 (Gene Youngblood, *Expanded Cinema* [New York: E.P. Dutton & Co., 1970], p 379); *middle center*: man with long pipe and light streaks projected onto chest and face, Los Angeles, CA, 1968 (photo: Paul Dembski); *middle right*: Haus-Rucker-Co., *Fly Head*, plastic space helmet with bug-eye goggles wired for deep exploration, Vienna, Austria, 1968; *lower*: sequence of projections made by Richard Aldcroft's Infinity Machine, 1966 (photos: *Psychedelic Art* [New York: Grove Press, 1968]).

p. 35: Abstract Patterns, 35mm slide by USCO.

p. 36: Ken Isaacs and his Knowledge Box, Illinois Institute of Technology, Chicago, Ill., 1962 (collection: Ken Isaacs).

p. 37: Stan VanDerBeek in front of the Movie-Drome, Stony Point, NY, 1964 (Douglas Davis, *Art and the Future*, [New York: Praeger Publishers, 1973], 50).

p. 38: *upper left*: USCO, *The Tabernacle*, diagram, 1966 (collection: Gerd Stern); *lower left*: USCO, Bob Dacey with concentric patterns, c. 1965 (collection: Gerd Stern); *right*: USCO (Jud Yalkut), film footage of USCO installation.

p. 39: *left and right*: USCO (Jud Yalkut) film footage of USCO installations; *middle*: USCO (Bob Dacey), *Tie-Died Cave,* Riverside Museum, New York, NY, 1966.

p. 40: USCO at work: Michael Callahan and Gerd Stern (collection: Gerd Stern, Adrienne and Michael Callahan, USCO Archive).

p. 41: *upper left and right*: USCO, *The Tabernacle*, installed in old church, Garnerville, NY, 1966; *middle*: USCO, *Seven Diffraction Hex*, 1967; *lower left, middle right, and lower right*: USCO collages (collection: Gerd Stern).

p. 42: *upper left*: Timothy Leary and his "Reincarnation of Jesus Christ" at the Yiddish-American Theater, New York, NY, October 1966 (photo: Gene Anthony); *upper right*: *Innertube*, video composition, Global Village Workshop (Rudi Stern and John Reilly), New York, NY, 1967 (photo: Jay Good); *line art*: USCO, Mandala, c. 1966 (collection Gerd Stern).

pp. 42–43: USCO, *Mandala* (collection: Gerd Stern).

p. 43: Jackie Cassen and Rudi Stern, "Death of the Mind," Psychedelic Religious Celebration #1, Village Theater, New York, NY, 1966 (Robert E.L. Masters and Jean Houston, *Psychedelic Art* [New York: Grove Press, 1968]).

p. 44: USCO, abstract slide (collection: Adrienne and Michael Callahan, USCO Archive).

p. 45: *upper*: Ugo La Pietra, *Tubular Environment for Contemplation*, 1969 (courtesy: American Craft Council); *lower right*: Stanley Landsman, *Untitled,* (Infinity Drawing), Magic Marker on paper, Aspen, Colorado, 1968 (collection: Mahnaz I. and Adam Bartos); *lower right*: USCO, abstract slide (collection: Adrienne and Michael Callahan, USCO Archive).

p. 46: Bob Goldstein's Lightworks Discotheque, New York, NY, 1966 (*Life*, September 9, 1966).

p. 47: USCO, "Satisfaction," "Time is Come," eighteen slides (clocks, insects, boots, go-go girls) from USCO light shows for The World Discotheque, Garden City, NY, 1966 (collection: Adrienne and Michael Callahan, USCO Archive).

p. 48: *upper left*: "New Madness at the Discotheque," *Life*, May 27, 1966, cover; *upper right*: The World Discotheque, Garden City, NY, 1966 (*Life*, May 27, 1966); *lower*: The World Discotheque, Garden City, NY, 1966 (photo: Ben Martin).

pp. 50–51: *line art*: Tony Martin, *The Game Room*, diagram of interactive installation, Howard Wise Gallery, New York, NY, 1968 (collection: Tony Martin).

p. 51: *upper*: Joshua White light show, Fillmore East, New York, NY, 1969 (photo: Amalie R. Rothschild); *lower right and left*: USCO, control panel for light shows, Maverick Systems, Michael Callahan, 1964 (collection: Adrienne and Michael Callahan, USCO archive).

p. 52: Ivan Chermayeff and Tom Geismar, poster for Electric Circus, New York, NY, 1967 (collection: Chermayeff and Geismar); *background*: USCO, abstract slide (collection: Adrienne and Michael Callahan, USCO Archive).

p. 53: *upper*: Tony Martin, "Ultramedia" light show at the Electric Circus, New York, NY, 1967 (photo: Anne Simpkin); *lower*: Electric Circus, showing aperture through tent-like screen, c. 1967, projected imagery by Tony Martin, screen by Charles Forberg (photo: Malcolm Varon).

pp. 54–55: Tony Martin, hand-made glass slides (2 x 2"), mixed media: string, tobacco, lace, butterfly wings, etc., used in combination with eight electronically controlled slide projectors for the Electric Circus, New York, NY, 1967–68 (collection: Tony Martin).

p. 56: *upper and lower*: Tony Martin, composite multi-projector images for Fillmore West and the Electric Circus, 1966–68 (collection: Tony Martin).p. 48: upper: Cerebrum club, New York, NY, 1969 (Life, April 4, 1969); lower: a balloon is slowly filled with helium at Cerebrum, 1969 (photo: John Veltri).

CHAPTER 3

p. 60: *Grok*, communal crash pad, Galahad's Pad, the East Village, New York, NY, 1967 (photo: Ben Martin).

p. 61: *background*: from Wolf Strache, *Forms and Patterns in Nature* (New York: Pantheon Books, 1956).

p. 62: *left*: topless women on street, San Francisco, 1966 (photo: Gene Anthony / Wolfgang's Vault); *right*: Fosso, "Americas Outlaws," *The East Village Other*, cover, vol. 2, no. 6, February 15–March 1, 1967 (collection: Alastair Gordon).

p. 63: *upper left*: East Village crash pad (photo: Larence Shustak); *upper right*: flower children, Haight-Ashbury (photo: Gene Anthony / Wolfgang's Vault); *lower left*: crash pad, Haight-Ashbury (photo: Richard Crone); *line art*: "The Astrological Future of Man," *San Francisco Oracle*.

pp. 64–65: *Electric Lotus Head Shop*, East Village, New York, NY, 1967 (photos: Don Snyder).

p. 67: Sitting on steps, Haight-Ashbury (photo: Gene Anthony / Wolfgang's Vault).

p. 68: *upper*: Free Clinic, Haight-Ashbury (photo: Gene Anthony / Wolfgang's Vault); *lower left and right*: in Panhandle Park, San Francisco, 1967 (photos: Richard Crone).

p. 69: *upper and lower left*: ads from *San Francisco Oracle*, vol. 1, no. 9, August 1967); *middle*: poster for the Trips Festival, 1966.

p. 70: Avalon Ballroom, San Francisco, 1967.

p. 71: W.S. Metcalf, peace/love collage, *Berkeley Barb*, cover (vol. 5, no. 18, issue 116, November 3–9, 1967).

p. 72: Multicolored façade, Haight-Ashbury (photo: Gene Anthony / Wolfgang's Vault).

p. 73: *upper*: dancing in Golden Gate Park, San Francisco (photo: Richard Crone); *lower*: summer solstice (photo: *The Modern Utopian*, "Communes U.S.A.," vol. 5, nos. 1, 2, 3 [San Francisco: Alternatives Foundations, 1971]).

pp. 74–75: Human Be-In, Golden Gate Park, San Francisco, Jaunary 14, 1967 (photo: Richard Crone).

p. 76: *Human Be-In*, 1967 (photo: Gene Anthony / Wolfgang's Vault).

p. 77: *upper left*: three friends (photo: Richard Crone); *upper right*: painted feet (photo: Chester Maydole, *Saturday Evening Post*, September 23, 1967, 27); *lower*: hippie hill, Golden Gate Park, San Francisco, CA, 1967 (photo: Richard Crone).

p. 78: *line art*: Eyes of Buddha, illustration from *San Francisco Oracle*.

p. 79: *Group Living*, Haight-Ashbury (photo: Gene Anthony / Wolfgang's Vault).

p. 80: *upper*: crash pad, Haight-Ashbury, 1967 (photo: Ted Streshinsky); *lower*: Morton's crash pad, Haight-Ashbury (*Look* magazine, August 22, 1967, 80); *center*: Bill Gallagher, "The Meaning of Life Is the Celebration of It," *San Francisco Oracle*.

p. 81: Sans Souci Temple, Los Angeles, CA, 1967 (*Time*, July 7, 1967).

p. 82: *Media Blitz*, book and magazine coverage of the hippie phenomenon, *upper left*: Delbert Earisman, *Hippies in Our Midst* (Philadelphia: Fortress Press, 1968); *upper middle*: hippies at Golden Gate Park, San Francisco, in "The Hippies," *Horizon*, vol. 10, no. 2, Spring 1968 (photo: Don Snyder); *upper right*: Haight-Ashbury crash pad penetrated by reporter William Hedgepeth, "Inside the Hippie Revolution," *Look* (August 22, 1967); *middle left*: *The Hippies* (New York: Time Inc., 1967); *middle center*: Burton H. Wolfe, *The Hippies* (New York: Signet, 1968); *middle right*: "The Hippie Cult," *Saturday Evening Post*, September 23, 1967; *lower left*: "The Hippies: Philosophy of a Subculture," *Time*, July 7, 1967; *lower middle*: "Inside the Hippie Revolution," *Look* (August 22, 1967); *lower right*: Jerry Hopkins, *The Hippie Papers*, (New York: Signet, 1968).

pp. 84–85: Galahad's Crash Pad, East Village, New York, NY (photos: Ben Martin).

CHAPTER 4

p. 86: Aleksandra Kasuba, *The Spectral Passage*, M.H. De Young Memorial Museum, San Francisco, CA, 1975.

p. 87: *background*: from Wolf Strache, *Forms and Patterns in Nature* (New York: Pantheon Books, 1956).

p. 88: *upper left*: Ted Hallman, "Centering Environment," 1969 (courtesy: American Crafts Council); *upper right*: Sim Van der Ryn, "Envirom," as seen in *The Last Whole Earth Catalog,* Brand, ed., June 1971); *lower*: John Storyk, "Relaxation Well," New York, NY, 1968.

p. 89: Neke Carson, *Man-Moon Fountain*, 1968 (courtesy: American Crafts Council).

p. 90: Wendell Castle, *Enclosed Reclining Environment for One,* Rochester, NY, 1969 (courtesy: American Crafts Council).

p. 91: *left and right*: Ugo La Pietra, *Plastic Environment for Experiencing Optical Phenomenon*, 1969 (courtesy: American Crafts Council).

p. 92: ALEPH (Sam Apple, Harry Fischman, Peter Heer, Jon Olson), *Stroboscopic Crystal Waterfall Environment*, New York, NY, 1969 (photo: Harry Fischman).

p. 93: *upper left*: Roberto Sebastian Matta, Malitte Seating System (for Gavina/Bologna), 1966; *upper right*: Verner Panton, "Phantasy Landscape," Cologne Furniture Fair, Germany, 1970; *lower left*: ALEPH, "Stroboscopic Waterfall"; *lower right*: Harry Fischman, "Egg Environment," 1969; *line art*: ALEPH, sectional diagram of Stroboscopic Crystal Waterfall Environment, New York, NY, 1969.

p. 94: *upper left and right, lower*: Tom Luckey, Rotating Barrel Room, Steele House, Warren, Vermont, 1967.

p. 95: Aleksandra Kasuba, *Sensorium, Walk-In Environment*, New York, NY, 1971.

p. 96: Aleksandra Kasuba, *Color Structure* (blue), Potsdam, NY, 1973.

p. 97: *upper*: Aleksandra Kasuba, *Stretched Fabric Environment for Teresa Sevilla*, New York, NY, 1970; *lower*: Kasuba, *Sensorium, Walk-In Environment*, New York, NY, 1971; *line art*: Kasuba, *The Spectral Passage*, M.H. De Young Memorial Museum, San Francisco, CA, 1975.

p. 98: Aleksandra Kasuba/Silvia Heyden, *Sleeping Bower, Walk-In Environment*, New York, NY, 1971.

p. 99: Aleksandra Kasuba, *Passageway and Group Shelter, Walk-In Environment*, New York, NY, 1971.

p. 100: Les Walter, *Super Cube*, New York, NY, 1967. (photo: Hans Namuth; source: Plumb, *Young Designs in Living*, [New York: The Viking Press, 1969] 25).

p. 101: Gamal El Zoghby, *Multi-Level Living Environment*, 1969 (photo: John T. Hill; source: Plumb, *Young Designs in Living*, [New York: The Viking Press, 1969] 138).

p. 102: *middle*: Jersey Devil, inflatable environment, Princeton, NJ, 1970 (photo: Steve Badanes); *background*: the architecture of soap bubbles (photo: Peter S. Steven, *Patterns in Nature,* [Boston: Little, Brown and Company, 1974], 168).

p. 103: Reyner Banham and Francois Dallegret, *The Environment Bubble,* 1965 (Renyer Banham, "A House is Not a Home," *Art in America*, April 1965).

p. 104: *Upper*: Jean Aubert, Utopie Group, *Travelling heater for 5,000 Spectators,* 1967; *lower right and left*: Aubert/Utopie, *Pneumatic House*, 1967.

p. 105: Quasar (Nguyen Manh Khanh), *Inflatable House*, Paris, 1968 (photo courtesy: American Crafts Council).

p. 106: Ant Farm: *Enviromints,* 1970 (courtesy: Ant Farm Archives, University of California, Berkeley Art Museum. Purchase made possible through a bequest from Thérèse Bonney by exchange, a partial gift of Chip Lord and Curtis Schreier, and gifts from an anonymous donor and Harrison Fraker).

p. 107: *upper*: Ant Farm, *The World's Largest Snake*, *Inflatocookbook*, 1970 (courtesy: Ant Farm Archives, University of California); *background*: Ant Farm, 50' x 50' inflatable, Freestone, California, 1970 (photo: Chip Lord).

p. 108: Ant Farm: *100' x 100' Pillow,* 1969; temporary installation, San Francisco, California (photo: Chip Lord).

p. 109: *upper and lower*: Ant Farm: *Dream Cloud*, tie-dyed parachute on the beach, Freeport, Texas, during "AstroDaze," 1969 (photo: Doug Michels).

p. 110: *upper*: Ant Farm, *Clean Air Pod*, University of California, Berkeley, 1970 (photo: Chip Lord); *lower left*: Ant Farm, *ICE 9* inflatable, "Truckstop Network," 1971; *middle right*: Ant Farm, *Spare Tire Inflatable* (inside *50 x 50' Pillow*), Freestone, California, 1970 (photo: Chip Lord); *lower right*: Ant Farm, *50 x 50' Pillow,* temporary installation at Saline Valley, California, for *Whole Earth Catalog* supplement, 1969 (photo: Curtis Schreier).

p. 111: Ant Farm, *50 x 50' Pillow,* 1969, temporary installation, Freestone, California, 1970 (photo: Chip Lord).

p. 112: Kenzo Tange, *Tokyo Bay Project*, 1960.

p. 113: *upper*: Paolo Soleri, "Novanoah," (page from *Visionary Cities: The Arcology of Paolo Soleri*, [New York: Praeger Publishers, 1970]); *lower left*: Soleri with plaster model of Babelnoah, Cosanti, Arizona, 1968; *lower right*: Paolo Soleri, *Babel IID*, 1969.

pp. 114–115: Paolo Soleri, sketches for Arcologies, 1967–1970.

p. 116: *upper left*: Soleri, *Hexahedron,* 1968; *upper right*: Cosanti drawing, 1964; *lower*: Soleri, *Ribcage Dam*, 1964.

p. 117: Paolo Soleri, Mesa Dam, 1965.

p. 118: *upper*: Chanéac, *Crater City* (site plan), 1968; *lower*: Günther Feuerstein, *Urban Utopia for Salzburg*, 1969.

p. 119: *upper right*: Chanéac, *Cellules Polyvalentes*, 1960; *lower right*: John Osajimas, *Congress Center,* Vienna, c. 1968;

p. 120: Haus-Rucker Co. (Klaus Pinter), *Downtown Megastructures,* 1971.

p. 121: *Upper*: Haus-Rucker Co., *Yellow Heart,* 1968 (photo courtesy: American Crafts Council); *lower*: Yona Friedman, *Osaka Board*, 1970.

p. 122: Haus-Rucker Co., *Yellow Heart,* 1968 (photo courtesy: American Crafts Council).

p. 123: *upper*: Haus-Rucker Co., projects, 1967–1970; *lower*: *Pneumacosm*, 1967.

CHAPTER 5

p. 124: Gathering, Strawberry Lake, Colorado, 1972 (photo: Paul Dembski).

p. 125: *background*: from Wolf Strache, *Forms and Patterns in Nature* (New York: Pantheon Books, 1956).

p. 126: *upper left*: "The Youth Communes," *Life* magazine, cover, July 18, 1969; *upper right*: Swami Kriyananda, *Cooperative Communities*, cover (Nevada City, CA: Ananda Publications, 1971); *lower left*: Abbie Hoffman, *Woodstock Nation*, cover (New York: Vintage Books, 1969); *lower middle*: Roy Ald, *The Youth Communes*, cover (New York: Tower Publications, 1970); *lower right*: Robert Houriet, *Getting Back Together* (New York: Avon Books, 1972).

pp. 128–129: Paradise Now, leaving the city, bound for New Mexico (photo: Paul Dembski).

pp. 130–131: On the road, converted trucks and school busses (all photos and line art: Jane

Pincus Lidz).

p. 132: Back to the Land, *upper*: Mother Earth collage, from *San Francisco Oracle,* vol. 1, no. 9, August 1967; *lower left*: farming at Morning Star (photo: Anders Holmquist, *The Free People* [New York: Outerbridge & Dienstfrey, 1969]); *lower right*: naked yoga at Morning Star (photo: The *Morning Star Scrapbook*, Unohoo, Coyote, Rick and the Mighty Avengers [Occidental, CA: Self-Published, 1973]).

p. 135: Roberta Price bringing in the harvest at Libré commune, Colorado, c. 1973 (photo: David Perkins, courtesy: Roberta Price).

p. 136: *upper*: shack at Wheeler's Ranch (photo: Bill Wheeler, courtesy: www.laurelrose.com); *lower:* simple bath, Morning Star East, Arroyo Seco, New Mexico, 1969 (photo: © Roberta Price, All Rights Reserved).

p. 137: *upper left*: Shack at Lorien Commune, Questa, New Mexico (photo: Rich Jamison); *upper right*: cabin at Wheeler's Ranch (photo: Bill Wheeler, courtesy, Roman Sender); *lower*: funky shelter, Peñasco, New Mexico, 1970 (photo: © Roberta Price, All Rights Reserved).

p. 138: Hippie farmer, Lorien Commune, Questa, New Mexico, 1969 (photo: © Dennis Stock/Magnum).

p. 139: *background*: from Wolf Strache, *Forms and Patterns in Nature* (New York: Pantheon Books, 1956).

pp. 140–141: Circle of hands around the meadow, Gila National Forest, New Mexico, 1975 (photo: Paul Dembski).

p. 142: Communal toothbrushes, Lama Foundation, New Mexico (photo: Richard Fairfield, *Communes: A Personal Tour,* Baltimore, MD: Penguin Books, 1972, p. 306).

p. 143: Gathering, Gila National Forest, New Mexico, 1975 (photo: Paul Dembski).

pp. 144–145: Talking Stick, Strawberry Lake, Colorado, July 2, 1972 (photo: Paul Dembski).

p. 146: Happy hippies (photo: "The Youth Communes," *Life* magazine, July 18, 1969).

p. 148: *Self-Reliance*, woman chopping wood, *Shelter*, Lloyd Kahn (ed.) (Bolinas, California: Shelter Publications, 1973); *line art*: "how to split a log," illustration from D.C. Beard, *Shelters, Shacks and Shanties* (New York: Charles Scribner's Sons, 1914).

p. 149: New Frontiers, *upper*: log house (photo: Barry Shapiro); *middle:* Jersey Devil, log sauna, Dumbarton, New Hampshire, 1973 (photo: Steve Badanes); *lower*: log shack interior (photo: Barry Shapiro).

p. 150: *Solux Manifesto*, USCO (Steve and Barbara Durkee), c. 1966 (collection: Gerd Stern).

p. 152*: upper*: Drop City, kitchen complex and theater dome (photo: Jack Fulton); *lower*: Hog Farm, *Mobile Dome*, Sunland-Tujunga, CA, 1968 (photo: Lisa Law).

p. 153: Wavy Gravy, *The Hog Farm and Friends*, cover (New York: Links Books, 1974); *line art*: dome variations, Lloyd Kahn (ed.), *Domebook Two* (Santa Barbara, CA: Mountain Books, 1971).

p. 154: Morning Star Commune, California, *upper left*: Lou Gottlieb among sunflowers, c. 1967 (photo: Don Snyder); *upper right*: tipi at Morning Star (photo: *Morning Star Scrapbook*); *lower*: morning yoga (photo: *Morning Star Scrapbook*); *line art:* Buddha, *San Francisco Oracle.*

p. 155: *Line art*: *Morning Star Scrapbook.*

p. 157: "Wake Up," *Morning Star Scrapbook.*

p. 159: *upper*: Morning Star gathering (photo: *The Modern Utopian,* "Communes U.S.A.," vol. 5, nos. 1, 2, 3 [San Francisco: Alternatives Foundations, 1971]); *lower left*: Meadowboat, Morning Star (*Time*, July 7, 1967); *middle left*: shack at Wheeler's Ranch (photo: *Morning Star Scrapbook*); *lower right*: Charlotte and Bryce in yurt, Wheeler's Ranch (photo: Brand, ed., *The Last Whole Earth Catalog*, June 1971).

p. 160: Pages from *Morning Star Scrapbook*, 1973.

p. 162: *upper left*: walking in woods (photo: Anders Holmquist); *upper right*: sunbathing, Morning Star (photo: Gene Anthony); *middle right*: shack at Wheeler's Ranch (photo: Bill Wheeler, courtesy Ramon Sender); *lower*: house at Wheeler's Ranch (photo: Bill Wheeler, courtesy Ramon Sender).

p. 163: *upper left, right and middle left*: hand-built shelters at Wheeler's Ranch (photos: Bill Wheeler, courtesy Ramon Sender); *middle right*: Cindy and Herb's Scotch Broom Room, Morning Star (photo: *Morning Star Scrapbook*); *lower*: Fern on the rocks with guitar, Devil's Lake, Wisconsin, 1972 (photo: Paul Dembski).

p. 164: *upper:* Alicia Bay Laurel, drawings of basic shelter (Tree House, Umbrella Dome, Hexagonal Cabin, Triangle House, Tent of Three Blankets, Arcology) illustration from Alicia Bay Laurel, *Living on the Earth: Celebrations, Storm Warnings, Formulas, Recipes, Rumors, and Country Dances Harvested by Alicia Bay Laurel* (New York: Random House, 1971); *lower left*: cover, *Living on the Earth.*

p. 165: Alicia Bay Laurel, "In the Morning," illustration from *Being of the Sun*, Ramon Sender and Alicia Bay Laurel (New York: Harper & Row, 1973), 73.

CHAPTER 6

p. 166: image, hands in middle of circle of hippies: photo: from Corinne McLaughlin and Gordon Davidson, Builders of the Dawn (Walpole, New Hampshire: Stillpoint Publishing, 1985).

p. 167: background: from Wolf Strache, *Forms and Patterns in Nature* (New York: Pantheon Books, 1956).

p. 168: *upper*: Paolo Soleri, Ceramic Apse, Arcosanti, Arizona, 1971 (photo: Terrence Moore); *lower*: Paolo Soleri and Mark Mills, Dome House, Cave Creek, Arizona, 1949 (photo: Mark Mills).

p. 169: Paolo Soleri, Ceramics Studio, Cosanti, Scottsdale, Arizona, 1957.

p. 170: Richard Buckminster Fuller, *Spherical Truss for Ford Motor Company,* 1953.

p. 171: Dome information page, *The Whole Earth Catalog*, Stewart Brand (ed.), Fall 1969, 19.

p. 172: *left:* Instructions on how to build a triacontahedron (*Domebook Two,* Lloyd Kahn (ed.), [Santa Barbara, CA: Mountain Books, 1971]); *upper right and lower right*: erecting a dome, from The Modern Utopian, "Communes U.S.A.," vol 5, nos. 1, 2, 3 (San Francisco: Alternatives Foundations, 1971).

p. 173: *upper*: from Dome Book Two Lloyd Kahn (ed.), (Santa Barbara, CA: Mountain Books, 1971); lower: Four-Dome Residence, San Diego, CA, 1972. (photo: Richard Davis); *line art*: Steve Baer, plan for Main Building, Lama Foundation, New Mexico.

p. 174: *upper*: Triple-Dome Complex, Drop City, Colorado, 1967; *lower*: tarring the first dome at Drop City, 1966; *line art*: Steve Baer, zome cluster, 1967.

p. 176: *upper*: Domes of Drop, Drop City, 1969 (photo: Clark Richert); *lower*: theater dome under construction, Drop City, 1966.

p. 177: *lower left*: second dome at Drop City (photo: Clark Richert); *lower right*: interior of dome, Drop City (photo: Clark Richert).

p. 178: *line art*: Steve Baer, sketch of chopping car tops, 1968 (*Dome Cookbook* [Corrales, N.M.: Lama Foundation, 1968]).

p. 179: First dome (duo-dodecahedron) at Drop City, 1966 (photo: Clark Richert).

pp. 180–181: Steve Baer, *Dome Cookbook,* (Corrales, N.M.: Lama Foundation, 1968), pp. 22, 13.1.

p. 182: Steve Baer, *Triple-Fused Cluster,* 1967.

p. 183: Solar-heated dome, Drop City, 1967 (photo: Clark Richert).

p. 184: Painted domes, Drop City (photos: Dean Fleming).

p. 185: Peter Rabbit, *Drop City* (New York: The Olympia Press, 1971).

pp. 186–187: *Zomeworks*, Steve Baer's bus, Manera Nueva, New Mexico, c. 1969 (photo: Jack Fulton).

p. 188: *upper right*: Jerry Burgland, Dome Adobe, Plactias, New Mexico, c. 1970 (photo: Jack Fulton); *middle*: Zome Adobe (Lee Johnson home), Placitas, New Mexico, c. 1970 (photo: Jack Fulton).

p. 189: *upper and lower:* Steve Baer, Solar-Heated Zome Cluster (Baer home), Corrales, New Mexico, 1971 (photo: Jack Fulton).

p. 190: What we love about our dome, Red Rock, Commune, Colorado, 1970 (Lloyd Kahn, *Shelter* [Bolinas, California: Shelter Publications, 1973]).

p. 192: Richard Wehrman, drawing of Libré Commune, Gardner, Colorado.

p. 193: Dwellings at Libré Commune, Gardner, Colorado, 1968–72; *upper left*: Gwen's House (photo: Dean Fleming); *upper right*: Peter Rabbit's Zome (photo: Dean Fleming); *middle*: Steve and Patty Raines Dome House (photo: © Roberta Price, All Rights Reserved); *middle left*: "V" House, Steven Vasey House (photo: Dean Fleming); *middle right*: Fleming Dome Home (photo: Dean Fleming); *lower*: Fleming Domes (photo: © Roberta Price, All Rights Reserved); *line art*: San Francisco Oracle.

p. 194: Tony Magar's Dome, Libré Commune, 1970 (photo: © Roberta Price, All Rights Reserved).

p. 195: Red Rock Dome under construction, Colorado 1970 (photo: © Roberta Price, All Rights Reserved).

p. 196: *upper and lower:* interior, Red Rock Dome, Colorado (photos: Jack Fulton).

p. 198: *Upper left:* "Eightfold Path," page from *Be Here Now*, Steve Durkee, Baba Ram Dass (San Cristobal, New Mexico, 1971); *lower left*: Consciousness Diagram, *San Francisco Oracle,* vol. 1, no. 9, August 1967, 28; Swami Kriyananda, *Temple Dome,* Ananda Meditation Retreat, California, 1967; *line art*: San Francisco Oracle.

p. 200: *upper*: Steve Durkee, Steve Baer, interior kitchen building, Lama Foundation, New Mexico, c. 1968; *lower*: Baghavan Das, Sunday morning drums and sitar, Lama Foundation, New Mexico, 1973 (photo: Paul Dembski).

p. 201: Page from *Seed,* Steve Durkee, ed. (San Cristobal, New Mexico: Lama Foundation, 1973).

p. 202: Baba Ram Dass chanting, Taos Community Auditorium, 1975 (photo: Paul Dembski).

p. 203: *Upper:* Zome roof of the center at sunset, Lama Foundation (photo: Barry Shapiro); *lower right*: man meditating (photo: Don Snyder); *lower left:* Kitchen Building, Lama Foundation (photo: Barry Shapiro).

p. 205: A school that bathes together stays together. Students and faculty sharing a tub in the Bathtub Dome, Pacific High School, California, 1969.

p. 206: The Student Run School (photo: Jack Fulton).

p. 208: *upper left*: cat and dome; *upper right*: Jay Baldwin in his Pillowdome; students and their dome, Pacific High (all photos: Jack Fulton); *bottom left, center and right*: from Dome Book Two Lloyd Kahn (ed.), (Santa Barbara, CA: Mountain Books, 1971).

p. 209: *upper:* Peter Calthorpe, *Zapoche Dome* under construction, Pacific High, 1971; *lower:* Lloyd Kahn, *Aluminum Triacon Dome*, under construction, Pacific High, 1971; *bottom left, center and right*: from Dome Book Two Lloyd Kahn (ed.), (Santa Barbara, CA: Mountain Books, 1971).

p. 210: *upper and lower:* Jay Baldwin, *Pillowdome*, Pacific High, 1970 (photos: Jack Fulton).

p. 211: Alan Schmidt, *the Om Dome*, Pacific High 1970 (photo: Jack Fulton).

pp. 212–213: Dome homes, Pacific High, 1971 (photos: Jack Fulton).

p. 214: Dome in the woods, Pacific High (photo: Jack

Fulton).
p. 215: Martin Bartlett, *Pod Dome*, Pacific High.
p. 216: *upper:* Steve Baer, Crystal Garnett Zome, Manera Nueva; *middle left*: Jim Anderson atop his Cedar Shake Dome, Washington State, 1970; *middle right*: Shingled Dome House, Woodstock, NY, 1969 (photo: Jonathan Elliott).
p. 217: Wholeo Dome is a 14-foot-diameter, 7-foot tall geodesic dome clad with curved, stained glass panels. Caroling completed the structure in 1974. *left:* Caroling in front of "Bump", Harmony Ranch, California, 1974 (photo: Gordon Adelman, courtesy wholeo.net); *upper right:* Bump seen from Wholeo Dome, 1974 (photo: Caroling, courtesy wholeo.net); *lower right*: Wholeo Dome, Harmony, 1974 (photo: Caroling, courtesy wholeo.net).
pp. 218–219: Interior view of Wholeo Dome, 1974, (photo, 1976: © Chuck Henrikson, courtesy wholeo.net).

CHAPTER 7

p. 220: Naked dancers, Rainbow Gathering, Gila National Forest, New Mexico, 1977 (photo: Paul Dembski).
p. 221: *background*: Wolf Strache, *Forms and Patterns in Nature* (New York: Pantheon Books, 1956).
p. 222: *upper left:* Ela's Mandala House, Sonoma County, California, c. 1969 (photo: Sally Bailey); *lower left*: "The Owl," houseboat, Sausalito, California, Chris Roberts; *line art*: Tipi-Snail House (Potter House), Mass-achusetts; *lower right*: shack, northern California (photo: Barry Shapiro).
p. 223: *upper left*: interior, pole roof house (photo: Barry Shapiro); *upper right*: The Madonna, house-boat, Sausalito, California, Chris Roberts; *line art*: Moving to the Country, *San Francisco Oracle*; *lower right*: shack, northern California (photo: Barry Shapiro).
p. 224: *upper*: Tipis under rainbow, New Buffalo Commune, Aroyo Hondo, New Mexico, 1967 (photo: Lisa Law); *lower left*: book cover, *The Indian Tipi*, Reginald and Gladys Laubin, (Norman, Oklahoma: University of Oklahoma Press, 1957) (photo: Bill Stone); *lower right*: tipi entrance, Evan Ravitz Tipi, Arroyo Seco, New Mexico (photo: Paul Dembski).
p. 225: *upper*: Tipi buddies, Jake, Evan Ravitz, and Ricky, Arroyo Seco, New Mexico (photo: Paul Dembski); *line art*: "How to Make a Tipi," *The Mother Earth News,* vol. 1, no. 1, January 1970, 36; *lower right*: interior of tipi, Woodstock, NY (photo: Jonathan Elliott); *line art*: from The Mother Earth News, January, 1970.
pp. 226–227: Shampoo, Gila National Forest, Arizona, July, 1977 (photo: Paul Dembski).
p. 228: *Upper left*: yurt under construction (photo: R. Ellis); *lower left and right*: Yurt City, Westlake Hills, Texas, Tao Design (Charles Harker, Betty Gaddis, Paul Gaddis, David Gaddis, Tom Hatch, Elizabeth Yndo), 1972 (photos: Charles Harker).
p. 229: *Upper left, right, middle*: Yurt City, Westlake Hills, Texas, Tao Design, 1972 (photos: Charles Harker); *lower*: guest yurt, Dickinsons Reach, Maine, William S. Coperthwaite, 1966.
p. 230: Working on Rock House, Libré Commune, Colorado, 1970 (photos: © Roberta Price, All Rights Reserved).
p. 232: *upper line art*: Paolo Soleri, studies for plant-like towers, *The Sketches of Paolo Soleri* (Cambridge, Mass: MIT Press, 1971), 73; *middle*: Soleri drawing in his studio, Cosanti Foundation, Scottsdale, Arizona, c. 1964; *lower line art*: P. Soleri, Axial Park, Mesa City, 1960.
p. 233: Paolo Soleri, silt cast architecture, North Studio, Cosanti Foundation, Scottsdale, Arizona, 1961 (photo: *Horizon,* vol. 12, no. 4, Autumn 1970).
p. 234: Teddy and his Mushroom House, California, c. 1970 (photo: Sally Bailey, from: *Dwelling, River.* [Albion, CA: Freestone Publishing Co., 1974], 147); *line art*: Teddy's Mushroom House, (draw-ing: Leona Walden, from: *Dwelling, River.* Albion, CA: Freestone Publishing Co., 1974, p. 145).
p. 235: Aleksandra Kasuba, Cocoon Dwelling, Whiz Bang City East, Woodstock, NY, 1972.
pp. 236–237: Aleksandra Kasuba, interior view of Cocoon Dwelling at night, Whiz Bang City East, Woodstock, New York, 1972.
pp. 238–239: Aleksandra Kasuba, Cocoon Dwelling, Whiz Bang City East, Woodstock, New York, 1972.
p. 240: Foam House, fabricated by students from the Yale School of Art and Architecture, New Haven, Connecticut, 1968 (photo: "Plastic as Plastic" exhibition, Museum of Contemporary Crafts, New York, NY, 1968–1969), *lower right*: Woodstock, NY (photo: Jonathan Elliott).
p. 241: *upper, lower right, and middle*: igloo house, Woodstock, NY (photo: Jonathan Elliott); *lower right*: polyurethane house near Woodstock, NY (photo: Jonathan Elliott).
p. 242: *Upper and lower*: James Hubbell, "Ilan-Lael", Hubbell Compound, Santa Ysabel, California, 1958–1970.
p. 243: James Hubbell, boys house bathroom, Hubbell Compound, Santa Ysabel, California, 1970.
p. 244: *Upper and lower*: James Hubbell, Waldorf School Library, Fairoaks, California, 1973 (photos: Robert Thiele).
p. 245: James Hubbell, Davidson House, Alpine, California, 1972 (photo: Jerry Oshinga).
p. 246: *upper*: John M. Johansen, *Spray-Form House*, 1959; *line art*: Frederick Keisler, *Endless House*; *lower*: Daniel Grataloup, Villa d'Anieres, Geneva, Switzerland, 1970.
p. 247: *upper*: Roger Dean, Organic City, 1970; *lower*: Mark Mills, "Limp Penis House" (Hass Residence) Carmel, California, 1969 (Weber Photo).
pp. 248–249: Bob De Buck, desert house, Truchas, New Mexico, 1969 (photo: Jack Fulton).
p. 250: *line art*: Charles Harker, Tao Design, floor plan, Earth House, Westlake Hills, Texas, 1970.
p. 251: Charles Harker, Tao Design, Earth House, Westlake Hills, Texas, 1970 (photos: Charles Harker).
p. 252: Spraying polyurethane walls, Earth House, Westlake Hills, Texas, 1970.
p. 253: Earth House, Westlake Hills, Texas, 1970.
p. 254: Charles Harker, Tao Design, front entry, Bloomhouse, Westlake Hills, Texas, 1973.
p. 255: Charles Harker, Tao Design, staircase, Bloomhouse, Westlake Hills, Texas, 1973.
p. 256: Strider, New Buffalo commune, Arroyo Hondo, New Mexico, 1970 (photo: © Roberta Price, All Rights Reserved).
p. 257: Adobe Structures, page from *Shelter*, Lloyd Kahn (ed.) (Bolinas, California: Shelter Publications, 1973), 43.
p. 258: *upper*: Dragon House (Sally Edelman resi-dence), New Mexico, 1970 (photo: Wayne McCall); *lower*: summer solstice meditation, New Buffalo commune, Arroyo Hondo, New Mexico, 1974 (photo: Paul Dembski).
p. 259: Adobe fireplace, Virginia Gray house, Santa Fe, NM, 1970 (photo: Wayne McCall).
pp. 260–261: *upper left*: Edward Allen, Mud House, (from: *Shelter*, Lloyd Kahn [Bolinas, California: Shelter Publications, 1973]); making adobe bricks, Reality Construction Company commune, Arroyo Seco, New Mexico, 1969 (photo: © Roberta Price, All Rights Reserved).
p. 263: *upper*: kitchen, Barry's house, Canyon, California, 1968; *lower left*: Barry's house; *lower right*: musician's house, California (photos: Barry Shapiro).
pp. 264–265: Self-build shelters, New York, California, New Mexico (photos: Barry Shapiro, John Elliott).
p. 266: Couple bathing in tree house bathtub, Canyon, California, 1971 (photo: Bruce Davidson/Magnum).
p. 267: *upper*: teahouse over stream; *lower*: hot tub, California (photos: Barry Shapiro).
pp. 268–269: Hot-tub culture, northern California, c. 1970–1972 (photos: Leon Elder, *Hot Tubs* [Santa Barbara, CA: Capra Press, 1973]).
p. 270: Driftwood, Hornby Island, British Columbia, Canada (photo: Blue Sky Archive, Bo Helliwell and Michael McNamara).
p. 271: Tim Biggins, Log-Rythmic House, Hornby Island, 1969; *line art*: Log-Rythmic House (photo: Blue Sky Archive, Bo Helliwell and Michael McNamara).
p. 272: *upper*: Vaugn and Betty's house, the "Shire," Hornby Island, 1968; *lower*: Lloyd House, "Leaf Retreat," Hornby Island, 1970 (all photos this page: Blue Sky Archive, Bo Helliwell and Michael McNamara).
p. 273: *line art*: development of Leaf Retreat from a single piece of driftwood; *middle left*: interior, Leaf Retreat; *lower left*: Wayne Ngan, studio door, Hornby Island, 1969; *lower right*: Tim Burrows, "Cliff-Top Mound," view from beach, 1972–1975 (all photos this page: Blue Sky Archive, Bo Helliwell and Michael McNamara).
p. 274: Tim Burrows, notes and sketch of "Cliff-Top Mound," (letter to Bo Helliwell), Hornby Island, 1976.
p. 275: Driftwood entry, Community Center, Hornby Island, 1974 (photo: Blue Sky Archive, Bo Helliwell and Michael McNamara).
p. 276: Dave Sellers, Bill Reienecke, Tack House/Sellers Residence, Prickly Mountain, Warren, Vermont, 1966–1970 (photo: Wayne Fuji).
p. 277: Dave Sellers, Bill Reienecke, Wadsworth House, Prickly Mountain, 1966 (photo: Alastair Gordon).
p. 278: *upper*: Dave Sellers, Bill Reienecke, Tack House/Sellers Residence, Prickly Mountain, Warren, Vermont, 1966–1970 (photo: Alastair Gordon); *lower*: swimming in Mad River, Warren, Vermont (photo: Bill Wadsworth).
p. 279: *upper left*: Dimetredon, Prickly Mountain, (photo: Alastair Gordon); *upper right*: Dave Sellers, Bill Reienecke, Tack House, Prickly Mountain, 1966; *lower left*: Jersey Devil, Helmet House, interior view, Goffstown, New Hampshire, 1974 (photo: Steve Badanes); *middle right*: Bill Wadsworth, Dave Sellers (fiddle), Carl Bates playing music in Tack House, Prickly Mountain, c. 1975 (photo courtesy: Bill Wadsworth); *lower right*: Helmet House, Goffstown, New Hampshire, 1974 (photo: Steve Badanes).
p. 280: Jersey Devil, Snail House, Forked River, New Jersey, 1972 (photo: Steve Badanes).
p. 281: John Ringel of Jersey Devil sitting on founda-tion, Snail House, 1972 (photo: Steve Badanes).

EPILOGUE

p. 282: *Hippie Under Plastic*, 1968 (photo: Anders Holmquist, *The Free People* [New York: Outerbridge and Dienstfrey, 1969]).
p. 284: *Let's Get Together and Build Domes*, graffiti, Drop City in ruin, 1970 (photo: Jack Fulton).
p. 286: *Through Triangle Door*, Drop City in Ruin (photo: Jack Fulton).
p. 287: *Get Hi I Do*, graffiti, Drop City in Ruin (photo: Jack Fulton).
p. 288: *Yab-Yum*, American Tantric #2, *San Francisco Oracle*, vol. 1, no. 7, April 1967 (photo: Paul Kagan, design: Hetty McGee).
p. 296: USCO slide, courtesy: Adrienne and Michael Callahan, USCO Archive.
p. 303: *upper*: Author with Holly and Richard, Paris, 1970 (photo: photo booth); *lower*: Author, Grenoble, France, 1970 (photo: Emily Goldstein).
p. 304: Drop City in ruin, 1972 (photo: Jack Fulton).

INDEX

ALASTAIR GORDON (above, Paris, 1970 is an award-winning critic, curator and author of numerous books including *Weekend Utopia, Naked Airport, Romantic Modernist,* and *Beach Houses: Andrew Geller*. He writes about design and the built environment for several different publications including *The New York Times, Architectural Digest* and Dwell. He lives in Pennsylvania with his wife and four children.

FIRST PUBLISHED IN THE UNITED STATES OF AMERICA BY
Rizzoli International Publications, Inc.
300 Park Avenue South
New York, NY 10010
www.rizzoliusa.com

FEATURED PHOTOGRAPHERS IN THIS BOOK ARE:
Gene Anthony (Wolfgang's Vault)
Paul Dembski
Jack Fulton
Ben Martin
Roberta Price

Spaced Out is a co-production of
Gordon De Vries Studio, LLC
www.gordondevriesstudio.com

DESIGN: Sara E. Stemen

EDITOR: Dung Ngo
COPY EDITORS: Alexandra Tart, Tricia Levy
EDITORIAL ASSISTANTS:
Henry Casey, Meera Deean
PRODUCTION: Maria Pia Gramaglia, Kaija Markoe

ISBN-13: 978-0-8478-3105-0
LCCN: 2007926997

2008 2009 2010 2011 / 10 9 8 7 6 5 4 3 2 1
PRINTED IN CHINA